In Pursuit of
PHANTOM BOMBERS

In Pursuit of
PHANTOM BOMBERS

Ravi Shanker

Shauryanker Kaushik

PRABHAT
PRAKASHAN

Published by
PRABHAT PRAKASHAN PVT. LTD.
4/19 Asaf Ali Road,
New Delhi-110 002 (INDIA)
e-mail: prabhatbooks@gmail.com

ISBN 978-93-5562-265-5
IN PURSUIT OF PHANTOM BOMBERS
by Shri Ravi Shanker & Shri Shauryanker Kaushik

Edition
First, 2024

Paperback Price
₹ 500.00 (Rupees Five Hundred only)

Cover Design
Shri Shauryanker Kaushik

Printed at
R-Tech Offset Printers, Delhi

The policeman is denounced by the public, criticised by preachers, ridiculed in the movies, berated by the newspapers and unsupported by prosecuting officers and judges. He is shunned by the respectable, hated by criminals, deceived by everyone, kicked around like a football by brainless or crooked politicians, exposed to countless dangers and temptations, condemned when he enforces the law and dismissed if he doesn't. His home life is made unhappy by long hours of duty; he is forced to endure every conceivable form of hardship. He is supposed to possess the qualifications of a soldier, doctor, lawyer, diplomat and educator with remunerations less than that of the daily laborer. But despite these obstacles, he has achieved a fair measure of success in protecting the lives and property of citizens and preserving the integrity of this nation."

—August Vollmer
Former Chief of Police,
Berkely, California

T.R. KAKKAR
IPS (Retd.)

D-284, Ramprastha,
(Opp. Vivek Vihar-Delhi)
P.O. Chander Nagar
Distt. Ghaziabad-201011 (U.P.)

Foreword

Unravelling Terror: A Year of Triumph over Adversity

In the annals of India's battle against terrorism, the year that unfolded in 1997-1998 stands as a testament to unwavering determination, resilience, and the relentless pursuit of justice. Pursued by a dedicated team within the Interstate Cell-Crime Branch Delhi, a dark and dangerous web of terror was meticulously dismantled, providing a glimmer of hope to those affected by a wave of terror that had gripped several regions. Several modules in Delhi, Uttar Pradesh, Punjab; Hyderabad, Mumbai, and Ahmedabad saw their nefarious designs shattered with the arrest of 26 terrorists, which included Pakistanis, Bangladeshis, and Burmese affiliated with the notorious Lashker-e-Toiba and ISL.

A staggering 42 bomb blasts had terrorized the regions of Delhi, Uttar Pradesh, Haryana, Punjab, Mumbai, and Hyderabad. However, with the arrest of these terrorists, the immediate threats to VVIP's and further loss of life was thwarted. Their possession yielded an alarming arsenal, i.e., RDXIPETN, improvised explosives, electric detonators, car bomb circuitry, hand grenades, fire arms, wireless sets, etc.

The path to success was. far from easy. The initial investigation yielded no actionable leads, and the continuous bomb blasts left a feeling of frustration. However, the team, under the leadership of Shri Karnal Singh IPS and led by Shri Ravi Shanker, the then ACP (The author of the book), was hastily formed. Every piece of evidence was meticulously analyzed, and the team worked in complete unison towards a common objective, despite the ever present threat of compromising the operation. The investigation led the team to various outstations across many states.

This remarkable chapter in the battle against terror serves as a testament to the indomitable spirit of a team whose relentless pursuit for justice, unwavering dedication, and commitment triumphed over adversity to protect society from those who posed a threat. The team's remarkable performance in both brainstorming sessions and field investigations ignited their extraordinary capabilities, leading to the unmasking of terror designees of LeT and ISI.

In the forthcoming pages of this book, readers will embark on a journey through a sequence of real investigations racing to detect and prevent various acts of terror across India. The team led by Shri Ravi Shanker in the field worked tirelessly, and was ably supervised by Shri Kamal Singh, the then DCP (crime). Then I happened to be the Commissioner of Police, Delhi and therefore I can emphatically say that this book will be a valuable guide for the present generation of police officers, who are much better equipped technologically today. Furthermore, the book holds immense learning for all stakeholders in government and non-government circles, especially when the scourge of terrorism looms large and menacingly over the world even to this day.

I wish the author well and appreciate his very sincere efforts to bring out his vast experience in the field of criminal Investigation.

With Best Wishes!

T.R. Kakkar
(IPS)

Prologue

In the year 1982, I joined Delhi Police as a Sub-Inspector and I got an out-of-turn promotion to the rank of Inspector in 1989. I got another out-of-turn promotion to the rank of Assistant Commissioner of Police in 1995. Thereafter, I was posted as an ACP (Operation) in the north-west district of Delhi. In May 1997, under some special circumstances, I was posted to the Interstate Cell (Crime Branch) in Delhi. When posted in the Interstate Cell (Crime Branch), I and my dedicated team were instrumental in neutralising several modules of terrorists belonging to Lashkar-e-Toiba, Hizbul Mujahideen, Harkatul Ansar, Babbar Khalsa International, Khalistan Commando Force, Khalistan Zindabad Force, Khalistan Liberation Force and modules of narco terror backed by Pakistan ISI and many mafia gangs.

Now I have decided to pen down my experiences and memories in a series. This is my first such attempt regarding a multistate operation spanning more than a year between 1997 and 1998. My team apprehended 26 trained terrorists of the Pakistan-based Lashkar-e-Toiba (eight Pakistanis, four Bangladeshis, one Burmese and 13 Indians) who were responsible for detonating more than 40 bombs in Delhi, Haryana, Punjab, Uttar Pradesh, Andhra Pradesh Maharashtra.

The Sessions Court in Delhi found all the accused guilty in a conspiracy case in which all of them were arrested. They were convicted and sentenced. However, Kamran, who was involved in 28 bomb explosions, was convicted in only two additional bombing cases of Karol Bagh because eyewitnesses were available, whereas in other cases there was no eyewitness available; thus, he was released.

In these two cases, viz. bomb blast in a sweet shop named Roshan-di-Kulfi and another just adjacent to that shop in Karol Bagh, Delhi. Kamran was convicted for life imprisonment and sentenced for 10 years. He decided to challenge the District Court decision in all the three cases. In one instance, in which he was awarded life imprisonment by the District Court. However the High Court of Delhi observed, while acquitting him, as under:

"Presence of appellant at the spot cannot be doubted but mere presence is not sufficient to bring home the guilt of the accused to the charge framed. There is no doubt also that the explosion took place soon after the accused left the seat. This fact too is not sufficient to conclusively infer that the accused had planted the bomb and thereafter left. There is evidence on record to show that the accused himself had partaken in eating 'golgappa' which must have taken some time. But there is nothing on record to suggest that the crude bomb blast was the handiwork of this accused. It may be the accused himself providentially escaped the consequences of the blast. Suspicion is at all no matter how grave is no substitute for evidence. The circumstances in this case do not form a chain of events strong enough to bring home the guilt of the accused."

In another case of a bomb blast, the Sessions Court granted capital punishment to Pakistani terrorist, namely Hussain. His conviction was confirmed by the Delhi High Court whose verdict he challenged. After 12 years, the Supreme Court of India ordered for retrial of the case. Later, he was acquitted in that case due to non-availability of eyewitnesses for cross-examination.

It is pertinent to mention the evidence recorded during the trail of an eyewitness who, without any doubt, identified the planter of the bomb (Hussain). Statement of the witness is reproduced below:

"Darshan Kumar, the conductor of the bus, deposed regarding one passenger who had boarded his bus from Paharganj bus stop along with a rexine bag for going to Nangloi, but instead of going up to Nangloi, he had gotten down from the bus at Karol Bagh, leaving his rexine bag underneath the seat that he had taken, which was near the seat of the conductor. The conductor had given a description of that passenger. As per the prosecution case, the explosion had taken place below that seat, which that passenger had occupied and underneath which, he had kept his rexine bag. Later, the bus conductor identified the accused, Hussain, who planted the bomb."

Not only this, Darshan Kumar was also present in the court on three dates for the cross-examination, but it was not done and deferred at the request of the accused Hussain. Even though the Supreme Court observed that the accused was not given a fair chance to defend himself by the District Judge and remanded the case for retrial, that too after 12 years, how can anyone think that a person who appeared in court three times in such adverse circumstances would come forward that way against a hardcore terrorist? Finally, as expected, the accused, Hussain, a Pakistani national, was acquitted and was thereafter deported to Pakistan.

As a supervisory officer of an investigating team which had worked tirelessly for months, neglecting our families and personal desires, sacrificing festival celebrations and risking our life with honest intentions, the acquittal of the accused was a shock and a source of sorrow for me. Although legal recourse was sought at the time but the result wasn't favourable. I had witnessed my fair share of violent crimes and acts of violence, but the Delhi bombing case was unprecedented in its scope. I knew from the instant the explosions shattered the city that this investigation would be the most difficult one in my career. Our mission was to uncover the truth behind the relentless surge of attacks that shook the city for more than a year.

Having witnessed the destruction and sorrow caused by these bombings firsthand, I understood the magnitude of the upcoming challenge. The complex terrorist network that spanned multiple states, including NCR, Uttar Pradesh (UP), Maharashtra, Gujarat, Hyderabad, West Bengal and internationally in Pakistan, Bangladesh and Nepal, presented formidable obstacles to our efforts.

After the release of Kamran, à prominent newspaper, *Hindustan Times*, published a series of press articles from 9 February to 4 March, 2012, portraying him as a victim of the judicial system. I was no stranger to such circumstances. However, years after my retirement, I learnt through an incidental conversation with a colleague that Kamran had been awarded Rs. 5,00,000 in compensation and that a human rights activist had written a book portraying him as a victim of the system. This revelation was incredibly disheartening and it only added to my grief. Regarding our judicial system's treatment of a terrorist, I have struggled with anger, emotional breakdowns and an overwhelming sense of helplessness in recent days.

Presently the Unlawful Activities (Prevention) Act (UAPA) is being used to try acts of terrorism but this Act is grossly inadequate in the face of strong political and non-political lobbies who jump into action in support of such terrorists. In recent years, the government has been able to prevent terrorist activities effectively but to root out the menace, much more is required.

In terror cases where incidents like bomb blasts, suicidal attacks, etc. caused by the terrorists, it is rare for any eyewitnesses to be left behind. Even if someone survives, they may not come forward to depose against the accused in the court of law due to fear of reprisals. If such a person does come forward, considering it is his moral duty to help the police and investigation, he may be declared hostile by the court when tricky questions are put by the defence counsel to an ordinary person Or, they may not come to court to depose due to deliberate prolonged trial on one pretext or another by the counsel of accused. Therefore, investigating terror cases become even more challenging, particularly in collecting and analysing every piece of evidence to ensure justice is served.

Above all, the entire judicial system is based on the principle – 'it is better that hundred guilty persons go free than that one innocent person be convicted.' Prosecution has to prove the case beyond any reasonable doubt. To prove the case, generally there are requirements of independent witnesses. But my straight question is: Is it easy to find such a person in this world where even near and dear ones do not come forward, either due to threats or reasons best known to them?

Undoubtedly, terror crime is an international crime, always conspiring in isolation in neighbouring countries, most of the time in Pakistan routed through Arab countries, Bangladesh, etc. There is no possibility to collect any evidence with respect to hatching the conspiracy in these countries. Pakistan motivates, trains and launches terrorists to carry out terrorist acts in India. Therefore, there is a remote possibility to link the accused with his masters in Pakistan, except through his own statement before a police officer (which is not admissible in the court of law) and circumstantial evidence collected during investigation. The outcome of investigation, i.e. the version of investigating officer, is entirely disregarded.

Terror crime is a special crime. Police are the only agency authorised by the State to investigate such cases but they are not believed by the courts. Is it not a joke? Outrightly rejecting the prosecution version and believing the arguments of the accused without any supporting evidence does not sound fair.

Need for Special Laws

In my perspective, and I believe many would concur: "Terror crimes should be addressed with specialised laws." In the past, India enacted terrorism laws, like Terrorist and Disruptive (Prevention) Activities (TADA) and Prevention of Terrorism Act (POTA), which to an extent addressed such crimes, but unfortunate political manoeuvrings led to their repeal. It is imperative to address terrorism with seriousness, employing specialised laws and agencies, such as NIA (National Investigating Agency). Equally important is safeguarding the rights of victims and the sovereignty of the State, rather than favouring the accused.

All these events prompted me to write about the case based on my memory, press clippings and notes taken during the investigation, interrogation of the arrested suspects, legally listening to 'telephonic conversations' with their Pakistani handlers and the presentations made by me for academic purposes. I take great pleasure in recounting a pivotal moment in my life's journey – an episode that is etched deeply in my memory. This is not an exhaustive account, but rather a personal reflection on the obstacles we encountered and how we tackled them during the year-long investigation.

Contents

1

Posting at Interstate Cell, Crime Branch Office, New Delhi

Delhi Police's two prestigious units - the Crime Branch and Special Cell - are such that every police officer whose temperament has been one of crime detection and investigation considers it a matter of pride to get posted. These units have been leaders in solving sensational and very important cases. So working in these units has been considered a matter of pride. After the Connaught Place encounter on 31 March, 1997, in which two businessmen were killed by the team of the Interstate Cell (Crime Branch), all senior officers who were operating this unit, including the Commissioner of Police, faced backlash and were transferred. The morale of the unit was very low. The command of the Delhi Police Commissioner was taken over by T.R. Kakkar, who then handed over the command of the Crime Branch to Karnal Singh in May 1997. Most of the police officers of the Interstate Cell (Crime Branch) were transferred out. Only a skeleton staff was available. Therefore, Karnal Singh, DCP, made up his mind to take me on transfer to head the Interstate Cell (Crime Branch), Delhi Police. In May 1997, he got my transfer done from CP, Delhi and expressed his confidence in me. Freedom was also given to select my team independently, due to which I got a team of reliable and hard working officers transferred to the Interstate Cell (Crime Branch).

Uphaar Cinema Tragedy

The Interstate Cell was not yet fully constituted when, on 13 June, the Uphaar Cinema tragedy took place, in which 59 people lost their lives. The owner, Sushil Ansal, etc. did not join in the police investigations. Moreover, their whereabouts were not known. The investigation of the Uphaar case was handed over to the crime branch, which was being done by ACP Jaipal Singh. There was no news of the Ansal brothers; possibly they were hiding in Mumbai.

A special team was constituted, consisting of Alok Kumar, Additional DCP, Pramod Kushwaha, ACP and myself posted as ACP, ISC, to trace the Ansals in Mumbai. After hard work of about 10 days on the basis of mobile phone data analysis, on 22 July, 1997 Sushil Ansal and Pranav Ansal were arrested in Mumbai and handed over to Jaipal, ACP, who was the chief investigator in the Uphaar Cinema incident. Since it took a long time in Mumbai, I went to Karnal Singh's office and asked him to permit us rest for a day or two.

Tasked to Rescue Kidnapped Child

I entered his office and saluted. Karnal Singh, while talking to someone on the phone, gestured towards the chair and signalled to me to sit. He put the receiver on the cradle of the phone and commended me for the job done.

Karnal: You and your team have done an excellent job. You know that there was great pressure from all quarters.

Ravi: Thank you, sir.

Before I could ask for rest for a day, Karnal continued: Sorry Ravi. I understand that your entire team needs some rest, but there is another case where you and your team is urgently required. Where is your team?

Ravi: They are outside your office, sir.

Karnal took the intercom and asked the PA, "Look, Ravi's team is standing outside; send them in." The team entered the office. Karnal Singh got up from his chair, congratulated the team and shook hands with the entire team.

Karnal, while sitting in the chair, addressed the team members, saying, "You need to immediately contact Ajay Kumar, ACP (heading the Anti-Extortion Cell), at RK Puram and assist him. In fact, a schoolboy was kidnapped forcibly from the Golf Link area. We have to solve this case and recover the boy unharmed. Had it not been such an emergent situation, I would have given you some leisure time."

The team started to stare at me.

Ravi (addressing the team members): Okay, you meet me at ISC, Chankyapuri; I will follow you.

However, it took about two months following the successful rescue of the child from western Uttar Pradesh to wrap up the investigation in Delhi, Uttar Pradesh and Himachal Pradesh.

Meanwhile, on 1 October, 1997, two bombs exploded and one live bomb was recovered in Sadar Bazar, and two bombs exploded in a train near Sahibabad, UP. Previously, there were several other blasts in Delhi, Haryana, Punjab and UP.

□

2
Simultaneous Explosions in Delhi and UP

Office of Gyanendra Singh Awana, ACP, Crime Branch, 1 October, 1997 at about 5:30 p.m.

A meeting was going on among the 1982 batchmates regarding the decision to organise an annual get-together party. Jai Kishan, Somendra Pal Tyagi and Gyanendra Awana, including myself were present.

Gyanendra: "Which venue will be suitable for the party?"

Jai Kishan: "I have visited two to three venues, but they are very expensive; we can't afford that."

Gyanendra: "Try to take the area SHO in loop."

Jai Kishan: "I did that. SHOs were with me. But you know the owners of the venue are crooks. They were deliberately asking for an amount that could not be negotiated."

Gyanendra: "Can the G.O.'s mess on Alipur Road serve as a suitable venue?"

Somender interrupted: "*Yaar* (friend), it might not be a convenient location for many of us, so it may not be the ideal choice."

"Hmmmm," all said together.

Jai Kishan: "Alright, let me give it another shot in the Karol Bagh area. And remember, as usual, Deshwal will be arranging the liquor."

"That's very nice of him," Gyanendra responded.

Meanwhile, as tea was being served, my driver, Ramswaroop, entered the office.

Ravi (on noticing Ramswaroop's entry): "*Arey Ramswaroop chalte hain yaar, chai to pi lene de ghar jaane ki kuchh zyada hi jaldi lagti hai*?" (Ramswaroop, you're always in a rush to get home. Allow me to enjoy the tea.)

Ramswaroop: "*Ke ghar janab ghar to ja liye yo bumb phaadva jaan de hai? Bhasudi hogi ek aur*." (Let's not discuss going home for now. We can head there when the bomber gives us the green light.)

I quickly came realise that another explosion had occurred elsewhere.

Ravi: "*Ab kahan phat gaya*?" (Where did it explode?)

Ramswaroop: "Sadar Bazar Market *mein, do phat gaye*?" (Two bombs exploded in Sadar Bazar.)

I set aside the tea and said, "*Pili yaar chaaye ab to khana bhi naseeb nahin hoga*." (Forget the tea; it looks like we won't be able to have dinner either.)

In the meantime, the WT set held by my driver Ramswaroop flashed a message.

Control room: "Juliet 4 (my call sign), Juliet 50 calling (Control room call sign)."

Ramswaroop: "Carry on, sir."

Control room: "Juliet 4, contact Juliet 1 (DCP Crime Call Sign) in his office without delay."

Ramswaroop: "Roger sir!"

I took the landline phone and contacted DCP (Crime), Karnal Singh.

Ravi: "Sir, I am in PHQ. I am coming to your office."

I put the phone on the cradle and left the office, waving my hand to the batchmates.

Blast Site

I entered the office of Karnal Singh and gave a salute. Rajendra Singh Ghumman, Additional DCP, Railways, Delhi was also present in the office. They, as I entered, jumped out of their chairs and immediately rushed out of the office to leave in Karnal Singh's ambassador car. My vehicles followed behind. On the way, we discussed the ongoing menace of bomb blasts in Delhi and adjoining states. During discussion, it also transpired that similar bombs had exploded on 14 March, 1997, somewhere in Jalandhar, and that after a gap of about three months, another blast took place on 20 June, 1997, in Punjab. To find out the details of those blasts, Karnal Singh directed Rajendra Singh Ghumman to visit the site and obtain the details from SSP, Jalandhar. Moreover, I was asked to revisit and collect fresh details of the bomb blast in Delhi and Haryana.

Meanwhile, we reached the spot, 12 Tooti Railway Bridge, Sadar Bazar, Delhi. The local police were also present. The spot was guarded by them. At the spot of the damaged tableau, a participant of a religious procession (Agarsen Jayanti) was standing. Inside and around the tableau, blood and *prasad* lay scattered. It transpired that a bomb had exploded in the hand of an artist who was playing Kevat (a character from the *Ramayana* epic). He was injured grievously along with others. The injured were shifted to a nearby hospital.

Another bomb had exploded under a table where the fruits and *prasad* were kept for distribution to the public, who had come to see the procession, as well as to the artistes participating in the procession. During the precautionary search, one live bomb was also detected in the same vicinity. The live bomb was diffused by the police. A tin container, a metal file cap, a cast iron shell with lid, improved explosive mixture consisting of potassium permanganate, potassium nitrate, sugar, almunium powder, black colour powder with iron rivets, were used as missiles in the IED. A case at PS, Sadar Bazar, Delhi was registered regarding this incident and investigation was taken up by the local police.

The bombs exploded within an interval of five minutes at 5:15 p.m. A total of about 30 people were grievously injured. Local inquiries also revealed that some devotees were also distributing *prasad* to the artistes who were taking part in the procession. The bomber posing as a devotee handed over a box containing the bomb to the artiste playing the role of Kevat.* As soon as the bomb was presented to Kevat, the bomb exploded and there was every possibility of the bomber getting injured in that blast.

Meanwhile, my team of Interstate Cell (Crime-Branch) had also reached the spot. They were directed to immediately rush to the hospital to gather details of the incident, interview the maximum number of the injured and find out surreptitiously if the bomber had been injured in the incident, since the bombs exploded within a short span of time.

On the spot, a message from the Police Commissioner was received on the wireless set for Karnal Singh to attend an emergency meeting with respect to the blast at the police headquarters. From the spot, Karnal Singh proceeded to the police headquarters after directing me and my team to remain present at the Interstate Cell, Chanakyapuri till the meeting was over.

ISC, Chanakyapuri, 10 p.m.

A brief was being taken from the officers who had gone to interview the injured. Meanwhile, another message was received from the Crime Control room regarding the bomb blast in the *'Golden Express'* train near Sahibabad, UP. At the same time, the telephone bell also started to ring. I picked up the phone and responded.

Ravi: "Hello, *Jai Hind*, sir."

Karnal (on the other side of the phone): "Ravi, have you received information about the bomb blasts in Sahibabad, UP, on the '*Golden Express*" train?"

Ravi: "Yes, sir, I just received that message."

Karnal: "You and your team leave the office and gather maximum details from the blast site. I will be arriving at your office early tomorrow morning to evaluate the situation."

Ravi: "Okay, sir, *Jai Hind!*"

Inspector Rajendra Bhatia (with a smiling face): "Let's go, sir. Now it seems we'll have to stay here for the next 10-15 days."

Constable Vinod: "Sir, why are we concerned about the UP case? Let UP Police handle their work."

Another officer: "Yes, sir, we have our own issues to deal with."

Ravi (smiling, got up from his chair): "Alright, we'll decide whose issue it is, later. For now, we need to follow the orders."

Harbir, ASI (sarcastically): "Vinod, your home is in that area. You can go home; we'll handle this case."

By that time, I alongwith Inspector Rajendra Bhatia, ASIs Harbir Singh, Ramesh Sharma and other team members had come down and left the office in a Tempo Traveller and one Gypsy.

It was late at night; it must have been around 1:00 a.m. when we reached Sahibabad at the bomb blast site. Senior officers of the Uttar Pradesh Police, FSL team and crime team had also reached the spot and were supervising the investigations. In that incident, two people had died and more than 20 were injured. The injured had already been shifted to the hospital. On inquiry, it was found that there were two blasts in coach number S-3 at around 8:22 p.m. last evening, when the train crossed pillar number 13/37 and was moving ahead of Sahibabad station. On further inquiry, it was discovered that after the bomb blast, when the train stopped, an unexploded bomb was recovered in the general coach under seat number 71. However the bomb exploded when the general coach was removed from the train and in which, two persons were injured. An Australian and a Japanese citizen were also among the injured; later, both of them succumbed to their injuries. Coach number S-3 was in a mutilated state. The quantum of blood and scattered damaged belongings like shoes, slippers, bags, eatables, etc. told the story of the impact of the blast and its aftermath.

It was being debated if a group of two or three persons were involved in the incident, out of which a young man of about 19 years of age, wearing a checked shirt, spoke a little bit of English. The Uttar Pradesh Police had taken a witness to the incident with them to help them in getting the portrait of the suspects made. In the evidence collected by the police from the spot, an iron disc, some pieces of pipe and other evidence like traces of explosives, blood samples, etc. were collected. Initially, a case was registered at PS, GRP, Sahibabad, UP. After gathering the required details and conducting inquiries on the spot, my team came back to Interstate Cell, Chanakyapuri at 5:30 in the morning and fell down to rest in their respective rooms.

□

3

Commissioner T.R. Kakkar's Trust in the Crime Branch of Delhi Police

The Special Cell was formed for the prevention of terrorist activities and the investigation of terror-related cases. It also works in tandem with Central Intelligence Departments (Ministry of Home Affairs, GoI). There was no clue about the bomb blasts that had been taking place continuously in Delhi and the National Capital Region since December 1996. Till then, several people had been killed and injured. Delhi police was not achieving any success in that regard. Due to this, an atmosphere of panic prevailed all over Delhi. Anger and mistrust in the police lay spread among the people. Police arrangements were increased from place to place in Delhi.

The Commissioner of Police of Delhi, T.R. Kakkar, was under a lot of pressure. Back-to-back meetings in PHQ, MHA, and District were going on. In such an exclusive meeting, the Commissioner of Police at PHQ, summoned Karnal Singh, DCP, Crime.

Kakkar: "Karnal, the prestige of the Delhi Police is at stake. Special Cell, with the help of the Intelligence Bureau, is doing their job and investigating these cases, but I want you to put all your resources at work independently and work out these cases as soon as possible."

Karnal: "Sir, my boys are already into it. I tasked ACP Ravi Shanker's Interstate Cell for that."

Kakkar: "Is he the same chap who solved the Tarun Puri kidnapping for ransom case? Uphaar cinema case?"

Karnal: "Yes, sir, I think that earlier, when he was posted as ACP (Operations) in the north-west district prior to his posting in the Crime Branch, he was gathering details of the previous blasts that had occurred in the NCR region."

Kakkar: "Oh, I see! Okay, take it seriously and brief me daily about the progress."

Karnal: "Sure, sir! Is there any information or clue with IB (Intelligence Bureau)?"

Kakkar: "They are totally blank. Not only IB, but even all the Central and state agencies are clueless."

Karnal: "Okay, sir, I would like to take your leave. Hope for the best; we will leave no stone unturned to solve these cases."

Shahidi Khalsa Force Owns Responsibility for Blast; 2.10.1997, 8:00 a.m.

While I was sound asleep in the rest room of my office, the mess boy entered. Initially, he attempted to wake me up by calling out, but when that had no effect, he softly nudged my leg.

Mess boy: "Sir, sir."

Ravi: "Bahadur *kya* problem *hai, thoda chain lene de*?"

(Bahadur, what's the issue? Can you let me have some peace? I need some rest.)

Mess boy: "Sir! DCP sir has arrived at the office."

Karnal: "Bahadur, no problem; let him rest. I will come later."

On hearing his voice, I came out of the restroom.

Ravi: "Good morning, sir. Apologies; we actually arrived at 5:30 a.m."

Karnal: "No problem, take your own time. I will come after lunch.".

Ravi: "No, no, sir. Please give me 15 or 20 minutes and I

will be ready. Will rest later."

Karnal: "Feel free to take your time. In the meantime, I will complete the morning briefing for Commissioner of Police and Additional Commissioner of Police, B.K. Gupta."

Approximately fifteen minutes later, I got ready and joined Karnal Singh. By that time, he too had concluded his briefing session with the Commissioner of Police and the Additional Commissioner.

Karnal: "Ravi!!! Last night, an organisation called Shahidi Khalsa Force claimed responsibility for the explosions by informing *Dainik Jagran* newspaper over the phone. Have you ever heard about this organisation before? I personally haven't heard of this group's name."

Ravi: "No, sir, I'm not familiar with this organisation either. It appears to be either a fictitious organisation or a recently established one. We can cross-check with the Central Intelligence Agency to confirm."

Karnal: "They also do not have any idea about this."

Ravi: "I think, sir, the culprits are trying to divert our attention."

Karnal: "You are correct. At this stage, since we have no leads on the suspects, our initial approach should be to gather information on Punjab terrorist organisations to understand their modus operandi. Oh, that reminds me, I need to send Rajendra Singh Ghumman to Punjab right away."

Karnal Singh promptly called his operator and instructed him to send a message to R.S. Ghumman, urging him to contact the Interstate Cell (Crime Branch) immediately. After a short while, R.S. Ghumman made the call and Karnal Singh instructed him to leave for Punjab without delay, to investigate the incident and find out if they had previously arrested anyone who used a similar tactic.

Ravi: "Have we traced the location of the phone call?"

Karnal: "No, in fact, the phone call was received on a landline number and the instrument did not have a CLI (calling line identification) feature. Now the Commissioner of Police has requested that all newspapers and media outlets must equip their instruments with the CLI feature."

Ravi: "Yes, sir, that was necessary."

Karnal: "The situation is very serious and it's the festival season. The Commissioner of Police is deeply concerned about this. He has asked me to handle these cases with utmost seriousness. First, let me know the details of the train blast."

I proceeded to provide the details of the train blast, which Karnal Singh had jotted down in his diary.

We then discussed previous blasts that had occurred in Delhi, Haryana and Punjab during 1996-97.

Karnal continued: "Ravi, you mentioned that you worked on these cases when you were posted as ACP (Operations) in the north-west district."

Ravi: "Yes, sir. There have been blasts in Haryana, such as at Sonipat, Rohtak, Panipat and Delhi, since December 1996. I visited most of the blast sites and gathered some details. (I took out a file from a rack in the office and began providing details of the blasts.) In Sonipat, a blast occurred on 28 December, 1996, around 5:20 p.m. at Bawa Cinema where 'Raja Hindustani' was being screened and another blast occurred about five minutes later at a nearby sweet shop."

Ravi (continuing): "In Rohtak, two blasts took place – one at Sabji Mandi and another on Kila Road, Rohtak, on 22 January, 1997, around 5:30 p.m. and 5:50 p.m., respectively. In the Sonipat blast, eight people were injured, while in the Rohtak blast, 17 people were injured. Similar low-explosive IEDs were used in the Rohtak, Sonipat, and Sadar Bazar, Delhi blasts. In Rohtak, a rickshaw-puller provided some physical details about the suspect and a sketch was prepared based on his description. However, the police have no leads in the Sonipat and Rohtak blasts."

Karnal: "What about the Panipat blast?"

Ravi: "In that case, a different modus operandi and IED were used. The blast occurred on a roadways bus on 1 February, 1997. The explosion involved a 2 kg. plastic container as well as potassium chlorate, potassium nitrate and splinters. The impact of the blast was more severe than the Sonipat and Rohtak blasts, resulting in one fatality and around 20 severe injured."

Karnal: "Is it possible that it's a different group, or could it be the same group deliberately using different tactics?"

Ravi: "It's possible, sir."

Karnal glanced at his wristwatch; it was 11:30 a.m. "Alright, Ravi, I need to leave for a meeting with the Commissioner of Police, Special Cell and the Intelligence Bureau. In the meantime, you should take some rest. We can discuss the details later in the evening."

Karnal Singh left the ISC office and I called my driver Ramswaroop to enter the office.

Ramswaroop: "Sir, several calls have come from home..."

Ravi: "Yes, of course, they must have. Okay Ramswaroop, you do one thing: go home and get my food immediately. In the meantime, I'll ask them to pack it."

After Ramswaroop left, I picked up the phone and dialled home. My wife, Sushma, answered: "*Ram, Ram! Ke khabar*?" (Greetings! how are you?)

Sushma: "You tell me. It's been two days and I have no news about you. When I call your office, they beat around the bush and you don't answer your mobile. Do they even pass on my messages to you?"

Ravi: "Yes, I do receive messages. Alright, forget it. I've sent Ramswaroop; please send the food."

Wife: "Okay, I will. Will you come home this evening or even today..."

Ravi: "There's a 50-50 chance. I'm busy right now; I'll let you know later. Okay, bye-bye."

I hung up the telephone.

I contacted Inspector Rajendra Bhatia and authorised the release of the team members with the exception of a small staff which had to report early the following morning. Additionally, I directed Inspector Rajendra Bhatia to attend an evening meeting with the DCP. About an hour later, Ramswaroop served the food, after which I went to take some rest.

□

4
Pursuing Leads: Tracking 'Sun Bearing' Information

At 7:30 p.m., Karnal Singh, DCP (Crime), reached Interstate office and started taking stock of the case from me. Rajendra Bhatia, Harbir Singh and Ramesh Sharma were also present.

Karnal: "Yes! This morning, you were briefing me on the details of the other bomb blasts that occurred in Delhi."

Ravi: "Sir, on the 4 January, 1997, around 5 p.m., two simultaneous explosions rocked GT Karnal Road, Mukarba Chowk, in Delhi. The first explosion took place on a passenger bus en route to Sonipat from Bulandshahar, while the second blast occurred in a jeep that had arrived from Badkhalsa, Sonipat. After disembarking its passengers, the jeep was expected to continue its journey towards Bhalgarh Chowk, Sonipat. These explosions resulted in one fatality and 10 people sustained injuries. The explosives used in both the incidents comprised a mixture of potassium chlorate and sugar."

Ravi continued: "However, sir, what's worth noting is that a bundle of discarded plastic wrappers from automotive ball bearings were reportedly found at the scene. According to the assessment of the Central Forensic Science Laboratory in Delhi, these wrappers might have been used as a cushion for the explosive device. In essence, they could be a component of the bomb."

Karnal: "What brand or manufacturer produced the bearing?"

Ravi: "Sun Bearing."

Karnal: "I believe we should initiate our investigation from this point. Let's go ahead and track down the producer and distributor of this product and inquire about the purpose of retaining the used wrappers. I suggest we pursue this lead without delay."

Ravi suggested, "Rajendra, I believe we should gather some leads from the spare parts market at Kashmiri Gate. Tomorrow morning, please go and find the dealer."

Rajendra Bhatia responded, "Certainly, sir."

Karnal then concluded, "That will be all for today. You may now be excused and we'll resume our work in the morning."

In unison, all the officers expressed their gratitude, saying, "Thank you, sir."

With a smile, Karnal Singh left the office and subsequently, the remaining staff members departed, leaving some personnel behind.

Next Morning

After extensive and diligent efforts, our team successfully located the dealer of the Sun Bearings and collected pertinent information. The dealer responsible for this particular brand was Ms Rohtak Sales and Corporation located in Mori Gate, Delhi. These bearings were primarily used in automobiles and the dealer distributed his products in Sonipat, Panipat, Rohtak and nearby towns where some of the bombings had occurred.

When the dealer was questioned about the purpose of retaining the used wrappers, he revealed that they were part of a promotional scheme. Mechanics received gifts, based on the number of wrappers they returned. Given the possibility of a mechanic, someone working at the workshop, or an associate's involvement, it was deemed necessary to investigate every mechanic and sub-dealer. This was a laborious and extensive task for our relatively small team, raising concern about the duration of our work. However, DCP Karnal Singh assured me that he would provide additional manpower and requested for a list of officers and subordinates for potential reassignment.

The open investigation approach did not seem promising, so we had to handle this task discreetly, having gained the dealer's trust. Inspector Rajendra Bhatia and his team were assigned the duty of identifying and questioning the technician who had gathered the wrappers but subsequently lost them, as the technician who collected the wrappers was unlikely to be the one who used them. There was a possibility that someone else had collected them and another individual, perhaps a colleague or an acquaintance, had utilised them. This required highly astute interrogation of the individuals involved, a task I was confident Rajendra and his team would handle adeptly.

Despite the inherent ambiguity of this endeavour, it was imperative to persevere. We had very few leads apart from a sketch of the suspect, created based on information provided by a rickshaw-puller in the Rohtak bomb blast case. We needed to concentrate our efforts on scenarios where even a one per cent chance of success existed, as that one per cent could potentially evolve into a hundred per cent. As the saying goes, '*Himmat-e-marda, maddad-e-khuda*' (if you make the effort, God will help), we took the leap.

On 4 October, 1997, ASI Ramesh Sharma reached the dealer's location at Mori Gate.

ASI Ramesh Sharma: "Sureshji (manager at dealer's shop), we require your assistance."

Suresh: "In what context, sir?"

Ramesh Sharma: "Regarding the bombings that occurred in Delhi, we need your support for the next five to six days."

Suresh: "How can we be of help, sir?"

Ramesh Sharma: "We will approach every dealer and workshop. Bring one or two of your employees along and gather the gifts you provide in exchange for wrappers received from the mechanics. While distributing the gifts, we will attempt to identify the suspect."

Suresh: "Sir, the owner is on his way, so it would be best if you speak with him. Whatever he decides, we will comply."

In the meantime, the business owner, Mr. Patel, arrived at the store and received a briefing from ASI Ramesh Sharma.

Mr. Patel: "Certainly, why not? We are prepared to assist in any way you require and this will also promote our business. (Laughs and turns to his servant) How many gifts do we have, Chhotu? Pack all the gifts, and Suresh, you should accompany Rameshji as well as a senior corporate representative needs to be present."

With all the gifts loaded into the Tempo Traveller, Suresh and Ramesh Sharma set off for Sonipat.

Inspector Rajendra Bhatia, along with the rest of the team, promptly travelled to Sonipat, where they led the operation with the sub-dealers. They devised an action plan during a discussion and acquired a comprehensive list of all the workshops. Thanks to a friend of ASI Ramesh Sharma, a suitable location for the team to stay was secured and the operation was to commence the following morning.

From 5 October, 1997 to 10 October, 1997, the team engaged with over 350 mechanics operating in workshops across Sonipat, Panipat, Rohtak and the surrounding areas, but failed to identify any suspects.

□

5
Coordinated Bus Explosions

10 October, 1997

Inspector Rajendra Bhatia and ASIs Harbir Singh and Ramesh Sharma met me to review the outcomes of the exercise conducted in Sonipat, Panipat, Rohtak, etc.

Rajendra Bhatia expressed concern: "We have contacted over 350 mechanics so far, but gathered nothing. This sounds like an activity that is futile. It is quite difficult to find the offender in the absence of a specific lead and there is a significant likelihood that the suspect is one of the 350 people we have questioned."

I responded, "Bhatiaji, I can understand. Nevertheless, it's crucial to collect information and conduct investigations because we can't predict when we might encounter data that could eventually be connected to someone we've interviewed."

Harbir ASI jokingly questioned, "Certainly, sir. Now, please advise us on the next step. Should we proceed with the survey at Shamli and Baghpat in UP where these bearings are also supplied?"

I suggested: "Let's move on and talk to DCP."

I, along with my team, arrived at the DCP's office at PHQ to discuss the further strategy.

Karnal inquired, "How are things progressing?"

I explained: "Sir, we've interviewed more than 350 mechanics, but none of them provided any leads. However, we can explore the criminal records at the pertinent police station to verify if there's any history of criminal activities among them?"

Karnal agreed, "Indeed, I concur. Additionally, we may appoint some clandestine sources there in an effort to collect information using human intelligence." Continuing, Karnal added, "Ravi, besides this, we should also consider tracing the telephone number from where the calls were made by the suspect to the newspapers. So we need to collect and analyse the STD booth record."

Expressing my concern, I stated, "Sir, I'm apprehensive because I believe MTNL doesn't monitor local phone conversations. Hence, how beneficial would this information be for our investigation?"

Karnal clarified: "Indeed, you're right that they don't retain records of local calls. Nevertheless, we should retain this information for potential future use..."

I proposed an alternative, "Certainly, one avenue to explore is the possibility that the perpetrator made calls to PTI and *Dainik Jagran* from an STD booth in a nearby UP district, like Ghaziabad, Noida, or Sahibabad, when claiming responsibility for the 1 October, 1997 blast, following the bombings in Delhi's Sadar Bazar and Sahibabad on a train. In such a scenario, identifying the booth is feasible, as every call from outside Delhi to a Delhi telephone number is categorised as an STD call, generating a record retained by the telephone exchange of the originating booth. Additionally, there's the potential that the culprit may have simultaneously contacted another person from that STD booth. This suggests there is still room for one more investigative step."

Karnal agreed, "I am aware of your intentions. Moreover, we should also search these numbers in Mobile Service Provider records."

I acknowledged, "You're absolutely correct, sir. We should get that information right away. If it indeed happened, it could be a highly significant development in our investigation."

With a sense of urgency, I addressed Harbir Singh, "I

am drafting a letter to the concerned BSNL office and mobile service provider. Tomorrow morning, you please personally deliver this request and also apprise them of the urgency of the case to get the details as soon as possible."

Harbir Singh asked, "What about the survey of Sun Bearing in Shamli and Baghpat, sir?"

Addressing the DCP, I suggested, "Sir, I think it would be prudent to temporarily suspend the survey as the telephone record appears to be of greater importance. Furthermore, we require additional manpower for a more comprehensive investigation. Sir, may I inquire about the status of my request for the officers to be transferred to the ISC?"

Karnal reassured, "The transfer request has obtained CP's approval. If there's been any oversight, please remind me as I thought the officers had already reported to you. Nonetheless, I will look into it and you can expect to have the officers with you by tomorrow."

I apologised, "I sincerely apologise."

Three simultaneous explosions occurred in buses at 8:10 p.m.

Meanwhile, the DCP operator entered the room and saluted before informing, "Sir, I regret to inform you that there have been three simultaneous explosions in buses: the first at Kingsway Camp at 7:35 p.m., the second at Sakti Sthal at 7:50 p.m. and the third at Chatta Rail at 8 p.m. The Commissioner of Police for Delhi is en route to the blast sites and he has requested for your presence there as well."

Karnal expressed frustration, "*Isne toh hadh hi kar di yaar! Aatank macha rakha hai! Chalo Ravi! Aap bhi mauka par pahooncho* team *lekar.*" (The bomber has unleashed terror and chaos across Delhi. Ravi, I need you and your team to accompany me to the explosion sites immediately.)

I addressed Ramesh Sharma, "You stay behind, Ramesh and make inquiry at each workshop you visited earlier. Check if any of their employees or mechanics were absent during the time of the explosions. If you find any such individuals missing, gather information about their whereabouts and report back to me."

We left the office for a comprehensive site inspection, examining each of the bomb blast sites sequentially. Local law enforcement people had swiftly secured and preserved all blast locations, cordoning off the areas and summoning emergency services. The DTC buses at each site bore the marks of destruction with shattered glass, debris and visible bloodstains. Prompt action ensured that the injured were promptly transported to the nearby hospitals.

During our minute-long inspection at each scene, meticulous attention was paid to gather crucial details and evidence. Eyewitnesses recounted their shock and disbelief at the abruptness of the attacks, describing chaotic scenes as individuals grappled with the reality and rushed to aid the injured. The aftermath of these blasts profoundly affected the city's collective psyche, leaving many residents apprehensive about the possibility of further attacks.

Site Inspections

Kingsway Camp

The first bomb blast occurred in a DTC bus at Kingsway Camp, a busy area in north Delhi. Eyewitnesses reported hearing a loud explosion followed by screams and chaos as people tried to evacuate the injured from the bus. Several people were injured in the blast and some of them were rushed to nearby hospitals for treatment.

One witness shared, "I was on my way home from work at about 19:30 when I heard a loud explosion. At first, I thought it was just a tyre burst, but then I saw people running towards a DTC bus. I ran towards the source of the sound and saw that DTC bus route No. 192 ISBT to Nathupura had been blown apart. There was smoke everywhere and several people were bleeding profusely. It was a horrific sight."

Shakti Sthal

The second blast took place at about 19:50 near Shakti Sthal, the *samadhi* (shrine) of our late Prime Minister Indra Gandhi, a tourist attraction in the city. This explosion occurred on another DTC bus route No. 302 ISBT to Khurinji and witnesses described seeing smoke rising and debris flying. Panic ensued as people tried to flee the scene and five persons were grievously injured in the blast.

A bystander recounted, "I was waiting for a bus when I heard a deafening explosion. I turned around and saw that a blast in the DTC bus had occurred and people were screaming for help. It was a terrible sight and I will never forget it."

Chatta Rail, Mori Gate

The third blast occurred at Chatta Rail, Mori Gate, another busy intersection in the city. One person at the scene shared, "I was standing at a tea-stall when I heard a loud explosion at about 20:00 hrs. At first I thought it was a gas cylinder blast, but then I saw people running in panic. I rushed towards the site and saw that a bomb had exploded on DTC bus route No. 622 from RK Puram to Krishna Nagar. There were pieces of metal and glass scattered around. I saw people bleeding profusely. It was a terrible sight and I couldn't believe that something like this had happened in our city."

The Commissioner of Police and DCP Karnal Singh, DCP North, DCP B.S. Bola, myself and other investigating teams of the local police and Special Cell, after visiting the blast sites of Kingsway Camp and Chatta Rail, gathered at Shakti Sthal for a detailed briefing by CP, Delhi, T.R. Kakkar.

CP addressed the team, "Alright, everyone, listen carefully. We need to secure the perimeter and get a visual of the damage. I want you and your team to gather as much evidence as possible. Karnal, I need you to start scouting the area for witnesses or anyone who may have seen something suspicious."

Karnal acknowledged, "Understood, sir. We'll start with the Kingsway Camp site and work our way through the others. We'll document everything we find and collect any potential evidence."

CP took Karnal aside and said, "Look, Karnal, I want you to take the lead on that investigation. The formal investigation will be done by the local police or Special Cell."

Karnal agreed, "Yes, sir, I'll get on it right away."

DCP (North) reported, "Sir, in all the three blast sites, we recovered identical pieces of cast iron cylinders, iron rivets, etc. It looks like it could be the bomb itself."

Karnal noted, "That could be a crucial piece of evidence for our investigation."

Meanwhile, an officer known for his ability to woo senior officers but not for significant contributions reported that he had found a witness who claimed to have seen someone suspicious at Shakti Sthal before the blast.

The officer, here named Patey Khan, reported, "Sir, we've already found witnesses who claim to have seen someone suspicious at Shakti Sthal before the blast. They described a man with a backpack and he seemed to be acting strangely." The senior bosses recognised the importance of this information and instructed him to take the lead on that investigation, gather more information and possibly identify the suspect.

CP instructed, "Good work. I want you to take the lead on that investigation. See if you can get more information and a possible ID of that suspect. Get a portrait prepared at the instance of the witness. By the way, where is that man?"

Patey Khan replied, "Sir? *Abhi to yahin tha mai dekh kar aa ta hoon*." (He was here just a minute ago; where has he gone? Let me check.)

CP directed, "Trace him and produce him before your DCP."

Patey Khan hurriedly left the meeting in search of the witness.

DCP (North) humorously muttered, "*Ab subahtak nahi milega ye ch***.*" (Now he will not turn up till morning, bloody fool.)

CP concluded, "Alright, team. We have a lot of work to do, but I have faith in each and every one of you. Let's work together to bring those responsible to justice."

B.S. Bola, DCP (Special Cell) assured, "Understood, sir. We'll work as quickly and efficiently as possible to gather all the evidence we can."

Karnal added, "I'll continue to scour the area for any other potential evidence."

CP instructed, "Okay. Keep me updated on any new development."

CP left the place and afterwards every DCP started tasking their team.

11 October, 1997; office of ISC

A meeting was underway among the officers of the Interstate Cell (Crime Branch) at Chanakyapuri; DCP Karnal Singh was the head. Inspector Subhash Tandon, Inspector Rajendra Bhatia and other subordinate officers were also present in the meeting to discuss a roadmap to be adopted in order to work out the cases where there was no eyewitness and no clue left by the bomber.

Despite various exercises conducted by our team members and other investigators, such as special cells, local police, etc., the police investigation was not heading anywhere. Intensive hotel checking and field inquiries were also made. During this period, police received several fake calls of bomb blasts, as well as information about the suspects for whom a reward was declared by the police. Under any circumstance, the police had to respond to those calls promptly, causing undue interruption in the police investigation. The entire police force, including law and order staff, investigation staff, and officers and men from the administrative staff who were generally not supposed to be in the field, was on its toes.

Karnal updated, "Ravi!! Situation is getting tenser. Chief Minister, Delhi, Sahib Singh Verma, is after CP; he has his own agenda, best known to him. Yesterday, he called CP, Delhi. CP took me along to that meeting. For the time being, we convinced him and explained to him about the investigation we are doing, but if there is any blast in the future, he will not remain silent."

I acknowledged, "Sir, after all, he is the CM of Delhi and to some extent, he is also answerable to the public. He cannot avoid public questioning by saying that the police are not under him."

Karnal agreed, "Yes, you are right. So, what can we do further? Even the exercise on Sun Bearing is not yielding any results."

I asked, "What happened to that witness Patey Khan was talking about?"

Karnal "Leave it, Ravi. You know his nature. You have to deploy your men to collect intelligence."

Ravi: "Sir."

After the meeting, Karnal Singh left the Interstate office and I conveyed the instructions to the team members for compliance.

The bomber had claimed responsibility for the blasts in the name of the Shahidi Khalsa Force. Inspector Dataram, reporting to the Interstate (Crime Branch), was tasked with scrutinising the interrogation reports of Punjab terrorists. Dataram reviewed the interrogation reports of the accused persons arrested in the 1985 transistor bomb blast cases and other terrorists of Babbar Khalsa International arrested thereafter until 1993. He prepared important notes after a thorough analysis, revealing that most terrorists were either killed or out on bail. The accused out on bail were identified and interviewed in connection with the recent bomb blast, but there was no clue.

On the other hand, my visit to all the prior bomb blast locations in Delhi gave me a vague idea that at least two groups were responsible for these crimes. This conclusion was drawn based on patterns and exhibits gathered from the bomb blast locations.

□

6

Explosions at Rani Bagh Market, Delhi

18 October, 1997, 8 p.m., My Residence

Information about Two Simultaneous bomb blasts at Rani Bagh Market

At approximately 8 p.m., as I prepared to take a bath, a sudden interruption shattered the tranquillity of my evening. Ramswaroop's urgent doorbell echoed through the house, coinciding with the shrill ring of the landline phone. Sushma, my wife, swiftly answered the call.

Sushma: "Hello."

Karnal: "Can I speak to Ravi? Karnal Singh here."

Sushma: "Good evening, sir. (She handed me the cordless phone in the bathroom.) Please hold on; DCP wishes to speak."

Ravi (in a hushed tone): "What's happening here? (to himself) Good evening, sir.

Karnal: "Ravi, get to Rani Bagh Market immediately. I'm on my way there."

Ravi: "Another one! Has a bomb detonated?"

Karnal: "Yes, Ravi, two simultaneously."

Ravi: "Alright, sir. My team and I are on our way there."

(Meanwhile, Ramswaroop entered the house.)

Ramswaroop: "Sir, please talk to DCP. There have been two bomb blasts in Rani Bagh Market."

Ravi: "Just spoke to him. You get ready; I am coming."

My mother, sensing the tension from another room, voiced her concern.

Mother: "*Ravindra ke ho gaya, bhai? Eeb to aaya tha, eeb phir chal pada kisi nokri se ya?*" (Ravindra! You just came and you are leaving again. What happened now?)

Ravi: "*Maa, kuch nahi kar sakta. 2 bomb aur phaat gaye. Jana padega.*" (What can I do, Mom? Two bombs detonated again.)

Mother: "*Satyanash ho iss satyanashi ka. Kye soch rakkhi hai isne, bhai, jaldi pakado isane, nahi to yo bahoot aatank macha dega?*" (May destruction befall this evil-doer. What is he thinking, son? Capture him soon, or he will cause a lot more terror.)

Ravi: "*Ma! Kisne pakadle kuch na pata lag raha. Bas dhool me lath mare raye hain hum.*" (Maa, we're trying our best. In spite of this, we know little about him.)

As I prepared to leave, my two-year-old son and daughters approached me. I gave my son a kiss before heading out.

Priyanka: "Oh, Papa, you never stay at home these days. We are upset with you since you did not keep your word to take us on a holiday."

Ravi: "What can I do, baby? I'm firmly stuck in this situation. We'll make it over the upcoming Christmas break, I swear."

Iteeh: "Papa, the procedure of your cases never ends. However, we have to travel somewhere for the holidays this December."

Ravi: "Okay, I swear. I'm running late, sweetie. We can talk about it later."

Sushma: "The food is ready. Have it before you depart."

Ravi: "Oh, I apologise for being late."

Sushma: "Okay, I am preparing a takeaway and eat the rice and dal while travelling."

Ravi: "Alright, please prepare two! Another one for Ramswaroop."

Sushma packed two lunch boxes and gave them to me. I hurriedly left. While en route to Rani Bagh, I conveyed a message through a wireless set to the duty officer of the

Interstate Cell (Crime Branch), directing Inspector Rajendra Bhatia and Inspector Subhash Tandon to reach the spot with their teams. On the way, I and Ramswaroop, the driver, finished the food by exchanging seats. It took about an hour to reach the spot. The DCP of north-west Delhi, along with the local SHO and ACP of their different units, were present at the spot. Meanwhile, CP, Delhi, DCP Karnal Singh, B.S. Bola and other senior officers also arrived on the spot. Places of occurrence were cordoned off. The injured were rushed to Bara Hindu Rao and Deen Dayal Upadhyay hospitals.

Upon investigation at the site, it was found that two bomb blasts had occurred in the bustling marketplace at 19:40 and 19:50, claiming one woman's life and injuring approximately 28 others. These incidents occurred within a span of 10 minutes, precisely opposite Shop Nos. 859 and 747. The date coincided with the eve of Karva Chauth, a day when married women observe a fast for the long life of their husbands. On that evening, women flocked to artistes temporarily stationed on a footpath to apply *mehendi* (henna tattoo) on their hands and feet. The market was densely crowded and the ensuing chaos left a lasting impact.

This marked the third in a series of low-intensity blasts that rocked the capital in October. Despite the suspected low intensity of the devices, the consequences were severe. Items including pieces of a tin box, rivets, torn black polythene and a tin piece containing powder-like material, debris and blood were scattered across the site.

Subsequent to the incident, the narrative continued with witnesses providing consistent accounts, following the directions and guidelines from senior officers. The standard drill, as per the standard operating procedure, was adhered to.

Follow-up Action

The origin of the telephone calls made by the bomber on 1st October remained untraceable. The subsequent call made to the media during another blast was traced to a makeshift booth at New Delhi railway station. Efforts to obtain telephone booth details from MTNL proved futile due to incomplete billing cycles.

Moreover, on the basis of cast iron shell pieces and unexploded bombs that were retrieved from the scene of the blast, more than 100 samples of cast iron cylinders were prepared and further distributed to local district police, Haryana Police, Punjab Police and bordering areas of western Uttar Pradesh in order to find out if any person had obtained identical cylinders from any factory or moulding unit in their area.

Further, to find out the probable mechanism of the bomb in preparing and detonating the bomb, CFSL (Central Forensic Science Laboratory), Delhi and FSL, Madhuban, Haryana, where the exhibits of the bomb blast cases of Sonipat, Rohtak and Panipat were sent, were contacted to know if there was any similarity with the exhibits seized in the Delhi blast cases. FSL, Madhuban prepared a bomb and gave us a demo of how the bombs were probably manufactured and detonated (details of preparing and blasting are not being given due to security reasons.) This exercise gave an idea of the outfit or organisation that could probably be involved in this series of blasts.

Investigations made on those lines, i.e. modus operandi, showed that the CBI had arrested a gang of terrorists in 1993 in connection with the bombings that occurred on 5 and 6 December, 1993, at Mumbai and six '*Rajdhani Express*' trains, under the leadership of Dr. Jalees Ansari. Abdul Karim Tunda, a specialist in creating IEDs (Improvised Explosive Device, i.e. bomb) by using chemicals openly available in the market, could be involved in those explosions.

In the year 1985, Tunda was making an IED, which exploded in the process and due to that, he lost his left hand. Improvised explosive material (low explosive) comprising potassium chlorate, ammonium nitrate, nitrogen benzoate, potassium permanganate, aluminium powder, sugar and other ingredients was utilised in all bombing attacks. It is crucial to note that a gang working in the Delhi-National Capital Region employed the same method of constructing explosives as Tunda. Similar explosives were found in previous blasts and sulphuric acid was used as the ignition source, leading us to speculate that 'Abdul Karim @ Tunda/Lashkar-e-Toiba' militants were actively involved in these incidents.

While Abdul Karim Tunda had vanished and Dr. Ansari and his crew were in jail, Abdul Karim Tunda had eluded capture and had relocated to Pakistan's Lahore. Police had arrested his brother Abdul Haq during subsequent action in the Hauj Rani neighbourhood of Delhi, in 1993. Our team questioned his siblings about the ongoing blast, but they found nothing.

According to an intelligence assessment, Abdul Karim Tunda was operating a clothing store in Lahore and maintained regular contact with ISI, the senior office-bearer of Lashkar-e-Toiba. Hafiz Saeed, Zaki-ur-Rehman and Khalisthani terrorists, especially the International Sikh Youth Federation (ISYF) led by Lakhbir Singh Rode, were all headquartered in Pakistan. In Pakistan, Tunda was known as Abdul Quddus, while in Bangladesh, he was known as Anwar. He was found to have travelled back and forth from Pakistan to Bangladesh and Nepal in conjunction with terrorist operations. He used to instruct terrorists from various groups in Pakistan on how to make bombs.

We were interested in learning more about Tunda's activities and connections, especially since the explosive material used in the current blast resembled that used in previous attacks that Tunda had been involved in.

□

7

Sinister Plans of Pakistan's ISI and Lashkar-e-Toiba

Pakistan's priority in the early 1980s was Punjab; nevertheless, the Kashmir issue was also on their radar at that time. Various terrorist organisations were active in Punjab. Babbar Khalsa International and the Khalistan Liberation Force were prominently active in Delhi and other parts of India. These outfits were responsible for committing prominent crimes, including killings of VVIPs and kidnappings of Romanian diplomats. After the suppression of Punjabi militancy to a major extent, the ISI felt the need to fill the vacuum. The ISI aided in the creation of numerous insurgent groups in Jammu & Kashmir in the late 1980s and early 1990s. Hence, the ISI started using the terrorist outfits that were active in Jammu & Kashmir in other parts of India. Those terrorist organisations successfully committed engineered terrorist actions and bomb blasts in Delhi and other parts of the country.

With the exception of the terrorist organisation Lashkar-e-Toiba, no discussion of any other is currently warranted because investigation at hand was related to this organisation. The Lashkar-e-Toiba terrorist outfit, initially concentrated only on Jammu & Kashmir; their main target being the secession of J&K from India. But after 1994, the chief of this outfit, Zakiur-Rehman, was given additional responsibility by the ISI to carry out terrorist acts across India.

In the year 1995, this militant outfit decided and hatched a bigger conspiracy to carry out terrorist acts in different parts of India, particularly in Delhi. Abdul Karim Tunda@ Abdul Kudoos@Babaji, who relocated to Lahore, Pakistan from India, following the 1993 train bombings, would provide specific training for manufacturing explosives using widely accessible chemicals. Since then, Zaki-ur-Rehman had been active in launching terrorist strikes across the rest of India, in addition to Jammu & Kashmir, using sleeper cells and cadres of SIMI, Jamait-e-Islami, Ahlehadis and Abdul Karim Tunda's contacts.

It is worth mentioning that in the aftermath of the Babri Masjid's demolition, a considerable number of people from the country fled to Pakistan and received training in training camps. After returning to India, the majority of them became hostile, due to various reasons. But they would never come forward to disclose any information in reference to terrorists or their movements or plans. However, some dedicated individuals proceeded to conduct over-the-ground activities and provide shelter to terrorist organisation modules.

Markaz-ul-Dawa/Lashkar-e-Toiba (LeT)

Markaz-ul-Dawa is the front organisation of terrorist oufit, LeT. The primary purpose of this organisation is to secede Jammu & Kashmir from Indian domination. They used to persuade and propel Kashmiri youngsters into terrorist activities in J&K. Markaz's chief is Hafiz Saeed. Zaki-ur-Rehman is the LeT's chief, in charge of terrorist recruitment and training in training camps in Afghanistan and Muzaffarabad. ISI and the Pak Army assist the organisation. Moreover, Zaki-ur-Rehman was monitoring and handling the operatives and different modules of the LeT setup in India. The commander in charge of launching the terrorists in India is Azam Cheema. After training them, he used to launch militants in India with the assistance of the Pakistan Rangers (Force deployed on Indo-Pak border) and the ISI. Terrorist Azam Cheema, one of the conspirators of 26/11 Mumbai attacks, died under suspicious circumstances in Faisalabad.

Identification-Motivation-Radicalisation

They begin by identifying a soft target who can be easily motivated in the name of distorting the idea of *jihad*. Radical religious leaders would then brainwash the individual by giving *takrir* in *masjids* under *markaz* after *namaz*. They also used to teach them that anyone who doesn't engage in *jihad* will end up in *dozakh* (hell) and that those who don't follow Islam or pray to Allah are *kafirs*, including Jews, Hindus and Christians. They must wage war on them (*jihad*). They used to radicalise them repeatedly to indoctrinate them as *Hadisi*, *Asani*, *Kafirs* and *Jihadis* and also explained that earlier *jihad* was done with swords, but the time has changed and now *jihad* will be done with bombs, pistols and bullets, and if the person dies while doing *jihad*, the death will be easier and peaceful and the person will find a place in *jannat* (heaven) and will get 72 *hoors* (extremely beautiful women) there. They insisted that nobody should be aware of their mission because if the police were to learn about it, the *kafirs* may kill them. They delivered extremely provocative lectures. They were always opposed to the TV culture and greatly propagated the use of *hijab* by Muslim women along-with certain other restrictions.

Training

After motivation and radicalisation, the recruit would be selected for training. The subject would be trained at their training centres, namely Maskar-e-Toiba, Maskar-e-Akasa of Distt. Kunur in Afghanistan and Maskar-Ummul-Qura in Muzaffarabad (PoK). The following levels of training would be imparted to the recruits:

Daur-e-Aam

Daur-e-Aam is imparted at Maskar-e-Toiba. It is a type of preparatory training in which each subject gets physical and preliminary arms training. Tents are pitched to accommodate the trainees. A mosque, family quarters and training staff quarters are also built there. Trainees are imparted theoretical knowledge in handling Kalashnikov rifles, rocket launchers, anti-aircraft guns, pistols, grenades, etc., supervised by ISI officers, namely Nissar Javed, Amir of Maskar-e-Toiba. Abu Mohsin, arms instructor Abu Zehabi trained people how to lay mines. Abdul Rehman trained them in handling a rocked launcher. Zaki-ur-Rehman, Lashkar-e-Toiba, Pakistan, hailing from Rivala Khurd, Punjab province, with an office (0092-5xxxx63) at Chelabandi, Muzaffarabad, PoK and other leaders of Lashkar-e-Toiba, visit during training and stress to keep the morale high. They give references from the Quran and Hadis and boost their morale. They also cite the names of Mohammad-bin-Qasim, Salauddin Ayubi and Tarik Bin, who adopted *jihad* as their ideal. After completion of this training, some of the recruits are chosen from this group for additional advanced training. The remaining are mostly used as overground workers or as sleeping cells.

Daur-e-Khas

This is a rigorous three-month training programme. Subjects include advanced weapons and raid/ambush tactics, among other things.

For Daur-e-Khas training, they are taken to training camp Maskar-e-Akasa, located in district Kunar, Afghanistan, at a distance of 6 kms. from training centre, Maskar-e-Toiba. Abu Saadh is head of the Maskar-e-Akasa. Each trainee selects the *kuniat* (new name adopted during training) of his or her choice affixing 'Abu' and disregards his original name. Each trainee is provided with a Kalashnikov rifle for three months. They are trained in handling and firing from pistols, Kalashnikov rifles, rocket launchers, machine guns, lobbering hand grenades, rock climbing, judo-karate, boxing, crawling, walking barefoot on hills at day and night, surviving without food for four-five days, a 60-km. road march, sudden attacks, city warfare, etc.

Hafiz Saeed (55/56 trs., 5'8", fair complexion, medium built) r/o Jeddah, Saudi Arabia, financer and founder member of Dawat-ul-Irshad visits the training camp to boost the morale of trainees for *jihad*. Zaki-ur-Rehman and his deputy Abdul Rehman Adakhal also visit the training camp in Afghanistan and stress the need to keep the morale high for *jihad* in Kashmir.

Explosives training, like making bombs with sophisticated and advanced technology, is given by Army officers and making IEDs through locally-available chemicals is imparted by Abdul Karim Tunda @Babaji after the completion of the training period.

Launch in India

After completion of training, the subject is launched in India by Commander Azam Cheema through a pre-identified porous border with Bangladeshi guides, who are well trained in crossing the border. At that time, fencing was not done in many places. Infiltration was usually done through Gilgit, Kargil and the Sialkot border using the Tawi river; Athmukam Muzaffarabad. Jammu & Kashmir side; Bhawalpur, Ziraf, Sriganganagar, Rajasthan side; and Navakot-Bhuj, Gujrat side. During this process, the Pakistan ISI, Army, Rangers, etc. assist them.

However, they predominantly infiltrated Bangladesh by obtaining genuine or fake visas from Pakistan to Dhaka. From there, they used to go to Jatrabadi, where Abdul Karim Tunda (Babaji) had established his base/hideout. Tunda, with the help of local Bangladeshi guides, would launch the terrorists in India. It has been found that terrorists used to infiltrate the Indo-Bangladesh border with the help of local contacts in North Dinajpur, a border district of India, reportedly having a base in Rajshahi, a border district in Bangladesh. They used to adopt the following route to infiltrate the Indo-Bangladesh border:

The bus ride from Dhaka to Rajshahi is about 350 kms. long. The bus ride from Rajshahi to Godagari is 35 kms. 1.5

kms. from Godagari to Farakka via rickshaw. Padma river motor boat (25-km. long river channel crossing). 1.5 kms. on foot from the Farakka riverbank, Kalikapur border and Lal Gola village. By bus, travel 80 and 250 kms. from Lal Gola to Malda or Kolkata, respectively.

Larger conspiracy by LeT and ISI.

The outfit had sent and formed modules in Delhi, western Uttar Pradesh, Dehradun, Malerkotla, Punjab, West Bengal, Mumbai and Hyderabad during 1995-1996. There was no specific intelligence from any intelligence agency regarding this conspiracy that emerged in Pakistan's Lahore in the early 1990s and 1996.

Since December 1996, till 18 October, 1997, these modules have carried out a number of bomb blasts in Delhi, Sonipat, Rohtak, Panipat (Haryana), Ludhiana, Jalandhar (Punjab) and Kanpur (UP), resulting in the deaths of 12 individuals and injury to more than 200.

In Sonipat, the bombs were planted in Bawa Cinema and the front of a sweet shop; in Rohtak, in Sabji Mandi; and at Kila Road in Panipat, in a bus at the bus stand. In these bomb explosions, one person was killed and 49 were injured.

In Ludhiana, two bombs were planted at a railway station; one of them was foolishly taken to the police station, where it exploded; and in Jalandhar, a bomb was planted at the reservation hall. In these blasts, seven people were killed and 15 were injured.

In Kanpur, a bomb was planted in front of Central Dharamshala, injuring six people.

As far as Delhi is concerned, the bombs were planted in busy market buses, in which one person was killed and about 67 were injured. However, some others that were planted did not explode at various locations, either due to a malfunctioning device or for other reasons.

Up until 18 October, 1997, within eight months, there were more than 20 incidents of bomb explosions caused by the modules present in the NCR and neighbouring areas of

UP, Haryana and Punjab. All these IEDs were manufactured with easily available chemicals, such as potassium chlorate, nitrobenzeen, urea, sulphuric acid, sugar, etc. and kept in cast iron cylinders with iron rivets to be used as splinters. Had there been high explosives used by them, the casualties and damage to property would have been stupendous. Since there was no clue about the conspirator or operator in the field to any law enforcement agency, there was always a threat of a blast at any time.

□

8

Explosion Echoes in Karol Bagh Market

26 October, 1997

Two concurrent explosions and one live bomb were detected in Karol Bagh. As the evening unfolded, I found myself in Kinari Bazar, Delhi, accompanied by my wife and sister-in-law for Diwali shopping. After completing our purchases, we were en route to the Jama Masjid police station where our vehicle was parked. It was around 7:30 p.m. when a call came through the Control room on my mobile phone.

Control room: "Sir, *Jai Hind*! There has been no response from your WT set."

Ravi: "Yes, it was malfunctioning, so I had sent it to the workshop. I had informed the Control room about this in the morning. Any messages?"

Control room: "The same message as before, sir."

Ravi: "Now where?"

Control room: "The incident has occurred in Karol Bagh, specifically at Roshan-di-Kulfi sweet shop."

Ravi: "Oh, my, that is a highly frequented market."

Control room: "Yes, sir. A significant number of people are injured. PCR vans and ambulances have already been dispatched for assistance. Additional CP, B.K. Guptaji, Karnal Singh Sahib and other senior officers are en route to the scene."

Ravi: "Very well, I am also en route. If there are any messages for me, kindly convey them to my mobile. Please inform Inspector Rajendra Bhatia and Subhash Tandon to join me with their teams at the incident site."

Control room: "Understood, sir."

Ravi: "Sushma, I am arranging a taxi for you to leave. I need to proceed to Karol Bagh, where explosions have occurred."

Sushma: "I am aware. I overheard your conversation. So, you won't be coming home tonight either."

Ravi: "My apologies, dear."

I organised a taxi for them and proceeded towards Karol Bagh. By 8:20 p.m., I arrived at Karol Bagh, where all the senior officers of Delhi police were present at the site. ACP Karol Bagh was briefing the situation to the senior officers present.

ACP Karol Bagh: "Sir, as you can see, regular announcements are being made. Heavy patrolling is in progress and just half an hour ago, the dog squad also conducted checks. Despite these precautions, the incident occurred. What more can we do?"

Ajay Kashyap, DCP (Central): "I concur. Detection is the most effective means of prevention. Sir, do we have any information about the perpetrator?"

Karnal: "Ajay, we currently lack intelligence regarding these incidents. We are relying on the available clues from the scene. Bola (DCP, Special Cell) may have some information as they are connected with IB. Nevertheless, we have deployed our confidential sources, but as of today, we have not obtained any credible information."

Ajay Kashyap looked at Bola.

B.S. Bola: "Sir, a specific group of individuals are under observation. We are also interrogating those recently apprehended in a separate case to unravel the mystery."

Meanwhile, Inspector Rajendra Bhatia and Inspector Subhash Tandon reported that they were instructed to proceed to RML and Ganga Ram Hospital for further inquiry from the injured and subsequently report to ISC.

It was revealed that the initial bomb explosion occurred at 7 p.m. at Roshan-di-Kulfi, followed by another in Gaffar Market near a famous *chhole-kulche* shop five minutes later. SI Sandeep Gupta, along with H.C. Makkhan Singh and other police officials, who were on patrol duty near the Hardhyan Singh Road and Ajmal Khan Road crossing around 7 p.m., heard the explosion and promptly arrived at the scene, namely Roshan-di-Kulfi. The SHO and ACP also reached the location. Numerous individuals suffered injuries in the blast and substantial damage was inflicted on the shop. The injured were transported to Dr. Ram Manohar Lohia Hospital and Sir Ganga Ram Hospital for medical attention. Kumari Sonia, daughter of G.S. Arora, a resident of Vasant Vihar, was declared dead by the doctors. The area was cordoned off and subjected to inspection.

One iron disc and pieces of seamless pipe, torn pieces of polythene bag and iron rippets were recovered inside the shop. In front of the shop, another bomb was defused. From the site, one litre of Nerolac paint container and pieces of newspaper were recovered. Ashok Kumar Soni, owner of the shop Roshan-di-Kulfi, informed that at about 7 p.m., he was present in his shop. At that time, there was a big rush of customers and eatables were served by the staff to the customers. Suddenly, an explosion took place and the entire shop was filled with smoke. Several people sustained injuries.

I noticed two significant substances at the crime scene – a seamless pipe with a disc attached to it and some pieces of Urdu newspapers.

Ravi (engaged in a discussion with B.K. Gupta and Karnal Singh): "Sir, the train blast in Sahibabad yielded the same type of seamless pipe and disc. Furthermore, during my previous visits to all the police stations to scrutinise the evidence collected by the investigating officers in each bomb blast at Delhi, I observed that some newspapers were attached to the container or shell of the bomb. The remnants of these newspapers were confiscated during the investigation."

Karnal: "Okay, I'd like to examine those. With their assistance, we may make further progress."

Ravi: "Sir, tomorrow, I will have those pieces of newspapers photographed and show them to you. But what could be the reason for wrapping the newspapers?"

Karnal: "In my opinion, they might be wrapped to distinguish the top and bottom parts of the IED to prevent any mishap. During the planting of the IED, tilting it upside down could trigger a chemical reaction, leading to the explosion of IED."

Ravi: "You're correct, sir. Let's explore this avenue as well."

After that, Additional CP briefed the team and provided some instructions before leaving the scene.

□

9

Media's Critical Dance

27 October, 1997

All newspapers and the dynamic digital media landscape were vehemently critical of the Delhi police. The reports conveyed:

Delhi Chief Minister, Sahib Singh Verma, who was attending a wedding, hurried to the hospitals upon learning of the news. Expressing his anger, the Chief Minister remarked that repeated blasts had turned the national capital into a 'jungle raj' and the Delhi government could no longer remain a passive observer. He pledged to convene a meeting with top police officials and meet the Union Home Minister, emphasising that accountability and performance of the Delhi Police would see improvement if the Delhi government were also given control over law and order. Verma stressed that it was high time for the Central Government to acknowledge this reality.

Even at the Centre level, there was significant concern. Prime Minister I.K. Gujral visited the hospital to meet those injured in the explosion. Pressured by Delhi's Chief Minister Sahib Singh, the Home Ministry summoned Delhi Police Commissioner T.R. Kakkar for a thorough review. Kakkar, who was in the United States attending a police chiefs' conference when the blasts occurred, had to address the serious concerns raised by the Home Ministry.

News reports exhibited strong criticism to the criminal

justice system, intelligence agencies and counter-terrorism organisations.

In the National Capital Territory (NCT), a relentless series of bomb blasts sent shockwaves across the country, leaving citizens and authorities grappling with the aftermath. Newspapers criticised the glaring deficiencies in the nation's intelligence apparatus and law enforcement, attributing the attacks to a failure in preventive measures.

In the ominous shadow of recent attacks, a political analyst declared: "It's crystal clear that our intelligence and law enforcement have faltered. These attacks, ominous and devastating, should never have happened. Over the past year, a relentless wave of assaults on civilians has unfolded, striking with chilling precision. It exposes the glaring weaknesses in India's counter-terrorism endeavours, painting a grim picture of our national security."

A security analyst, adding a sense of urgency, remarked, "This group operates with alarming ease on our soil, thriving on the disjointed efforts of intelligence agencies and the police. We're in desperate need of a synchronised and aggressive strategy to combat this escalating terrorism threat. The clock is ticking and the stakes have never been higher."

The tense situation in the NCT persisted, with heightened security measures and a wary public. Despite government assurances of decisive action, scepticism lingered regarding the effectiveness of measures to prevent future attacks.

Expressed by a different political analyst, the sentiment underscored the necessity for decisive action from the government. "It's imperative that the government takes tangible measures to tackle the underlying causes of terrorism and fortify our intelligence and law enforcement capabilities," the analyst urged. "Failing to do so will result in the perpetuation of these attacks and the public will bear the brunt of the consequences."

Evening Meeting in ISC; Inquiries from Injured Persons in Hospitals

One injured Vikas revealed that on 26 October, 1997, he, together with his family members and neighbours, went to Karol Bagh for shopping. While at Karol Bagh, they went to Roshan-di-Kulfi, Ajmal Khan Road. At Roshan-di-Kulfi, there was a rush for seats, which necessitated some waiting. After some time, a seat fell vacant in the third row on the left side, probably at the second or third table. The seat had been vacated by a young boy aged about 19 years with a permanent cut mark on the cheek. He had finished having *golgappas.* After four or five minutes that young boy vacated the seat and while he and the party had taken their seats, a blast occurred. This caused injuries to him, his mother, his wife and daughter and many others. Smt. Sushma Narula lost her legs in this blast.

More than that, a woman shopper, namely Sonia Arora, r/o Vasant Vihar, was killed and 33 others were injured.

When the first explosion took place, 40 to 50 people were seated.

The second explosion occurred in close proximity to a *chhole-kulche* stall in Gaffar Market, but fortunately, it resulted in minimal damage as the crowd that had gathered had recently dispersed. Another witness reported scenes of chaos and confusion as the blasts rocked the area, "There was a loud explosion and people started running in all directions. I saw smoke and dust everywhere," said Sanjay Sharma, a shopkeeper in the market. "It was terrifying."

Ravi (when the description of the suspect and specific identification mark were disclosed by a witness): "Ramesh, we should immediately check with CRO if previously any such criminal with the same identification mark was arrested in any case."

Karnal: "Do it without wasting any time."

The prints of the newspapers seized were laid out for DCP Karnal Singh to inspect.

Karnal: "Ravi, mobilise your team to trace the newspapers' dates, editions and circulation areas."

Ravi: "Subhash, Rajendra (glancing at them, present in the meeting)."

Subhash: "I've got it, sir."

Ravi (handing printouts to Subhash): "Make it quick."

Rajendra: "Consider it done, sir."

Karnal: "Proceed with it. Ravi, stay here."

Karnal: "Ravi!! Additional DCP Rajendra Singh dropped a bombshell. Remember the cast-iron cylinder we sent to Punjab?"

Ravi: "Sir..."

Karnal: "He received Intel from SSP Jalandhar that one Nissar Ahmed and associates linked to Abdul Karim Tunda and Lakhbir Singh Rode of the International Sikh Youth Federation were arrested in Punjab. Same type of cylinders and bomb-making chemicals were found from their possession. The kicker? Nissar Ahmed was released in 1996 and the bombings started soon after."

Ravi: "This is crucial. He's our guy. We need to trace him asap."

Karnal: "Let's wait for the CP's approval. We'll coordinate with IB and set things up in J & K to aid your team."

28 October, 1997, Evening

Inspectors Subhash Tandon, Bhatia, Harbir Singh, Ramesh Sharma and the team arrived at ISC after verifying the newspaper cuttings.

Subhash (while showing the newspaper cutting): "Sir, this is from *Times of India*, but the edition is unconfirmed (shows cuttings). *Navbharat Times* is UP edition because the Delhi edition has different news on the back. This was published in the UP edition."

Ravi: "What about the others?"

Rajendra: "Similarly, we traced the newspapers and editions."

Bhatia continued: "*Punjab Kesari*, UP edition, *Amar Ujala*, UP edition, and *Hind Samachar*, Ambala edition. *Hind Samachar*, Urdu newspaper circulates around 1,000 copies, mainly in Saharanpur, Dehradun, Roorkee and parts of western UP. It's also sold in Ballimaran and Farash Khana, Delhi, besides railway stations and bus stands."

Ravi: "It suggests that bombs might be made in western Uttar Pradesh.

All in unison: "Yes, sir."

Karnal Singh, DCP, walked in and asked, "What's happening, Ravi?"

I briefed him on the newspaper development.

Karnal: "Good, now we focus, especially on western UP."

Ravi: "Sir, even in west UP, we can narrow our search."

Karnal: "How?"

Ravi: "*Hind Samachar* used frequently by bombers has only 1,000 copies in circulation. We can identify subscribers, mainly in Saharanpur and Roorkee and check their backgrounds, any links to Tunda or associates. I'll provide Tunda's associates' dossier for reference."

Subhash: "Sir, there are subscribers in Ballimaran and Farash Khana, Delhi. However, vendors sell newspapers at railway stations in western Uttar Pradesh; can't be identified."

Karnal: "It might be vague, but let's take a chance. What do you say, boys?"

Constable Vinod: "We'll do what you order, sir."

Karnal: "Tighten your belts. When are you sending them, Ravi?"

Ravi: "Sir (interrupted by Rajendra).

Rajendra: "Sir, there's an important case in the High Court tomorrow; I'll leave in the evening."

Ravi: "Oh, Rajendra, no issue!"

Ravi to Karnal: "Sir, let's keep this survey a secret."

Karnal: "How?"

Ravi: "Conduct a survey as a newspaper agent, interview subscribers about their paper choices, etc. I will draft a questionnaire for that so that we could extract maximum personal information from them."

Karnal: "Okay, do it and show it to me."

Ravi: "But sir, have you discussed Nisar's information received from Punjab with the CP? We should prioritise that before the survey."

Karnal: "I discussed it with CP during a review with Special Cell and Intelligence Bureau."

Ravi: "What did he say?"

Karnal: "Special Cell cleverly interfered and convinced the CP to handle it with IB and moreover, they had taken Additional DCP Rajendra Singh from our team to theirs."

Ravi (in vain): "And?"

Karnal: "I resisted, but IB pressured CP by saying that dealing with terrorism is in their charter. CP, under pressure, had to accept."

Ravi: "Sir, *kheer khae bandri* (monkey), *dande khaye reech* (bear)" (The hardworking suffers the punishment and the cunning enjoys the fruits of his labour.)

Karnal: "Nothing can be done now; let's focus on the newspaper survey."

Karnal Singh left the office. It took an hour to prepare the questionnaire. I instructed my staff officer to send it with the morning diary to Karnal Singh for approval. After that, I left the office. The remaining team members gathered in front of the duty officer's office on the ground floor and engaged in a lively discussion.

Vinod (Constable): "*Janab ya to pher pichhwade mein lathi aagi.*" (Sir, it looks like we might face some challenges again.)

Rishi Pal (Constable): "*Teri to jahan ko jave vahi ku mauj hai. Teri to rishtedari hai Saharanpur, 5 ungaliyan ghee mein rahngee.*" (Your influence spreads wherever you go. You have your relatives in Saharanpur; Saharanpur will be in the palm of your hand.)

Ashok, ASI: *Vinod bhai dhayaan rakhiyo barati bhi sath*

mein honge." (Vinod, be mindful; we will also accompany you.)

Subhash Tandon: "Alright, let's all get ready; we have preparations to make for tomorrow."

30 October to 5 November, 1997

A covert mission unfolded as Inspector Rajendra Bhatia and his team ventured into the dark alleys of Saharanpur, UP, to unveil the mysteries concealed within the folds of *Hind Samachar* newspapers. In the shadowy hours, they infiltrated the heart of the distribution network, targeting the place where vendors and hawkers exchanged these newespapers.

Zeroing in on approximately 20 elusive hawkers who peddled *Hind Samachar* in the labyrinth of Saharanpur, the team embarked on a high-stake pursuit. Tracking these shadowy figures led them to the enigmatic subscribers, shrouded in the morning mist. Days turned into nights as the team, like silent phantoms, interviewed these subscribers, extending their inquiries to the unsuspecting neighbours, unravelling the secrets that lurked behind closed doors.

The operation unfolded over a week, casting its net wider into the territories of Saharanpur, Dehradun and Roorkee. More than 650 subscribers fell under the team's intense scrutiny as they delved into incomplete police records and undertook covert field inquiries. Yet, the echoes of success remained elusive. Other hawkers and vendors emerged from the shadows, peddling newspapers openly in bustling markets, bus stands and railway stations. The labyrinth seemed impenetrable, yielding no fruits to their relentless pursuit.

6 November, 1997

As the night skies whispered their secrets, a message from Inspector Rajendra Bhatia signalled the culmination of the operation. In the early dawn, I hastened to Saharanpur, eager to assess the aftermath of the team's intricate dance with the shadows. A somber consensus emerged in the detailed discussion – the survey bore no fruit. Despite the team's unwavering dedication, the case remained a riddle without a clue. A decision was made to close this chapter and retreat to Delhi, granting the exhausted team a respite.

I told the team members: "I know you all must be thoroughly exhausted. Come, let me show you a better place where we can unwind together."

Ashok, ASI: "Sir, leave it; we're in the mood to head home."

Anil Dureja, SI: "Sir, Ashok is right. By the way, where are you taking us?"

Ravi: "Let's head to Kaudiyala. It's a nice place. I'll treat you all to beer and I'll personally cook and serve *pulao* for you. Even I feel like having a beer today." (The team was given a cook and utensils for cooking, when they left to conduct the survey.)

H.C. Vinod: "Sir, with your permission, why not, brother? We'll all go; after all, we'll reach home by evening."

We left for Kaudiyala and on the way, we purchased beer. After crossing Shivpuri, a suitable spot was located and the vehicle was stopped. Noticing some wood lying there, we prepared a temporary wooden stove. I prepared *pulao* for the team members, who enjoyed it with beer. Some songs were sung by H.C. Vinod and others. It was a great time for the team members. However, Inspector Rajendra Bhatia did not consume beer; he left after some time to explore the area along the bank of the Ganga river and hurriedly came back.

Rajendra: "Sir, let's leave this place quickly."

Ravi: "What happened, Bhatia Sahib? You seem troubled."

Rajendra: "Sir, the place where we're having fun is actually a cremation ground and the wood we used for cooking is leftover funeral pyre wood that is brought for burning bodies."

Some team members laughed, while others became serious.

Dureja: "Oh, sir, this is a real predicament. How did you find out, Bhatia sir?"

Rajendra: "While wandering towards the village, I met an elderly villager who asked me if we had made a vow to cook and eat at the cremation ground. I clarified that we were here for a picnic. He then revealed that the area was a cremation ground. Realising the potential conflict with the villagers if they saw us drinking beer there, I decided it was time to leave."

Ravi: "Alright, let's pack up, collect all the empty beer bottles and heed Bhatia Sahib's advice."

Following that, the team swiftly packed their belongings and embarked on the drive back to Delhi. Several team members were dropped off at their homes with instructions to resume work after a day of well-deserved rest.

□

10
Old Delhi as the Pulsating Core of Turmoil!

While the Special Cell focused on investigating the Nissar angle, my objective was to delve into the background of Nissar Ahmed and his associates without disrupting the Special Cell's ongoing operation involving him. To achieve this, I examined the interrogation reports compiled by the Punjab Police. These reports revealed that prior to his 1996 arrest, Nissar Ahmed maintained regular contact with Lakhbir Singh Rode, a high-ranking member based in Canada, of the ISYF (International Sikh Youth Federation) and the nephew of Jarnail Singh Bhindranwale. The ISYF was known to be associated with the pan-Islamic terrorist group, particularly with LeT. There were indications that leaders of ISYF had engaged in discussions with Abdul Karim Tunda, exploring the possibility of joint action.

Nissar was in continuous communication with Abdul Karim Tunda before his imprisonment. Nissar and Tunda first met at a mosque in Pan Mandi, Delhi. According to the interrogation accounts of other Lashkar-e-Toiba terrorists, Mohsin alias Pappu, a Pakistani citizen, was a friend of Tunda and Lakhbir Singh Rode. When Mohsin alias Pappu was in India, he mentioned meeting an elderly man and one Pakistani, namely Hussain, in Pan Mandi, Sadar Bazar. It was further found that they often spoke on the phone with their boss in Pakistan. Additionally, they always took responsibility for any action they took, either before or right away, to prevent another organisation from taking unfair credit for it.

Since the Special Cell was asked to pursue Nissar's case, the Crime Branch team felt compelled not to take any initiative to conduct any field investigations. Therefore, my team and I started gathering intelligence based on their phone call patterns prior to or after the blast.

To check if the bomber had called anyone in Pakistan or any other phone number in India shortly before or after the calls to PTI and *Dainik Jagran*, a detailed study of the STD booth record was conducted. But at the crucial moment, no such call was recorded.

Old Delhi, especially the walled-city region, was determined to be the epicentre of these blasts after locating the blast sites. The scale of every explosion in Delhi was shown on a map to choose a new course of action.

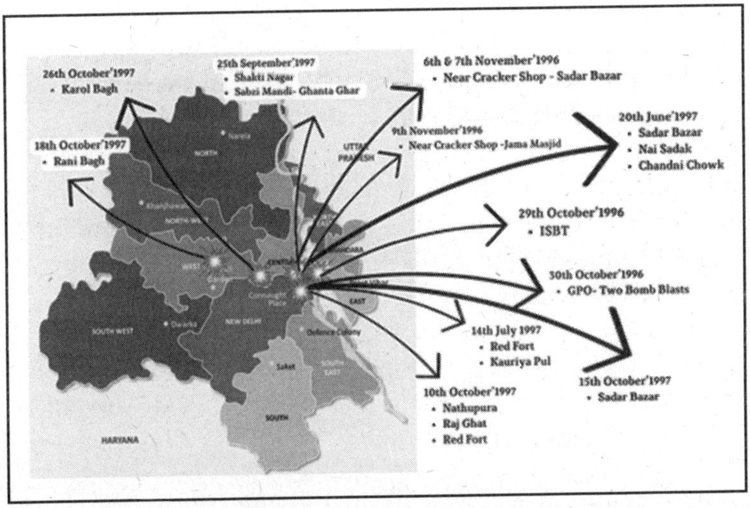

Enquiries from the earmarked area of walled city hotels and guest houses were made and records were collected. The following conclusions were drawn on the basis of the investigation that the Crime Branch had conducted up to that point.

Hypothesis

The majority of explosives were made in western Uttar Pradesh. The analysis and review of newspaper clippings showed that western Uttar Pradesh was the primary location for the manufacture of explosives. The bomber was either a Delhi resident or he came to Delhi with a partially-assembled bomb to reduce risk and the bomb's final assembly was completed close to the blast site, which was either his hideout or where he had been staying on the day of the explosion in a guest house or hotel.

Since the blast's epicentre was in the walled city area, the local police were requested to conduct a door-to-door survey, verify suspects and keep a close eye on both convicted criminals and budding criminals. They also received the bomber's description and a portrait created by the witnesses. To discover the bomber's hiding place, we also developed secret sources in that area. In the event that bombers came entered a hotel, it was imperative to ensure that every individual or group visiting the hotel from the outside did so on each day of the explosion. For this purpose, the records of each guest house in the walled city area were to be obtained and analysed. This was a tremendously difficult assignment that could only be completed with the aid of technical and scientific knowledge. However, DCP Karnal Singh issued orders to DCP (North) and DCP (Central) to gather records of hotels and guest houses for the relevant dates and forward them to my office. Since no technical personnel capable of using computers effectively was assigned to ISC, I made a request to Karnal Singh.

Ravi: "Sir, as we need to devise a programme in this respect, we don't have any technical personnel who could create a computer programme to carry out this activity. Additionally, data entry operators are needed because thousands of names with identical spellings must be entered."

Karnal: "Yes, we must act quickly."

He summoned ACP CRO, Awana to his office and gave him a buzzer.

ACP Awana saluted as he entered the office. "Sir *hukum*," said Awana.

Karnal: "At least three extra computers and data entry operators will have to be delivered right away to the ISC (Crime Branch), along with an officer who can create a programme in accordance with the logic or parameters provided to him."

Awana: "Yes, sir. I have two such computers that can be provided right now and I'll look for one more. Two data input operators and Sandeep Malhotra will report to Ravi by tomorrow."

"Thank you, Awana," said Ravi. Following that, Awana and I left Karnal Singh's office.

ISC, 10 November, 1997

The police stations started sending information about the guest house entries to ISC as directed. Only six to seven police stations were taking this exercise seriously and had sent the necessary records; however, it was also not certain that the records sent by them were complete. Since there were hotels operating without a licence, it was possible that the police station withheld that record out of concern. For my satisfaction, I passed the direction to Subhash to send our men to verify the information that the concerned SHO supplied as well. Meanwhile, two Intel 386 computers were brought by SI, Sandeep Malhotra, but these had limited hard disc and RAM storage areas. The speed of these computers was very slow. However, we had to accommodate the available stuff. Constable Devender and one more data entry operator also reported from CRO. Rajendra Bhatia was asked to supervise the data input procedure, whereas Subhash Tandon was requested to undertake field investigation and double-check the information that had been given by SHOs. The record was so voluminous that one room was completely filled with guest house records and it took more than 15 days to feed the record.

Five People Identified for Visiting Hotel on Days of Bomb Blasts

More than 65,000 entries were supplied into the computer throughout the course of this procedure, which was finished in around two weeks. Sandeep Malhotra created a programme to identify the names of regular people who visited the area on the day of each explosion. According to this exercise, a group of five people who used to stay at a guest house in Chandni Chowk were shortlisted. The guest house was located here and a random watch was maintained on this hotel.

Meanwhile, in the evening of 30 November, 1997, two simultaneous bomb blasts occurred in Chandni Chowk, Delhi that allegedly killed three people and wounded 69 others. As soon as the call was received at ISC, we headed straight towards the hotel to check on the whereabouts of those five people. The squad stopped as it got close to the hotel.

Ravi: "Subhash! Sneak up to the hotel lobby and check the registration to see whether that group has checked in yet or not."

Subhash: "Alright, sir. (Subhash ascended the stairs and quickly returned) Sir, today the same group has checked in, but at present, they are not available in the hotel."

Ravi: "Alright, give the hotel employees your trust and remain there. Send a signal as soon as they arrive."

Subhash walked upstairs with a sub-inspector and after around 30 minutes, Subhash signalled.

The team arrived at the guest house right away and picked them up. All of them were sent to Interstate Cell. Media representatives present at the bomb detonation scene witnessed the Crime Branch's operation. Numerous media representatives were very familiar with me; they began pursuing our vehicles and followed us to ISC. There was a hue and cry all over the media and the Police Department that the Crime Branch had picked up the bomber and the case was solved. However, after detailed questioning of Fayaz Akram,

Suhail, Shaukat and Akhtar, it was discovered that they were all businessmen and residents of Faizabad, Uttar Pradesh. They were all without any involvement. They used to dwell at Chandni Chowk and were regular visitors due to their glass bangle business. By chance, their dates fell on the day of each explosion. All of them were discharged the next morning after receiving the go-ahead from seniors.

Karnal Singh said, "How coincidental was that? Without a doubt, it was a logical exercise," and CP acknowledged this.

Ravi: "Really, it was a great sensation for about six or seven hours. Anyway, sir, do you have any details regarding Nissar? What took place?"

Karnal: "Oh, sure. He was picked up by Special Cell, but he wasn't involved, as I failed to mention."

"Thank God," said Rakesh Dixit. Interestingly, Karnal and I looked at Dixit in a surprised manner.

Ravi: "What's up Rakesh? Is Nissar somewhat related to you?"

Rakesh: "No, sir, it's just that those Special Cell guys were a bit too clever; that's why I responded like that."

Everyone chuckled.

Karnal: "Don't say it like that. If the case had been resolved, both our challenges and the public's distress would have seen some alleviation."

Rakesh: "Sir, you're absolutely right but the information we had was taken from us by them. I was talking about their cleverness."

Subhash: "Rest assured, Dixit, only we can solve the case."

Karnal: "I agree! The spirit is like this. I have complete faith in your team; you can and will succeed. Okay, keep the morale high; anyway, you may take rest tonight."

The team members walked outside the office, talking about Nissar as well. While they were discussing the Nissar episode, I observed that they had forgotten the anguish of the unsuccessful process of about two months when they learned that Nissar, who was identified by our team and was picked up by Special Cell after cleverly manipulating the seniors, was not found involved in the case.

Karnal: "Ravi, did you visit the spot yesterday?"

Ravi: "No, sir, yesterday we were busy with this operation. But today, early in the morning, I went there and after that, I went to inspect the exhibits in the police station."

Karnal: "What's your opinion?"

Ravi: "Sir, did you notice the impact of the blasts and the craters formed in the road in front of shops No. 1848 and 1895? Those were about one foot in diameter and 6 to 8 inches deep. This indicates the use of high explosives, like RDX or PETN. Furthermore, splinters and tin containers (Lactogen and Fargo Mental) were used. The damage was probably done by shockwaves."

Karnal: "I also think so. Either this is some other group or the present group has received the RDX, etc."

Ravi: "Sir, if this is the case, there could be a third group active in the city. They will create havoc. We left the office in a state of disappointment and frustration."

□

11

HUMANINT and TECHINT

The role of intelligence agencies, particularly at the central level while dealing with cases involving terrorism, is extremely important for both the prevention of crime and post-crime investigation. In the present scenario, the intelligence agency may have been successful in gathering strategic and psychological intelligence from open sources, peripheral secret sources, questioning of terrorists who were detained or who had surrendered and examination of confiscated papers. Still, there had been a paucity of intelligence that was either preventative or tactical.

This shortage is primarily due to the difficulty in infiltrating terrorist organisations to gather intelligence and obtain technical information regarding their communications infrastructure. Obtaining precise preventive intelligence is typically possible only through the use of moles planted in important positions within terrorist organisations and through the surveillance of their communications. Additionally, surrendered terrorists, couriers and overground workers, among others, may supply such intelligence; however, the likelihood of this happening was extremely low and not as plausible as depicted in Hollywood/Bollywood movies.

HUMANINT (Information given/received through human source): Terrorist groups are notoriously difficult to infiltrate. Infiltrating terrorist groups is much more challenging than infiltrating hostile States and this ethical problem is not well received by the public. If a government agency intends to plant a mole within a terrorist organisation, it is very difficult to prepare a person for that task, given the great risk of detection and danger to his life.

Even if, by any means, he manages to identify and insert a dedicated patriot as a 'mole' within the terrorist organisation, the leadership of that organisation might instruct the mole to carry out a terror act involving human lives, possibly targeting security officers as a means to test their loyalty and motivation. In such a scenario, if the mole were to approach the intelligence officer handling their operation and inquire about the necessity of killing to establish credibility with the organisation's higher-ups, the officer would find himself in a challenging situation, torn between giving a heads-up to the mole or maintaining the source's cover. While security groups can employ deceptive tactics to catch criminals, resorting to killing someone to apprehend a killer is a moral boundary that should never be crossed.

The second proposition involved recruiting a terrorist who was already a member of the targeted organisation. To achieve this, it was crucial to enlist an officer from the same racial or religious community as the intended terrorist and his organisation. The qualifications for this role included finding an officer who was dedicated and rare, possessing the ability to prioritise national interest over religious solidarity. This task was challenging, as individuals in this position must overcome concerns about potentially abandoning their religious ties and contend with fears regarding personal and family security.

All these actions are required to be done by a specialised unit or agency, such as the Central Intelligence Bureau's Research Analysis Wing in our case, when obtaining human intelligence to uncover the conspiracy or activities of terrorist organisations. This is because the modules sent and settled in India would never be introduced to each other due to fear of detection. State police would never be able to do this due to various other exigencies, like routine investigations, law and order, VIP duties and so on. They, however, come into play after the detection of the case. Nevertheless, the undeniable inevitability of 'chance detection and arrest' stands as an indomitable force that commands acknowledgment. Countless poignant examples within the realm of police work underscore its significance. In February 1996, among a few other instances of human intelligence received during our duties, a significant event occurred when my team apprehended four Kashmiri terrorists associated with Hizbul Mujahideen. This led to the resolution of a high-profile bomb blast case in Sadar Bazar, with a substantial cache of arms and explosives discovered in Jammu & Kashmir. Despite challenges, such as stone pelting and resistance from local residents, the successful outcome was attributed to the strategic deployment of human intelligence. This case serves as concrete evidence of the unpredictable nature of security operations and emphasises the crucial role of timely and actionable information in preventing potential threats. I plan to explore this particular case more extensively in my upcoming book.

I must emphasise that despite diligently pursuing all accessible leads and conducting the investigation based on some hypothetical grounds, we encountered no information from any human source. Even though our expectations were not high in that regard, lack of human intelligence in the current situation made reliance on the prospect of such fortuitous opportunities impractical. Consequently, the only viable option moving forward was to place reliance on TECHINT. Another method for gathering precise preventive intelligence is to penetrate the target organisation's communication system.

In the past, terrorists used couriers as a method of communication. It was difficult to penetrate the system without questioning the courier. As the scope of their activities broadened, terrorists are now more frequently employing contemporary modes of communication, such as telephones, fax machines, electronic mail, the World Wide Web and others.

If intelligence agencies are able to crack their codes and figure out their communications routine, then they will be able to detect the target.

Terrorists, learning from their past failures, adapt their future strategies by changing their modus operandi and abandoning their contact numbers, internet communication addresses and other previous communication systems. They frequently change the phone numbers as a precaution and communicate with each other in coded language to foil the efforts of intelligence services.

Every time there is a blast, innocent lives are lost and families are left shattered. We were working tirelessly under the guidance of Karnal Singh, DCP, to gather evidence and track down any leads, but the perpetrators seemed to always be one step ahead of us. It was becoming increasingly difficult to keep the morale of the team high in case they didn't catch the culprits soon. The police would lose the public's trust and faith in their abilities to protect them.

Analysis of Telephone Calls to Pakistan

Up till December 1997, the investigation team diligently pursued all potential leads and gathered evidence to identify and bring to justice those responsible for the bomb blasts. Despite their efforts, the team was unable to crack the case. Moreover, in the discussion between the Commissioner of Police and Karnal Singh, it transpired that the Special Cell was also unable to crack any leads despite all-out support from intelligence agencies. So, what would be the next course of action? This was the main discussion going on in my office among Karnal Singh, Additional DCP Alok Kumar, myself and the inspectors of Interstate Cell.

Ravi: "Sir, since it is clear from the perusal of interrogation reports of LeT operatives that they used to talk to their handler either prior to or after the blast, now is the time to shift our investigation towards 'technical intelligence'."

Alok: "Do we have any?"

Ravi: "No, sir, we have to generate."

Karnal: "How?"

Ravi: "We have to find out common numbers dialled from the Sadar Bazar area on priority to Pakistan on the day of the blast or prior to that for at least two or three days."

Alok Kumar: "Ravi, unlike other exercises, this would also be a long and highly hypothetical exercise."

Ravi: "You are absolutely right, sir, but, sir, we don't have any information at hand and sitting idle will not serve any purpose. By doing this, at least we will remain involved in the investigation."

Karnal: "I agree with Ravi. We should do this exercise since we do not have any leads."

Alok: "Okay sir, let's do it as there is a saying, '*kabhi kabhi tukka bhi teer ho jaye aur fatey jo doodh to paneer ho jaye.*' (Sometimes a random shot hits the target too! And when luck strikes, even milk can turn into cheese.)

Karnal: "*Kaal kare so aaj kar, aaj kare so ab, pal me parley hoigi bahuri karega kab*?" (Do tomorrow's work today, do today's work now. If you procrastinate, when will you get things done?)

Ravi to Dataram: "*Chadja beta sooli par bhali karenge Ram, bulao jara sandeep ko mere dataram.*" (by saying this, I asked Dataram to call Sandeep.)

The tense atmosphere lightened for a while. Inspector Dataram stood up to inform Sandeep Malhotra.

Ravi: "Sir, we have collected the records of all STD booths in Sadar Bazar and adjoining areas up to October 31st. We are expecting the records up to November 30th within the next three to four days from the telephone exchanges."

Sandeep (SI) (entered the room): "*Jai Hind*, sir."

Karnal: "Sandeep, we need to conduct an exercise to identify common numbers for Pakistan in MTNL records on different dates. Ravi will provide you with the details. How much time do you anticipate it will take?"

Sandeep: "Sir, we have received the records in text format,

which I need to convert to Fox Base. I am already on the job. Formatting will be completed within two to three days. After that, we can proceed with the exercise."

Karnal: "Do it quickly. You know the urgency."

Sandeep: "Sir, we have only one computer on which we can work. It is an Intel 386 computer with limited hard disk and RAM storage. Moreover, the speed of this computer is very slow."

Ravi: "Sir, can we acquire a latest model?"

Karnal: "Ravi, you know the process of procurement. Anyway, try to get it through your personal contacts and I will also make an attempt."

Sandeep: "Leave it, sir. I have trained Constable Devender; he will work during the night and I will be there during the day, or vice versa."

Karnal: "Good, Sandeep. Try to expedite it. We have to deal with these limitations."

After this, Karnal Singh left the office and Sandeep Malhotra and I resumed the job. The records of various booths in the walled city area were collected and analysed with the help of computers. Sandeep Malhotra and Devender worked day and night together. Some team members who were temporarily borrowed from other units started whispering.

"*Baba baith gaya ab nahi uthega*." (The boss has sat down; now he won't get up.)

"*Ab to ugrawadi ko computer se nikal kar uthega*." (Now, he will root out the extremists from the computer.)

"*Aisa bhi kahin hota hoga*?" (Could it be possible?)

"*Sheikh Chilli jaisi harkat hai*." (It's a foolish act like Sheikh Chilli.)

"*Bhai mai to kisi bhahne se chuttee le raha hoon, phir yahan nahi wapas aaunga*." (Brother, I am taking leave on some pretext; then I won't come back here.)

"*Meri to shaadi hai, mujhe to koi problem nahi hogi chuttee ki*." (I am getting married; I won't have any problem in taking leave.)

"*Mujhe lagta hai iski* (ACP) *bibi se nahi banti.*" (I think he (ACP) doesn't get along well with his wife.)

However, with the help of computers, after brainstorming day and night, we selected about 23 phone numbers from Pakistan and Dhaka that were dialled from the Sadar Bazar area three days prior to and on the day of the blasts during the months of October and November 1997. In order to probe further, it was necessary to obtain the previous records of at least six months for the identified 23 phone numbers. MTNL staff were contacted to provide records of how many other booths in Delhi these phone numbers were dialled from. MTNL staff revealed that it would take more than six months, as there were as many as 143 exchanges in Delhi. Then the team approached Bhikaji Cama Place's centralised billing unit. With the technical expertise of SI Sandeep Malhotra and certain modifications in the hardware of Delhi Police's computers, achieving compatibility with the MTNL computer system, the team was able to obtain the records of entire Delhi within a week. The data collected from Bhikaji Cama Place was voluminous and in text format, which was again converted into Foxbase software for the purpose of analysis.

After the analysis of Pak phone numbers, 12 suspected Pak phone numbers were identified. Sandeep Malhotra and I, with the help of computers, brainstormed for days and were able to narrow down on 12 phone numbers in Pakistan that could have been linked to terrorists. These phone numbers were dialled from different STD booths in South Delhi, walled city and the Adarsh Nagar area.

It was necessary to track down and gather more information about the caller of those numbers to determine whether the team's hypothetical analysis was on the right track. Though it was also a herculean task because most of the numbers were dialled from PCOs, to conduct inquiries regarding the person who had made the calls on Pak's phone numbers, Inspector Rajindra Bhatia and his team were deployed in the Adarsh Nagar area. Another team, headed by me and including Inspector Subhash Tandon and Inspector Dataram, stationed themselves in the Sadar Bazar area. As no call was made on these telephone numbers since 30 July, 1997, from the South district, no one was deployed in the South district. During the field inquiries supported by technical analysis by Sandeep Malhotra, I was able to zero in on two more suspicious numbers of Pakistan dialled from two STD numbers of Sadar Bazar, Delhi.

□

12

Another Explosion on a Bus

Meanwhile, on 30 December, 1997, at about 6:20 p.m., a Blueline bus with the registration number DL-IP-3088, carrying passengers from Ajmeri Gate to Nangloi, stopped at the Rampura bus stop on Rohtak Road for passengers to disembark. The moment the bus stopped, an explosion occurred inside, causing its floor to be ripped apart. Four passengers, namely Ms. Tapoti, Taj Mohammad, Narain Jha and Rajiv Verma lost their lives, and 24 other passengers, including the bus conductor, sustained injuries due to the explosion. Two policemen on duty at that time stopped at the blast site. After informing the local police station, the police team arrived on the spot. The crime team and bomb disposal squad were also summoned and the damaged bus was inspected. Debris was lifted and sealed on the spot. Based on the statement of Head Constable Suresh, one of the two policemen on duty at the Rampura bus stop, a case was registered at Punjabi Bagh police station under Section 307 IPC and Sections 3, 4 and 5 of the Explosive Substances Act. Section 302 of the IPC was added due to the deaths of some of the injured on the day of the incident itself. During the investigation, debris collected from the bomb blast site and damaged pieces of the bus contained explosive mixtures of chlorate, nitrate, sulphate and sugar. A mixture of these chemicals is used for making explosives and bombs and the mixture could have been initiated by the action of sulphuric acid.

After the site inspection by our team, a meeting in ISC on December 31st in the early morning was ongoing among the officers of the Crime Branch in my office. Karnal Singh was taking stock of the investigation until that day by the team.

Ravi: "Sir, as you know, we have already shortlisted 12 numbers from Pakistan during the initial phase of technical analysis and later, after field inquiries supported by technical analysis, we were able to zero in on two more suspicious Pak numbers dialled from two STD numbers of Sadar Bazar, Delhi. Still, it is necessary to hear the conversation between the caller and receiver in Pakistan. However, it is very difficult to monitor all the booths or put thousands of telephone booths under observation. So it is required to put these called telephone numbers (Pakistan phone) under observation. All international calls are routed through VSNL; therefore, I contacted VSNL to provide us with the facility, but they expressed their inability to provide it. However, IB must have some via media to tackle the monitoring of Pak numbers."

Karnal: "I think they must be on the job."

Ravi: "But, I don't think so. If they had been doing this, there would have been some result. However, I am sure they must have the latest numbers of the outfit."

Karnal: "If they are monitoring through some software or spyware, they will not disclose it. Their work is entirely different."

Alok: "Sir, is it not possible to get those latest numbers from the Intelligence Bureau? At least we can try to explore them further."

Karnal: "Let me try it through CP, Delhi."

ACP Awana: "Sir, if they have those numbers, then what are they doing with them?"

Karnal: "I can't say anything. They are not answerable to the Delhi Police."

ACP Awana: "Anyway, sir, I have a very good contact in IB at the senior level. If you allow me, I can talk to him if he could provide those numbers to us."

Karnal: "That would be okay. I don't mind. Talk to him. I will also try this through CP."

ACP Awana: "Just a minute, sir. I have dialled his number."

ACP Awana: "Good afternoon, sir."

IB officer: "Hi, Awana. How are you?"

ACP Awana: "Fine, sir. Will you please do us a favour?"

IB officer: "Of course, if it is in my purview."

ACP Awana: "Sir, we understand that you may have the latest number of LeT. Can you please forward those numbers to us since those numbers are required for investigation purposes?"

IB officer: "I think Special Cell is doing that investigation and we have already provided them with those numbers."

ACP Awana: "You are right, sir, but we are also doing that as per the orders of CP, Delhi. It would be nice if you could also provide us with those numbers."

IB officer: "There is no issue, but you have to send an e-mail requesting this, referring to orders of CP through DCP (Crime)."

ACP Awana: "Thank you very much, sir." (holding the conversation, Awana asks DCP Crime if he wanted to talk to him.)

Karnal agreed.

Awana (continued): "Sir, I am with DCP Sahib; he would like to talk to you."

Karnal: "Hello, how are you?"

IB officer: "Not okay. You can imagine the pressure we are facing due to these blasts."

Karnal: "The same situation is here; everyone is in a fix about what to do and what will happen the next day. Who knows? It would be another blast any time. Anyway, is it possible to send us the latest LeT outfit numbers?"

IB officer: "Of course, Karnal, please drop me an e-mail. I'll do it just now."

Karnal: "Okay, thank you very much. I am sending the mail. Please SMS your e-mail address."

After disconnecting the phone, an SMS was received on his mobile phone. Awana drafted it and sent it to IB; within no time, IB officer reverted back.

Karnal: "So quick. Ravi download it and give it to Sandeep; will check these numbers in the available records immediately."

Ravi: "Okay, sir, let me take out the printout of the e-mail from Sandeep's room."

I entered Sandeep's room and asked him, "Sandeep, this is the list we received from IB. This list contains the latest numbers. First of all, show me the numbers we have shortlisted."

Sandeep gave me a list of 14 numbers, out of which two were most significant and I selected them during the exercise. We started tallying the list and stopped at a number that was mentioned in both the lists. Sandeep and I exclaimed with joy, "Yeeeeeeeeeesss."

Karnal Singh and Alok Kumar peered through a small window that was between my room and the computer room.

Karnal: "Ravi, what happened? *Bahut khush ho rahe ho*? (Ravi, what happened? You seem very happy.)

Ravi: "*Sar tukka teer ho gaya. Dudh phatke paneer ho gaya*." (It was a lucky shot; we hit the bull's eye; like milk turning into cheese with a bang.)

Immediately, I placed both the lists before Karnal Singh.

Sandeep: "Sir, this is the number that is also on our list. As per the IB list, this number is installed in the office of Lashkar-e-Toiba in Muzaffarabad, PoK."

Alok: "Great, at least it can be said, *'agar kisi cheez ko tum shiddat se chaho, to puri kaynat tumhe us se milane ki koshish me lag jati hai.'*" (Great, at least it can be said, 'if you ardently desire something, the whole universe conspires to help you to achieve it.')

Karnal: "Alok, *aaj to bahut shayari kar rahe ho*?" (Alok, today you are reciting a lot of poetry, aren't you?)

Ravi: "Sandeep, please check it afresh in the entire records of MTNL."

Sandeep: "Okay, sir."

It took an hour to check the entire record of STDs. Sandeep was full of enthusiasm and after analysing it through the window, he conveyed, "Sir, this number is dialled from an STD booth in Sadar Bazar, apart from Adarsh Nagar Sabji Mandi."

Karnal: "Take a printout of the relevant dates for the STD booth at the Sadar Bazar."

Sandeep: "I have already checked and one more piece of good news is that this number is dialled from Sadar Bazar with the other three numbers, out of which two we have already zeroed down during the verification of the 12 suspected numbers of Pakistan."

Sandeep took out the prints of both booths and placed them before Karnal Singh. Karnal perused the record:

Pakistan Calls Details made from Phone No. 0113xxxx78

S. No.	Date	Time (hrs.)	Pak number	Duration	Charged call
884	27/06/97	1252	009242xxxx768	315	157
885	27/06/97	1254	009242xxxx768	25	13
1739	05/09/97	1241	009242xxxx004	47	24
3138	29/09/97	2305	009242xxxx004	176	68
1800	17/11/97	1948	009242xxxx004	32	16
1877	19/11/97	1120	009242xxxx004	34	17
1893	19/11/97	1841	009242xxxx004	97	48
2068	23/11/97	1054	009242xxxx004	40	20
2069	23/11/97	1059	009242xxxx004	70	35
2070	23/11/97	1100	009242xxxx004	21	10

S. No.	Date	Time (hrs.)	Pak number	Duration	Charged call
2071	23/11/97	1102	0092xxxx563	54	27
2072	23/11/97	1105	0092xxxx563	111	56
2073	23/11/97	1108	009242xxxx004	71	36
2074	23/11/97	1114	009242xxxx747	45	23
2075	23/11/97	1115	009242xxxx768	42	21
2076	23/11/97	1120	009242xxxx768	224	112
2160	24/11/97	2118	009242xxxx747	03	01

From Telephone No. 0113xxx272

S. No.	Date	Time (hrs.)	Pak number	Duration	Charged call
1073	28/06/97	1109	009242xxxx768	07	03
1074	28/06/97	1111	009242xxxx768	67	33
1075	28/06/97	1131	009242xxxx768	224	112
1078	28/06/97	1157	009242xxxx768	348	174
1243	02/07/97	1056	009242xxxx768	29	14
759	16/10/97	2138	009242xxxx004	223	112
760	16/10/97	2150	009242xxxx004	67	34
1134	23/10/97	2127	009242xxxx004	138	69
1590	14/11/97	2132	009242xxxx747	18	09
1591	14/11/97	2134	009242xxxx747	61	31
1592	14/11/97	2136	009242xxxx004	13	06
1593	14/11/97	2142	009242xxxx004	297	148

S. No.	Date	Time (hrs.)	Pak number	Duration	Charged call
2254	30/11/97	1006	009242xxxx004	88	44
2255	30/11/97	1010	009242xxxx004	173	86
2256	30/11/97	1011	009242xxxx004	02	10
121	05/12/97	2010	009242xxxx004	11	05
268	08/12/97	1014	009242xxxx004	218	109
565	13/12/97	1939	009242xxxx004	54	27
566	13/12/97	1942	009242xxxx004	58	29
567	13/12/97	1947	009242xxxx004	187	93

Ravi: "Sir, you can see the pattern of the calls in both the call details. I am sure all these numbers were dialled by one person and I am 100% sure he is our man. Sir, look at call Sl. No. 2071 and 2072. This is the common number in our shortlisted and IB lists. Had he not dialled this number, with the numbers mentioned from Sl. No. 2068 to 2076 on that day and time, then it would have been very difficult to track the new numbers. Sandeep! Search for these three numbers as well."

Sandeep: "I have already given the command on the computer; it will take about 15 to 20 minutes."

Karnal: "Excellent, Ravi. Good job, Sandeep."

Ravi: "Thank you, sir, but Sandeep and Devender worked day and night. Hats off to them!"

Sandeep: "Sir, ACP *Sahib bhi poore mahine me kewal 3 ya 4 baar ghar gaye honge.*" (Sir, ACP Sahib must have only gone home three or four times in the entire month.)

Alok: "I still can't believe it."

Karnal and Alok gave tight hugs to me and Sandeep. "Sir, Ravi never gives up, does he?"

Karnal: "I have full confidence in him and always admire his style of working."

Alok: "No doubt."

Karnal: "No doubt it's an excellent discovery of three new contact numbers from Pak, but without hearing the conversation between the Indian guy and his Pakistani counterpart, this is of no use."

Alok: "Agreed, the caller is at liberty to use any STD booth and it is not possible to put the entire Delhi telephones on observation."

Ravi: "Exactly, sir. That is why the observation of the called number with listening facilities is strongly recommended. In any case, the New Year has begun and I wish you a happy New Year. Let us hope that this year we will be able to overcome the constant trauma and risk of bomb blasts. God just gave his first indication to us."

All in one voice chanted, "HAPPY NEW YEAR."

The meeting dispersed at about 2:30 a.m.

□

13
Unveiling New Trails: Follow-up Leads

Around 9 a.m. on 1 January, 1998, I pressed the buzzer to alert the duty officer and summoned Subhash Tondon and his team. Subhash entered the room along with his team members.

Subhash: "Sir, *hukum*." (Any order, please.)

Ravi: "Please be seated. Subhash, do you know two STD telephone numbers in Sadar Bazar from where calls to three suspected Pak numbers originated? Have you obtained the addresses of these numbers?"

Subash: "Yes sir!"

Ravi: "Okay, then, take your men and try to gather intelligence around the booth secretly regarding the caller. I am sure we can find something important because the pattern of phone calls over the past six months indicates the frequent use of that STD booth by the suspect."

Subhash: "I also think so. I am taking Dixit and Ramesh with me. Okay, sir, *Jai Hind*."

Ravi: "All the best."

Subhash, Ramesh and Dixit left ISC.

Sadar Bazar, Teliwara

Subhash, Rakesh Dixit and Ramesh Sharma identify the PCO in question.

Dixit to Subhash: "Sir, we'll have to talk to the booth owner."

Ramesh: "Absolutely, sir."

Subhash: "You're right, but if the owner of the booth reveals our identity to the caller, the whole plan might go wrong."

Dixit: "Sir, Jain Sahib is a respected person and he seems like a family man. When we instil some fear in his mind, he won't talk."

Ramesh: "Scaring him too much won't be good. It could force him to seek advice from his lawyer."

Subhash: "What should we do now?"

Dixit: "Leave it to me; I'll handle it on my own."

Subhash: "Without talking to the ACP, I don't think it's right to talk to him."

Dixit: "Then do it; what's the problem?"

Subhash: "You do it, Dixit; I'm confused."

Dixit: "Alright, I'll do it now and I'll talk to ACP from his PCO as well."

Ramesh: "Sir, Dixit will surely get the information from the PCO; don't worry."

Dixit: "Okay, let me talk to ACP Sahib first. Let's see what his opinion is."

Subhash: "Alright, talk to him and come back; we'll be waiting outside."

Dixit came to the booth and started dialling the telephone number.

Jain: "Wait a moment, brother, first register the entry."

Dixit: "Since when did you introduce this system?"

Jain: "For the last two months, ever since these blasts started happening. What's the phone number you want to call?"

Dixit: "Okay, let me write any number in the register and if I dial another number..".

Jain: "Brother, there's a display in front of me; I can see everything."

Dixit mentioned the phone number of the ISC and dialled

my office number. I picked up the phone: "Hello."

Conversation between me and Dixit started in a guarded language.

Dixit: "Hello, brother."

Ravi (looking at the phone screen): Yes, Dixit, are you talking from Jain's booth itself?" (Laughing.)

Dixit: "Brother, this party seems to be sound. We can talk to him and there's no other way; we've been stuck for a long time."

Ravi: "See, the party should be reliable. We don't want to lose money."

Dixit: "Brother, integrity isn't written on one's forehead, but it becomes evident through actions and conversations. But this party seems to be genuine."

Ravi: "What does Subhash say?"

Dixit: "He's not saying anything; he seems confused."

Ravi: I know business is risky. Have to take it! Risk *lene ka maza hi alag hai.*" (The pleasure of taking risks is something else.)

Dixit: "Yes, brother."

Ravi: "Look, son! All four businesses (previous exercises) have failed. Don't sink the last capital. Besides, no other viable option is visible."

Dixit: "Should I talk to the party then?"

Ravi: "*Jai mata di*! Do your prayers and quickly bring the blessings and offerings of the goddess. And explain the terms and conditions to the party well. Don't scare them too much; handle everything with love."

Dixit: "Alright, brother, I'll go and talk to them."

Late in the evening, Inspectors Subash, Rakesh Dixit and Ramesh Sharma arrived at the office. Their body language was entirely different; it seemed as if they had achieved something significant.

Subhash (extending a sweet box): "Sir, *mithaai khao*."

Ravi: "First, tell me the good news."

Subhash: "*Wahe Guruji da Khalsa, Wahe Guruji di fateh*. Sir, we are on right track."

Ravi: "Oh, my dear, tell me quickly; I can't even enjoy the sweets."

Subhash: "We discreetly interviewed Jain, the owner of the PCO. He is very cooperative. During the discussion, he revealed crucial information. According to him, a Muslim boy named Kamran, residing nearby, dialled all these phone numbers. He has maintained the record in his register. The most important information he provided was that Kamran used to talk to someone named Babaji."

Hearing this information, I jumped out of the chair and shouted with joy, "Hurray! This is our man."

Upon hearing the excitement, other staff members gathered around my room.

Rajendra Bhatia: "What happened, sir?"

Ravi: "Bhatia Sahib, you will get to know it soon. Oh, let's talk later; first let me enjoy *kachori* and *jalebi*. (begins to play a beat on the table.) Dixit!! Bhatia!!!, Treat others as well and that's enough for today. Pack up; come to the office early tomorrow."

Dispersal happened around 10 p.m.

I reached home in a very happy mood. Sushma opened the main door.

Ravi: "Ram! Ram!"

Sushma: "You didn't inform that you were coming home today. Why do you look so happy? Seems like you've caught someone?"

Ravi: "Yes, think of it that way. I haven't caught him yet, but my sixth sense is telling me that we've cracked the case. Just need to catch the culprit somehow. Maa – is she asleep?"

Sushma: "No, as soon as she heard the sound of the Gypsy, she started making noise, 'Open the door, Sushma, Ravinder is here'. In fact, I fell asleep." (One can imagine a mother's instinct!)

Ravi (entering Mother's room): "Maa!"

Mother: "*Beta*, you came, after many days. Tell me, did you meet any success or not?"

Ravi: "Maa, it seems like we'll catch him soon."

Mother: "That's good to hear. Okay, take your time, eat and rest."

Ravi: "Alright, Maa."

Sushma served dinner. Meanwhile, both our daughters, who were sleeping, came to know about my arrival. Priyanka: "Dad, why do you come after so many days? Especially when the office is so close. It's just a five-minute drive."

Iteeh: "This is not fair. You've even stopped coming home, let alone taking us out."

Ravi: "I will be free soon, Okay! Now go to sleep; I have to leave early in the morning. When do your schools reopen? Oh, belated happy New Year to you all! Maa, happy New Year."

Mother: "Yes, *beta*, to you too."

After eating dinner, Ravi went to bed.

Next morning, 2 January, 1998

Ramswaroop arrived. Ramswaroop: "*Jai Hind*, sir!"

Ravi: "*Jai Hind*!! Let's go after having breakfast."

Both daughters wished me a happy New Year once again while going to school. After hearing Ramswaroop's voice, my mother called him.

Ramswaroop was a confidant of my mother. Through him, she always used to get information and cross-check the activities that she came to know through me.

Ramswaroop: "Ram! Ram! *Mataji*."

Mother: "Ram! Ram! Come and sit. (In a raised voice) Sushma, make tea for Ramswaroop."

Sushma gave him the tea.

Mother: "Ramswaroop, did you catch anyone?"

Ramswaroop: "No, *Mataji*, not yet. But it seems we'll catch him soon."

Ravi (enters the room): Maa, something secretive is going on. Did you have your tea, Ramswaroop? Let's go quickly. Okay, Maa, I'm leaving." (touches her feet.)

Mother: "Stay happy, take care of yourself."

Ravi: "Sure, Maa! Bye, Sushma!"

I hugged and kissed my son and left for the office.

□

14
Major Breakthrough

Inspectors Subhash, Rajendra, Dataram, Dixit, ASI Ramesh Sharma and other police personnel were present in my office (Interstate Cell). Meanwhile, Karnal Singh also joined in. Discussion about last evening's developments was the main issue.

Karnal: "This seems to be an enthusiastic development. Did you show the portrait to him?"

Dixit: "Yes, sir, he recognised it and said that it resembles 90 per cent of his face and also has a cut mark on his face, which corroborated the version of a witness in the Karol Bagh case. His age is also similar. And, above all, he told me that the subject used to talk with one Babaji in Pakistan."

Ravi: "Babaji, Abdul Karim Tunda, sir."

Karnal: "Yes, I know. Additionally, Kamran resides in the same area as Jain had suspected."

Dixit: "Sir, he himself introduced Jain with this name."

Karnal: "Immediately deploy sources to trace him."

Ravi: "Dataram Sahib, you immediately collect the voter list of that area to find out if anyone by the name of Kamran is living in that area."

Dixit: "You select two or three boys who do not look like policemen and try to find his house. Subhash, you supervise the operation and this time there is no open inquiry. It should be done in a very discreet manner, with patience and perseverance."

Karnal: "Yes, the team should not be exposed under any circumstances. Do it very patiently with a professional approach."

Karnal: "Ravi, come with me and let us update the Additional CP and CP about this development."

Ravi: "Sir, not today. I think we should do some more homework; otherwise, they will start grilling us. Sir, we want some working autonomy."

Karnal: "Okay, as you wish. I am leaving then; you continue."

Ravi: "Okay, sir, *Jai Hind*! I am also going to Sadar Bazar with Subhash."

Dixit: "Sir, what will you do by going to Sadar?"

Ravi: "I'll talk to Jain; maybe we can gather some more information."

Dixit: "Sir, if you go and meet him, he won't give us weightage. It's up to you. The rest is your decision."

Ravi: "I get your point, Dixit. Okay, you proceed."

Team dispatched.

At about 6:30 p.m., I received a telephone call from Additional CP, B.K. Gupta's office. I picked up the call.

PA to additional CP: "Sir, Karnal Singh wants to talk to you."

Ravi: "Okay, connect me." (B.K. Gupta picks up the phone.)

B.K. Gupta: "Excellent job, Ravi. It was expected only from you. Karnal just informed me of the way you and your team were able to make a very important breakthrough."

Ravi: "Thank you, sir; it was only due to the hard work and perseverance of my team and the guidance of my DCP."

B.K. Gupta: "That's true and I know you always give credit to your team, being well aware of your work for the last three years. You have done remarkable investigations previously, be it the Sadar Bazar bomb blast in 1996, the Tarun Puri kidnapping, or the arrest of Ansals from Bombay. Good job, Ravi. Karnal wants to talk to you."

B.K. Gupta gave the telephone to Karnal Singh.

Karnal: "Hello, Ravi."

Ravi: Finally you could not resist yourself, sir. I knew it was very difficult to hold such important information. Anyway, it is all for the best."

Karnal: "Any further leads about Kamran?"

Ravi: "No, sir, Subhash's team is on the job."

Karnal: "Guptaji wants to interact with your team tomorrow morning at 9:30. Ask all of them to gather in your office."

Ravi: "Okay sir."

After disconnecting the phone, Ravi called the duty officer and directed him to convey the message to all team members. Next morning (3 January, 9:30), Additional CP, B.K. Gupta and Karnal Singh came to ISC to brief and encourage the team. Team members were gathered outside the office. Inspector Dataram (gave command): "Team, *Savdhan!*" B.K. Gupta: "*Vishram, aaram se*. Today, in this delicate and challenging situation, I want to express my gratitude for your hard work. Your determination is commendable. Now we have crucial leads that can lead us to the perpetrators of the bomb blast. Although the journey ahead may be difficult, remember that enthusiasm, and even fear, is a natural part of it. But I believe that we can overcome any challenge. I trust all of you to be successful in this crucial task. We are moving forward with every lead. We must succeed in this work, keeping faith in ourselves. We have overcome challenges before. Our past record proves it. I am pleased to be the leader of such a dedicated team. Let's go out there and make a difference! Any doubt, Team?"

"No, sir," everyone shouted.

After briefing the team members, Additional CPs, B.K. Gupta and Karnal Singh, shook hands with each member of the team and left ISC. I came to the computer room for further analysis after assigning the tasks to each team.

6 January, 1998

Discreet watch over the hideout of Kamran. Since the whole probe was very secret and highly confidential, reliable secret sources were deployed in the Sadar Bazar area. One of the sources was able to locate Kamran's hideout. It was a rented house. The house was locked. The source contacted Rakesh Dixit, who was asked by me to handle him.

Rakesh Dixit to source: "Since when has the house been locked?"

Source: "It's been almost a month.

Rakesh: "Any idea where he has gone?"

Source: "I don't know where he has gone, but I came to know that he has gone to fetch his mother."

Dixit: "Alright, keep an eye on him and find out where his mother lives. Has he been alone until now?"

Source: "It seems so."

Dixit: "Okay, our team will stay permanently in Sadar Bazar. Let us know immediately when he arrives."

Source: "Sir, I won't meet any member of your team; I'll only inform you. I have your phone number. I'll call you as soon as he arrives."

Dixit: "Yes, that's fine. You don't need to come to me; just inform me over the phone. If you can't reach me, ACP Sahib's phone number is with you. Inform him without delay."

Source: "Okay, sir. Can I get some money? I need to buy medicine for my mother."

Dixit (gave Rs1,000/-): "If you need more, let me know. I'll arrange for it later."

Source: "Sir, instead of a reward, help my son get a job."

Dixit: "He got a job two months ago through ACP Sahib, right? What happened then?"

Source: "No, sir, it was the elder one. This one is younger and has only passed the 10th grade."

Dixit: "Okay, I'll talk to ACP Sahib and try to arrange something. Don't worry; it will be sorted."

Source: "Thank you, sir. I'm grateful for your help."

Dixit released the source after the briefing. Considering past developments, teams were permanently deployed in the

Sadar Bazar area 24x7. I went to Sadar Bazar to check their setup.

Dixit: "Sir, not more than two people will stay in one place and they will rotate."

Ravi: "Absolutely right."

Subhash: "Sir, arrange for some money from the Secret Source Fund."

Ravi: "Alright, I'll talk to the additional CP today and get some funds sent."

Subhash: "Sir, one more thing. Our informer has a son who has passed the tenth grade."

Ravi: "I'll see what I can do. I'll talk to DCP or Additional CP about a job, maybe in the Home Guard and for the time being I'll set him up in my friend's business."

Dixit: "Yes, sir, he's been working hard with dedication."

Ravi: "Okay, I'm heading out. Take care."

Need for observation on Pak number was felt. That was a very crucial stage. At that time, we were urgently required to watch the Pak numbers. We were stuck again because we still were solely dependent on traditional policing. It was hard to believe that in this high-tech modern era, observation on the called number was not possible. If that was done, it would have been a bonus. Moreover, it was more important to dig out the network of the outfit prior to the apprehension of culprits so that the simultaneous raids on other associates could be organised to avoid any slip in the operation. Therefore I again requested Karnal Singh to take up the issue at the ministry level. After that, he disscussed this issue with his friend Sunil Saxena DGM, MTNL.

A meeting was fixed with him at Karol Bagh Exchange in the morning, the next day.

At Sunil Saxena's (DGM, MTNL) office next morning, i.e. 7 January, 1998, I met Sunil Saxena and apprised him of the case and our requirement and the importance of observation on the called number for us.

Sunil: "I get your point, Karnal."

Karnal: "Sunil, please help us. If you will help, then we are sure that we will be able to crack the case. Sunil, why is VSNL not doing this? I don't know, but I am going to take up the matter at the ministry level, but you know, it's very urgent, and if you are able to do this, we can present our case at a higher level more strongly."

Sunil: "Okay, I think you would also like to record the conversation."

Karnal: "If it is possible."

Sunil: "Wait a minute, let me check an instrument on my inventory list."

Sunil Saxena took out a file from his drawer and inspected it. Sunil: "Yes, it is there. Okay, Karnal, give me the list of the numbers and a formal request for monitoring those numbers."

Karnal: "Ravi!"

Ravi: "Sir, I will send it in the afternoon."

Karnal: "How much time will it take, Sunil?"

Sunil: "In fact, calls to Pakistan are routed through two other TAXTs (Trunk Automatic Exchange Tandem Switch) besides our TAXT to VSNL. Now we have to make arrangements so that both TAXT will send all the calls to Pakistan to our TAXT to ensure that no call goes unnoticed. It depends on other exchanges as to how much time they will take."

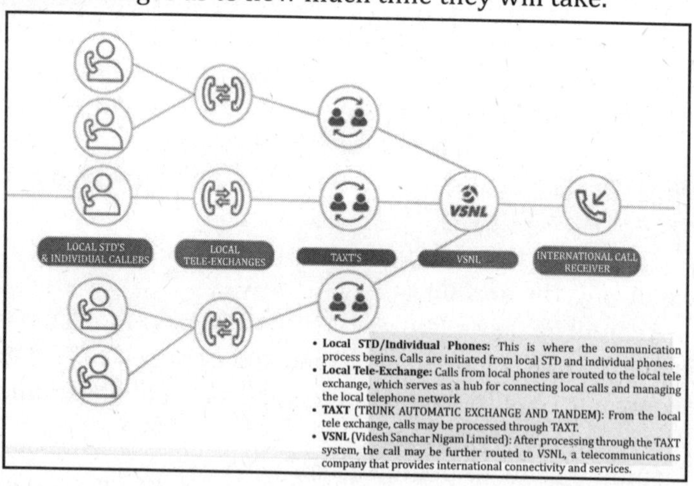

Karnal: “Sunil, please talk to them and apprise them of the urgency.”

Sunil: “Sure, you need not worry; if all things remain normal, then by tomorrow afternoon it will be done.”

Karnal: “Thanks Sunil. I would like to take your leave. Ravi will send you the details and requests for monitoring.”

We left the MTNL office. Walking towards our vehicles, I said, “Where there is a will, there is a way. Sir, it would have been easy for him as well to ignore us like the VSNL guys.”

Karnal: “You are right!!”

From Karol Bagh, I went to ISC and Karnal reached PHQ, ISC, Chanakyapuri. Sandeep prepared a formal request for monitoring with the listening facility of Pakistani 15 telephone numbers addressing DGM, Karol Bagh, MTNL and sent it through ASI Harbir Singh to Sunil Saxena, Karol Bagh Exchange.

□

15
Explosion and Further Surveillance

9 January, 1998

Secret sources deployed to develop further information about Kamran revealed his real name as Aamir Khan. Kamran and his mother had shifted from Sadar Bazar, Delhi, in 1990 to Karachi, Pakistan where Kamran's brother and sister were already settled. Kamran came to India last year. Initially, he was residing with his aunt somewhere in the Azad Market area. Recently, he had taken up a house on rent in Teliwara, Sadar Bazar, Delhi. As per the information, he had been in Karachi for about a month. The informer further revealed that Kamran had started a printing and dyeing factory in Pilkhuwa district, Hapur, UP. This information corroborated our survey regarding the newspaper pieces recovered from the bomb blast sites that led us to a strong suspicion that the bombs were being manufactured there with chemicals used in printing and dyeing. We couldn't afford to let this slip through our fingers. This information could be the key to unravelling the whole plot. We needed to act swiftly, gather all the necessary resources to follow up on this lead and mobilise the team to ensure we left no stone unturned. We had to work hard on this. In the afternoon, a discussion in this regard was on-going at PHQ, Delhi.

Karnal: "I'm proud of each and every one of you. Despite the setbacks, you've shown unwavering dedication and commitment. Now it's time to channel that energy and focus it on this new lead."

Ravi (solemnly): "Agreed. We'll analyse every piece of information, follow every lead and bring these terrorists to justice. This new lead has given us a renewed sense of purpose."

Alok: Let's go, Team. It's time to close this chapter and bring an end to these heinous acts. Together, we can make a difference."

Bomb Explosion near Income-Tax Office, New Delhi

The discussion was going on at about 2:00 p.m. A loud sound of explosions was heard. We all jumped out of the chairs and peered out of the window. A huge puff of smoke and dust arose across the road towards the Revenue Block income-tax office. A whirlwind of emotions swirled within our minds: the haunting images of devastation, the echoes of screams and the relentless ticking of the clock urging us to act swiftly. A pervasive sense of hopelessness kept us rooted to our place.

We immediately rushed to the spot. Without wasting any time, the injured were shifted to the nearest hospitals with the help of the police and the public. Nearly 55 people were seriously injured. The site was immediately cordoned and the Crime team and CFSL team were summoned for their expert opinions. During the inquiry, it was found that the bomb was planted in a fruit rickshaw, which was parked about 10 minutes before the bomb exploded. Later, one of the injured succumbed to his injuries. A case at the police station, IP Estate, was registered but was later transferred to the CBI.

However, a late-night meeting was called at PHQ among the officers of the MHA Research Analysis Wing, the Intelligence Bureau and the Special Cell of the Delhi police and the CBI. In that meeting, again the Crime Branch was not asked to participate. But it was not important for us since we were working on a very authentic lead. Karnal Singh held a meeting of all the officers of the ISC at Chanakyapuri late at night. As the entire team stood amidst the chaos and devastation caused by yet another bomb blast, a mix of frustration, anger and determination coursed through our veins. The relentless pursuit of justice had become an arduous journey – one that seemed to lead down a never-ending labyrinth of uncertainty and despair. But all our efforts had thus far fallen short, leaving us with a sense of helplessness. The weight of responsibility and the lives at stake had never been heavier on our shoulders. Each blast added another layer of guilt and remorse, amplifying the urgency to put an end to the reign of terror.

Ravi: "Sir, as per a source, Kamran has not been traced to his house for the last month. He is reported to be in Pakistan, but the blasts are still continuing. I suspect that some other group is also active because the last three blasts, dated November 30, December 30 and the present one, are not identical to previous blasts."

Karnal: "I agree with you."

Ravi: "Anyway, we will not give up and try to find out if there is another group, but as of now, we have to exploit all our resources to apprehend Kamran."

Ravi: "Subhash, did you send Rakesh Dixit to verify the whereabouts of Kamran?"

Subhash: "Yes, sir, he has checked. Kamran's house is still locked."

Karnal: "Rajendra, what is the position of phone monitoring in Karol Bagh?"

Rajendra: "Finally, it started about an hour ago."

Alok: "Thank God. Ravi, depute your man round-the-clock in exchange."

Ravi: "Sir, I have already given the instructions."

Rajendra: "Sir, as far as I could make out, Kamran is not coming to his house, as the posters were released in the wake of the coming Republic Day celebration. Out of the four terrorists whose portraits were released, one was a perfect depiction of Kamran's description given by our source."

Alok: "Yes, it could be. Moreover, the circulation of the description of the Karol Bagh suspect could be another reason."

Karnal: "Okay, Ravi, let's concentrate on Kamran and ask Sandeep to further analyse the data."

Alok: "Sir, it is high time to approach MHA for their intervention in the matter of phone monitoring at VSNL."

Karnal: "Alright, Alok. I will talk to CP in the morning

The meeting ended.

11 January, 1998; Meeting with Commissioner of Police in PHQ

Karnal: "Sir, we finally located the suspect's hideout. He's apparently been living a low-profile life, blending in with the common folk."

T.R. Kakkar: "That's really a great breakthrough! Well done, Ravi. Have we been able to keep an eye on him?"

Ravi: "Yes, sir, our team has been monitoring his hideout for the past two to three days, thanks to a secret source. It seems his house is currently locked up, indicating he might be away."

T.R. Kakkar: "Any leads on his whereabouts?"

Ravi: "According to the latest intelligence, it's been reported that he has travelled to Pakistan to bring his mother back from Karachi to India, but I think he has gone to plan further operations with his handler."

T.R. Kakkar: "Agreed. But how do we proceed when his house is locked? Is there any possibility of planting surveillance equipment?"

Karnal: "Unfortunately, it seems unlikely. We'll have to rely on other means to gather more information. We can try to trace his communication channels, monitor his online activities and track his movements. That is why facilities for international observation are urgently required."

T.R. Kakkar: "But you told me that it had already been started?"

Karnal: "Yes, sir, it is, but this is in the Karol Bagh Exchange, which is only able to monitor calls generated from Delhi, whereas VSNL can monitor it on a pan-India basis."

Ravi: "Moreover, I suspect that there may be another module active in the region responsible for the last three blasts. Monitoring at VSNL could provide us with further leads if that module is from the same terrorist outfit."

T.R. Kakkar: "That's a challenging situation. With a national celebration approaching, we can't afford any mistakes. We need to keep the public safe and prevent any potential attacks. Okay, I am going to discuss the matter with the Home Secretary and coordinate with VSNL in the evening. Time is of essence here, so we need to act swiftly and decisively."

Karnal: "Agreed, sir. We'll do everything in our power to apprehend the suspect and neutralise any threat that he poses. The safety of the public is our top priority and we won't rest until we've successfully dealt with this situation."

T.R. Kakkar: "All the best, Karnal. Excellent job, Ravi. Keep it up."

Ravi: "Thanks, sir. Rest assured, we will stay focused and maintain vigilance. We'll keep our eyes peeled for any further updates and take the necessary action accordingly. Our team is well-prepared and we'll get the job done."

T.R. Kakkar: "That's the spirit, Ravi. Together, we'll ensure a safe and secure Republic Day celebration for everyone. Let's remain alert and ready to respond to any developments swiftly and effectively. Okay Karnal, I will let you know in the evening about monitoring in VSNL."

Karnal: "Thanks, sir. We will take your leave."

At about 4 p.m. I was sitting in my office with Sandeep Malhotra, analysing telephone data. I received a call from ASI Harbir Singh, who was deputed to monitor the calls in the Karol Bagh Exchange.

Ravi: "Any significant news?"

Harbir: "Sir, we just received a call. It's on that Muzaffarabad number."

Ravi: "The same number many people use like a PCO?"

Harbir: "Yes, exactly. It's that number. Someone named Gulam Mohammed Bhatt was talking and he mentioned that he came to attend a book fair here in Delhi and he's asking his Pak counterpart to send 10 books to him."

Ravi: "He's ordering books from Pakistan to Delhi? He's trying to fool us. He's probably asking for something else. By the way, these people also refer pistols as 'books', right? Like, one 'book' also means 1 lakh rupees. Can you play the call on the telephone?"

Harbir: "Sir, if I play it from my mobile, there might be some disturbance and there's no landline phone nearby. I'm sitting in the switch-room."

Ravi: "Is anyone there with you? If someone is there, send me the recording."

Harbir: "Yes, sir, Rishipal is with me. I'll send it right away."

Ravi: "Okay, Harbir, backtrack this call and find out where it originated from."

Harbir: "I've already informed the New Delhi TAXT; we'll get to know in the next 10 or 15 minutes."

After about half an hour, a call from Harbir Singh was received.

Harbir: "Sir, note down the number. The call was made from a mobile and it originated in Delhi itself."

I noted down the caller's number and gave it to Sandeep to obtain the details immediately from the service provider. Meanwhile, Rishipal brought the cassette and we listened to the conversation between Gulam Mohammed and a person in Pakistan. Sandeep contacted the service provider and asked for the details.

Sandeep: "They will send the details up to January 9th because they are updating their records tonight and today's details we will be able to get tomorrow afternoon only."

Ravi: "Okay, until then, at least we can find out his contacts and profile from available call details. Also, ask them to send his CAF (the form filled out by the customer at the time of taking the connection)."

Call details were received in the evening. After perusing

the call details, it was revealed that it was a postpaid number in the name of Ghulam Mohammed Butt, who was about 60-years old and a resident of J&K. Meanwhile, Karnal Singh also reached the office after learning about the call. He also listened to the call.

Karnal: "Ravi, the sound of the recording is very poor; what do you think? Is he our man?"

Ravi: "I don't think so. First of all, I doubt that any terrorist will use a postpaid mobile. But he seems to be an on-the-ground worker; he probably is demanding money from Pakistan through *hawala*."

Karnal: "So, should we go after him?"

Ravi: "Sir, we already have a very good input; we should not waste our time. Our priority is to do that first, but this man should also be probed as to why he is contacting Pakistan and getting money. I think it is in national interest that we convey this information to the Intelligence Bureau through CP, Delhi."

Karnal: "I agree. Prepare a note on behalf of CP, Delhi and give it to me; I will forward it to MHA for action."

A note was prepared and handed over to Karnal Singh.

Karnal: "At least we have some satisfaction that the monitoring system is working. Okay, Ravi, let me know if something new emerges."

Ravi: "Sorry, sir, one more important thing I would like to convey to you is that at any time we could encounter terrorists. Many of us have been out of firing practice for a considerable time. I think we should go for firing practice. Secondly, we require some bullet-proof jackets of superior quality that can be worn under sweaters or coats. Thirdly, some pistols are also needed. Fourthly, many team members do not have mobile phones, which is the topmost requirement for us because we cannot carry wireless sets openly at the time of surveillance on the field. And finally, an alert commando team should be at our disposal round the clock."

Karnal: "Okay, Ravi, I cannot commit to you about bullet-proof jackets because Delhi Police do not have these in stock and you know the procedure for purchase. However, as far as mobile phones are concerned, PHQ has purchased mobile phones for senior officers in districts and units. I will talk to CP, if, instead of distributing to them, that can be diverted to us for the time being. I think it will be managed. As far as pistols and other things are concerned, it will be done. You can start fire practice on Monday."

Ravi: "Thank you, sir."

Karnal: "Okay, Ravi, take care."

Ravi: "Goodnight, sir."

I directed the duty officer to call all team members to remain present for the briefing at 9:00 a.m. the next day. After that, I left the office.

□

16

Specialised Training and Preparedness for Combat

Next morning, 12 January, 1998, the briefing started

Ravi: "Please pay attention to my words. In some extraordinary situations during the operation of arresting terrorists at their hideout, we have our commando team readily available, but we have to be prepared for a situation when we cordon off their hideout and stop them from escaping until our specialised team arrives."

In a different scenario, when engaging with a terrorist covertly integrated into the public, our response hinges on a combination of proficient marksmanship and swift instincts to navigate the evolving situation. Hence, regular firing practice sessions become imperative for all involved, ensuring that each member is well-equipped to handle such critical situations effectively.

Dataram: "Sir, I agree. Some of us are not proficient with firearms and facing armed terrorists without proper practice is a significant risk."

Ravi: I understand your concern. We cannot compromise on the safety and success of this operation. We need to ensure everyone is proficient with their weapons. I have arranged additional training sessions."

Vinod: "Sir, I have something to discuss with you regarding the upcoming operation."

Ravi: "What is it, Vinod? Speak up."

Vinod: "Well, sir, I am concerned about our readiness for the operation. I know you and your team are familiar with such situations and have successfully overcome them while dealing with Babbar Khalsa terrorists at Paschim Vihar and a more arduous situation in Kashmir recently, but many of us have never been in a situation where we have had to face armed terrorists."

Ashok, ASI: "Sir, what if we encounter terrorists who open fire? We need to be prepared for that scenario as well."

Ravi: Ashok, I am sure that most of you have conducted raids on notorious criminals and, at times, faced fiery encounters. It is nothing but the same thing. Trust your instincts. Remember, teamwork and communication were crucial at that time. We are a team and we have each other's backs."

Rajendra: "Sir, I believe we should conduct a mock operation to simulate real-life conditions. It would help us assess our readiness and identify any areas that need improvement."

Ravi: That's a valid suggestion, Rajendra. Let's organise a realistic training exercise at the New Police Lines to simulate a high-pressure situation. It will boost our confidence."

Dataram: "Thank you, sir. We appreciate your understanding and guidance. We will put in our best efforts to be fully prepared for the operation."

Ravi: "Remember, the safety of innocent lives is in our hands. We cannot afford any mistakes. Train hard, support each other and let's ensure this mission is a success."

Dixit : "Yes, sir, let's hope the terrorists are just as terrible at aiming as we are."

Ravi: "I wouldn't count on that but we'll rely on our training and teamwork to get through this. Stay sharp, everyone!"

ASI Kishan Lal: I'll make sure to give my best during this practice session, sir. I don't want to let my teammates down."

Ravi: "That's the spirit, Kishan. Dedication and teamwork are vital. We have each other's backs. Let's focus on improving our accuracy and coordination. Train hard and we'll face any challenge that comes our way."

Subhash: "Sir, we won't disappoint you. We'll train relentlessly and be ready to face whatever comes our way. We are all ready. *Koi shaque, jawano*." All in one voice: "No sir."

Ravi: "It's good to hear. Remember, your safety and the safety of civilians are our top priorities. Let's make every shot count and ensure that we can protect and serve with unwavering determination. Okay Dataramji, we will start it tomorrow morning. We will meet at the New Police Lines at 8:00 a.m. Disperse."

13 January, 1998 to 18 January, 1998

Firing practice and crisp training sessions were organised at NPL by a commando inspector during this period, in batches, so that ongoing surveillance on Kamran's hideout and observation of international calls were not disturbed. Inspector Dataram supervised these training sessions. Karnal Singh was able to procure, after convincing the Commissioner of Police, mobile phones purchased by PHQ for the use of the team members on an ad-hoc basis. The required arms and ammunition were also procured. But during this on January 14, an unfortunate incident occurred with Inspector Rajendra Bhatia. His father expired. I was present in the office when a call was received from Inspector Rajendra Bhatia regarding the death of his father.

Rajendra: "Sir, today it is not possible for me to attend the training programme and firing practice because my father has expired."

Ravi: "Oh no, very sad. What was his age and what happened? Was he sick?"

Rajendra remained silent. Ravi: "Rajendra, please inform me about the time and place of the cremation."

Rajendra: "Sure, sir."

The phone was disconnected immediately. I informed Karnal Singh about the death. I, along with Karnal Singh, Alok Kumar and some team members, attended the cremation. At the time of cremation, Karnal Singh allowed Rajendra Bhatia to stay on leave until the last rites of his father were over.

□

17
Identifying Elusive Caller to Pakistani Number

After attending the cremation of Rajendra Bhatia's father, on way to ISC, a call was received on my mobile from Harbir Singh, who was tasked with monitoring the observation of Pakistani phone numbers.

Harbir: "Sir, just now there was an attempt to call on Tunda's number, but no conversation took place."

Ravi: "Did you inform the Sadar Bazar team?"

Harbir: "No one is picking up the phone."

Meanwhile, Dixit's call was waiting on my mobile. Harbir disconnected and I took Dixit's waiting call.

Ravi: "Speak, Dixit."

Dixit: "Sir, a guy just tried Tunda's number from Jain's PCO but Jain told me that this guy wasn't Kamran. We are tracking him."

Ravi: "Very good, check where he goes and who he meets. It's possible he might meet Kamran. He shouldn't suspect anything."

Dixit: "Okay, sir, I'll talk to you later."

I reported this call to Karnal Singh. Dixit called me again.

Dixit: "Sir, he has entered the mosque in Pan Mandi."

Ravi: "Alright, keep an eye on him discreetly. If there are any new development, let me know. Try to find out from your sources who this person is."

Dixit: "Okay, sir, I'll try."

I conveyed a message to Subhash to maintain surveillance over that suspect until further directions. If possible, send Head Constable Hasrat Ali into the mosque in plain clothes and try to gather more information. Kamran's house was still locked.

By this time we reached the Interstate Cell, Chanakyapuri.

Ravi: "Sir, I think he has entered the same mosque that was disclosed by Nissar Ahmed and Mohsin Malik @Pappu and others when they were arrested along with Nissar by Punjab Police previously."

Alok responded, "But the Special Cell recently picked Nissar up and gave him a clean chit."

Karnal remarked, "What they have done, we are not aware of. Otherwise, it is not easy to break a subject until you have some solid evidence. Anyway, let's concentrate on our work."

I added, "Sir, as far as I recollect, the name of one Hussain, a Pakistani terrorist, was also mentioned in the interrogation of Mohsin Malik @ Pappu, and Nissar Ahmed."

Karnal inquired, "In what context?"

I replied, "Let me check the brief of their interrogation." (I picked up a file and consulted.) "Yes, sir, Hussain stayed in this mosque for some time. The reference of one Abdul Wahid and Abdul Majid also came up in their interrogation reports. The Intelligence Report of 1996 has been available to the Special Cell since then. The Special Cell previously questioned Abdul Majid and his father, Abdul Wahid, who were residing and managing the affairs of the mosque, but they were unable to produce any useful information. Sir, I think we should maintain a secret watch at this place and try to gather information."

Karnal considered, "It is also possible that this fellow was sent by Kamran himself to check on the police activities."

Alok agreed, "Absolutely, sir. We should not touch him until we get something solid against him or until the arrival of Kamran."

Hussain's identity remained unknown to us. But, dear readers, rest assured, you have the privilege of learning about him before we did. Up until his arrest in this case, we were completely in the dark about him.

Hussain Background (Around 1992)

Hussain, a 28-year-old Pakistani living in district Okara, frequently visited the mosque to hear *taqreers* (religious discourses). He became fascinated by the *taqreers* delivered by members of Lashkar-e-Toiba. Hussain used to perform his *namaz* (prayer) in Jama Masjid Ahle Hadis Jandraka and actively participated in all Lashkar-e-Toiba religious events.

After Lashkar-e-Toiba's annual gathering in Lahore in November 1992, Hussain decided to travel to Afghanistan for training. He participated in the Daur-e-Aam and enrolled in a three-month Daura-e-Khas training programme. Nassir Javed Ameer of Maskar-e-Toiba, along with individuals like Hafiz Saeed, Hafiz Yahya, Zaki-ur-Rehman, Nasir Rehmani and Shahbuddin Sharudi Hussain delivered *takreer* during the training.

As directed, Hussain gathered in Chela-Pandi, Muzaffarabad, after completing his training. In June 1994, he and 16 others took a bus from there to Gilgit (Kashmir). The individuals who would cross the border were chosen by Azam Cheema, the launching commander of the organisation. After a 24-hour journey, they reached Gilgit and spent 14-15 days in a government facility run by ISI, close to the police station.

During their stay, another group of 60-70 boys from Hizbul Mujahideen visited, leading to conflicts between the two organisations due to differing sects of Islam. ISI separated both groups at night to avoid potential problems. After 14-15 days, ISI officers and Azam Cheema arrived and they headed towards the Indo-Pak border.

After a lengthy trek through a thick forest, they reached the Indian border. Around five in the morning, they began to cross the Indian border, arriving at Pajipura after crossing the frozen river *nallah* and ascending a hill near Margand village in the Kangan area of Kashmir, India. Several lads were already residing in 'hide' in that area and this group had carried out several actions there.

Eight individuals, including Hussain, were dispatched to Badgam before being taken to downtown Srinagar. This led to crackdowns in the Kashmir Valley as they moved around in concealment. Their squad, well-prepared with hand grenades, rifles and other weaponry, ultimately remained in a group of three.

In August 1995, Hussain decided to sell his rifle for Rs. 35,000 and leave the area due to the increasing risk. He landed in Delhi in September 1995 and initially resided with Abdul Salam until January 1996. Later, he joined the Tablighi Jamaat in Nizamuddin and went on excursions with them. Later he enrolled himself in Maulvi Abdul Mazid's *madrasa* in Pan Mandi, Sadar Bazar, Delhi. There, he encountered Ammar, a Pakistani, who wore a Casio watch with a compass, leading Hussain to believe he might be a member of Lashkar-e-Toiba as each of the terrorists belonging to LeT were provided with such watches before they were planted in India. During that period, the police conducted an inquiry-visit to the Pan Mandi mosque following the arrest of Mosin@Pappu and his associates in Punjab.

However, Hussain left the *madrasa* to avoid police interrogation, learning later that Ammar was a student at Mama Masjid near Riazul-Uloom-Nadesa, Delhi. Hussain informed Ammar about his connections with Zaki-ur-Rehman from Lashkar-e-Toiba. Ammar verified this information and Zaki-ur-Rehman directed Ammar to send Hussain to Pakistan after the outfit declared him a deserter. Ammar arranged for Hussain to board a train for Howrah and on the way, he met Abu-Saeed, a Lashkar-e-Toiba terrorist, who was in his batch during training.

They travelled to Dhaka, stayed at Abdul Karim@Babaji's hideout in Jatrabari, Bangladesh, where Hussain met Babaji and expressed his intention to visit Pakistan as directed by Zaki-ur-Rehman. Hussain remained with Babaji, met other operatives of LeT at Babaji's hideout and learned how to make bombs. Babaji instructed him to travel back to India with LeT operatives and meet Abdul Baki in Pan Mandi, Sadar Bazar, where Hussain previously took admission upon arriving in Delhi from Kashmir.

15 January, 1998

Karnal and I were present at the Interstate Cell in Chanakyapuri, discussing an ad hoc substitute for Rajendra Bhatia when we learned that Rajendra Bhatia had already joined the office.

Meanwhile, Rajendra entered the room and saluted.

Karnal (surprised to see Bhatia): I think you should be at your home at this juncture. If you needed anything from us, you should have conveyed it through the telephone; it would have been done."

Rajendra: "No, sir, I don't require anything; rather, I have joined duty. This operation is more important than anything else. Nation first, sir."

Ravi: "We all salute you, Rajendra. It is so great of you, and really, you have solved our problem as well."

Rajendra: "Sir, it is my duty where there is no sort of greatness. Okay, sir, I am going to attend firing and training practice."

Karnal: "Ravi, this is the first time I have come across such a responsible officer."

Ravi: "No doubt, sir. Sir, what happened about the monitoring at VSNL?"

Karnal: "I have to meet Nikhil Kumar, Special Secretary IS (Internal Security) tomorrow morning in this regard."

Ravi: "Did you see any seriousness at the ministry level in such a grave situation?"

Karnal: "There are many other priorities on their agenda. Anyway, I will let you know after the discussion with Nikhil Kumar tomorrow."

On 16 January, 1998, Karnal Singh met Nikhil Kumar and

apprised him of the requirement for observation at VSNL. Nikhil Kumar immediately directed the concerned officer in Sanchar Bhavan's Ministry of Communication to facilitate the Crime Branch and make arrangements for the observation of Pakistani numbers at VSNL.

Finally, on 18 January, 1998, the monitoring at VSNL started on Pakistan number. This was the first time such a facility was explored and activated at the initiative of the Crime Branch. Even the Indian intelligence agencies did not visualise this aspect until then. This facility in the near future proved to be a game-changer in the collection of intelligence regarding the activities of terrorist outfits and notorious gangs based abroad and their network in India, which would further assist in neutralising these terrorist outfits.

□

18

Anticipating '*Acche Din*': Lucknow and Ludhiana Unveiled

21 January, 1998

During this time, ASI Hasrat Ali went to the mosque at Pan Mandi, Sadar Bazar to gather some information randomly. Abdul Majid, who had six sons and four daughters, was the manager of that Ahle Hadees mosque. His three daughters were living in Karachi and the young boy (the subject) was the fourth son of Abdul Majid. He had been running a general store in Sarai Khalil, Sadar Bazar for the last three years. During the last month of 1996, the subject, whose name was Abdul Baki, went to Pakistan and came back in February 1997.

Abdul Baki's house, the Mosque Paan Mandi, was under constant surveillance. Following the arrest of Nissar Ahmed and his friends, the Punjab Police had previously questioned the residents of Paan Mandi. Following their narrow escape from a police investigation, they were understandably cautious. This time around, it was crucial to have concrete proof to present them during interrogation and because of that, Abdul Baki escaped detection during earlier investigations. However, their actions were randomly and covertly reviewed. I relied heavily on INTEL gathered from informants embedded within the mosque and who developed intimacy with Abdul Majid, the father of Abdul Baki. A week before the Republic Day celebration, a large police presence was maintained in Delhi, particularly around the Sadar Bazar area. This provided our team with excellent cover for deploying uniformed personnel at the Sadar Bazar mosque.

During these events, on the 21 January, I was in the Sadar Bazar neighbourhood. Vinod Kumar, who had been assigned to VSNL to listen to calls from Pakistan, called in.

Vinod: "Sir, just received a call from Lucknow on Babaji's number. I'll send you the cassette and call details."

Ravi: "Oh, very good, quickly send it to the office."

Vinod: "Consider it done; the guy is already on his way to the office."

Ravi: "Okay, Vinod. Very good. Just stay alert."

Vinod: "Sir, don't worry. I won't let a single call go unnoticed."

Ravi: "That's why I've kept you on the job. Very good, I'll disconnect now."

I immediately shared the news of the conversation with Karnal Singh. Karnal Singh stopped work and headed to ISC as well. By that time, not only had we reached ISC, but the policeman had also arrived with a tape of the call. After playing the cassette, it was discovered that a man named Harun, speaking with a Bengali accent, was chatting with a man named Babaji (Abdul Karim Tunda).

Harun: "*Salaam walekum*, Babaji." (Peace be upon you, Babaji.)

Babaji: "*Walaikum salaam. Kaise ho aur Musa kaisa hai*?" (And unto you peace. How are you and how is Musa?)

Harun: "*Allah ke fazal se sab theek hai, Babaji, lekin yahan par ghoomne phirne mein kafi pareshani uthani pad rahi hai, isliye hum chahte hain ki ek nayi cycle le le.*" (By the grace of Allah, everything is fine, Babaji, but there is a lot of trouble in moving around here. That's why we want to buy a new bicycle.)

Babaji: "*Han, han, theek hai le lo aur acchi tarah se sabhi jagahon ko dekh lo, iske baad main batata hoon ki kya karna hai.*" (Yes, yes, that's fine. Purchase the bicycle and look around carefully everywhere. After that, I'll let you know what to do.)

Harun: "*Allah hafiz, phone rakhta hun.*"

The details of the mysterious phone call were unravelling, indicating that it originated from Lucknow TAXT. The calling number's specifics were shrouded in secrecy, as VSNL had not provided them, claiming it was to save space in the hardware.

My instincts tingled with anticipation as I discussed the situation with Karnal Singh. The need to probe deeper and trace the calling number led to a decision – Lucknow was the next destination.

"Sir, I have to go with the team. It's crucial," I insisted, feeling the urgency in the air.

Karnal nodded, recognising the gravity of the situation. Time was of essence and the investigation required my direct involvement.

In the midst of it, the duty officer interrupted with a message from my home.

Duty Officer: "Sir, there's a call from home; Madam wants to discuss something important."

Ravi: "I'll be right back to take the ca ll."

Karnal intervened: "It might be something important; go ahead and talk."

Ravi: "I know what it is. Sir, excuse me."

I picked up the phone and responded: "Hello *ji sarkar*."

Sushma: "Where have you been? It's been two days since you came home. Sister and brother-in-law and all the kids are here, waiting for you. I asked you before planning the programme."

Ravi: "Yes, I know, but work has become such that I can't avoid it at all. Sorry, I'll see what I can do. You all go ahead; I'll figure something out."

Sushma: "Okay, just come for 10-15 minutes. Sister is waiting for you. She has come from so far after so many days."

Ravi: "Okay, let me see. You hang up."

Sushma: "Just come, there's nothing to see; just come."

Karnal Singh again intervened: "Is there something urgent? If there is, go ahead, I'll handle it."

Ravi: "Sir, it's my wedding anniversary today and my sisters are at home, so she called to check if I can make it."

Karnal: "Congratulations! I'll handle things here. Since it's already decided, you're going to Lucknow in the morning. Plan your celebration; everyone is waiting for your company."

Karnal Singh left the office. I instructed Subhash Tandon and ASI Ramesh Dabas to accompany a small team to Lucknow, arriving at New Delhi railway station at 4:30 a.m. to arrange for tickets. I then left the office and went home to join the celebration.

22 January, 1998; BSNL Office, Lucknow

On 22 January, 1998, Srivastava, PA to the General Manager of BSNL, Lucknow, welcomed us. The General Manager was not present in his office. Srivastava promptly offered all possible assistance after speaking with the GM over the phone. Because the information was to be gathered from seven telephone exchanges in Lucknow, Srivastava assured us that the record would be available the following afternoon. We spent the night with Subhash Tandon's maternal uncle. Srivastava called in the morning and informed me that the information was ready. We went to the BSNL office, collected and examined the information. The Pak number was discovered to have been contacted from an STD booth in the Dolly Ganj region. An inquiry from the STD booth revealed that the phone number was dialled by a youngster of about 20 years of age. He who was accompanied by another boy of the same age. They were dressed like labourers and spoke in Bengali. Booth records were also obtained, studied and verified. Apart from the Pak number discovered at that booth, no other questionable numbers were found. However, it was decided to check for Pakistani numbers in Lucknow's entire six-month record. Srivastava was given a formal request. I then left Lucknow, leaving Subhash and his team behind to gather additional information.

A six-month database was obtained, revealing that two Pakistani numbers mentioned in the list had been dialled from two different STD booths in Lucknow since November 1997. An investigation of STD booth records showed one new Bangladesh telephone number, which Harun and Musa dialled on 24 January. Because the search results were received on 28 January, the conversation at this number could not be intercepted. This number, along with other Pakistani phone numbers in Lucknow, was kept under surveillance.

2 February, 1998

Nevertheless, *'acche din'* were ahead, but the national celebration began and passed quietly with the blessings of God, much to the delight of the entire Delhi Police force. Meanwhile, Harun and Musa arrived in Ludhiana; perhaps the directions were given by Babaji on 24 January when they would have contacted the Bangladesh phone number, which we came to know on 28 January, after processing the BSNL, Lucknow record. After reaching Ludhiana, they dialled Babaji's number from the Ludhiana railway station.

Harun: "*Salaam walekum, Harun bol raha hun Ludhiana se. Aap kaun bol rahe hain*?" (Hello, this is Harun speaking from Ludhiana. Who am I speaking to?)

Arif: "*Walekum salaam*, Arif, *bol raha hun*." He responded from Pakistan.

"*Abbu abhi yahan per nahin hai, 10-12 din baad call karna tab tak aap Ludhiana mein hi ghumen*." (Hello, Arif, this side. Abu is not here right now; call after 10-12 days. Until then, you can explore Ludhiana.)

Harun: "*Theek hai Arif bhai, aap Babaji ko bata dena ki hum Ludhiana pahunch gaye hain. Apki badi meherbani hogi, Allah Hafiz, Arif*." (Alright, Arif Bhai, please inform Babaji that we have reached Ludhiana. Your help will be greatly appreciated. *Allah Hafiz*.)

"*Allah Hafiz, aap apna khyal rakhna*." (Take care. *Allah*

Hafiz.) I was apprised of the phone call. As a result, Rajendra Bhatia's team travelled to Ludhiana.

3 February, 1998

When Inspector Rajendra Bhatia reached Ludhiana, he immediately got down to work. Phone numbers from Bangladesh and Pakistan were monitored. Additionally, the Ludhiana exchange records were examined to identify the booth from which the call on 2 February, 1998, was placed. In addition, it was requested that the last six months' worth of telephone exchange records in the area be searched to identify any suspected Pak or Bangladesh numbers dialled from that region. All the teams that would be stationed in phone exchanges follow a Standard Operating Procedure (SOP) briefed by me when a call is made on a suspect number of Pakistan. SI Sandeep Malhotra was given the duty to collect, examine and compile all the data from the relevant TAXT and exchanges when he received any information from the exchanges to find out the additional numbers related to the outfit.

Inspector Rajendra Bhatia and his staff were on the scene, ready for the next call. I made it plain to the squad that their objective was to identify Harun and Musa and keep them under surveillance, without compromising their identity until Kamran returned to his hideout. Some police officials deployed at Lucknow were also relocated to Ludhiana for assistance. At that point in time, the operation was spread in Delhi, UP and Punjab.

Teams were stationed at the following locations:

- STD booth of Jain at Sadar Bazar, Delhi.
- Kamran's house in Teliwara, Sadar Bazar, Delhi.
- Abdul Bakis hideout is Paan Mandi, Sadar Bazar, Delhi.
- Telephone Exchange, Lucknow, UP.
- Field Ganj, Ludhiana, Punjab.
- Ludhiana TAXT Punjab.
- Karol Bagh TAXT Delhi.
- VSNL (Videsh Sanchar Nigam Ltd.), Delhi.

I was coordinating with each team from my office in Interstate Cell at Chanakyapuri throughout the day. I couldn't afford to leave the office. This was a critical stage; any error in the procedure would have brought the entire operation to a halt. Every move had to be highly considered and prudent. At the time, the suspects were receiving orders from their handler in Pakistan, and most of their communication routes were being monitored to acquire as much information as possible about the suspects and the presence of additional modules in India. Listening in on their conversation was highly advisable for this purpose.

As a result, each team member's patience was sought, so they were given a clear directive: "At any cost, the team would not afford to expose itself." Not only did the officers give their best, but also their family, relatives and friends were extending all possible assistance in this operation.

In Sadar Bazar, Dataram's friend made arrangements for secret locations for the teams. Inspector Subhash Tandon's maternal uncle supplied logistics and support in Lucknow. In Ludhiana, Ramesh Sharma's brother-in-law and a friend of his in Sonipat; in Rohtak, Satpal Singh ASI's family; and in Saharanpur, the in-laws of head constable Vinod Kumar extended their support in the form of food, places to stay, mobile phones, vehicles and sometimes physical support when there was a need for manpower. Friends and relatives have fed and housed dozens of police officers in their homes on numerous occasions. In reality, the crew was severely underfunded; moreover, they could not afford to remain public and use official cars to prevent any exposure.

11 February, 1998

However, there was no conversation on any of the numbers under observation after 2 February and until 10 February. At that point, it was necessary to maintain the morale of the team members, who had been in the field for more than two weeks, neglecting their families. Therefore, it was critical to recognise and praise their efforts and dedication. They were constantly briefed to establish trust and keep them focused on their goal in the event of a sudden change in their job due to any operational requirement. However, the entire team was confident in their line of investigation because all independent leads and inputs uncovered during the investigation pointed fingers at: 'Abdul Karim Tunda, @Babaji' and 'Kamran'. According to information received from VSNL Delhi, a call was attempted to Babaji's number on 11 February, 1998, but no one answered in Pakistan. The team stationed at VSNL, Delhi was instructed to promptly communicate the information to the officer stationed at Ludhiana TAXT. I then contacted Ludhiana TAXT where Inspector Rajendra Bhatia's team was deployed.

Ravi to Satyavan (Head Constable): "Have you checked if any calls were made to Babaji's number?"

Satyavan: "Yes, sir and I have also obtained the STD booth's number and have provided it to Bhatia Sahib, who is present in Field Ganj. It will take him about 10-15 minutes to reach there."

Ravi: "Very good, Satyavan. Now tell me, is there any provision here through which we can cut the ongoing call?"

Satyavan: "I'll have to check with Lakhani Sahib (a senior employee in BSNL); he is sitting with me."

Ravi: "Please connect me with Lakhani Sahib."

Satyavan handed over the telephone to Lakhani.

Lakhani: "Good evening, sir."

Ravi: "Good evening, Lakhaniji. How are you? Bhatia has been speaking very highly of you. Will you please tell me if there is any facility to interrupt an ongoing call in your exchange?"

Lakhani: "Yes, sir, we can do it."

Ravi: "So I request that if the subject again tries to contact Pakistan and the call is matured, kindly disconnect the call in between, which would probably inspire him to dial again from the same booth. In this way, we can gain some time to reach there and identify the caller."

Lakhani: "I get your point very well, sir. Now you don't have to worry about this. I will handle it, rest assured."

Ravi: "Thank you, Lakhani Sahib. It's so nice of you. Can I have your number?"

Lakhani: "Of course, sir, please note it down."

Ravi: "Okay, Lakhani Sahib. Thanks."

Inspector Rajendra Bhatia called me after roughly 30 minutes.

Rajendra: "Sir, we've found the booth in Field Ganj. Can you perhaps allow me to contact the owner of the STD booth?"

Ravi: "What do you think? In my opinion, we should wait for a while; it will be pretty early."

Rajendra: "All right, sir, we'll wait for the next call. In the meantime, we're gathering the phone numbers of other STD booths in the area to avoid a delay in acquiring the booth's address."

Ravi: "That's fantastic! This is a wise decision. Okay, I'll contact you later. Best wishes."

15 February, 1998

However, no calls were made or attempted on Babaji's numbers following that until 6 a.m. on 15 February, 1998, when a call was received at VSNL. Harun contacted Arif in Pakistan, according to SI Anil Kumar stationed at VSNL. Arif, son of Babaji, requested that Harun would contact Babaji in the evening, after two or three days. I verified from Rajendra Bhatia about that: "Is there any movement?"

Rajendra: "Sir, we were late by 10 minutes. Because Satyavan was not present when the call was received, we only learned about it after 10 minutes."

Ravi: "Where has he gone?"

Rajendra: "In the washroom, sir. Moreover, BSNL staff were also not present in the exchange. Satyavan came to know about this call after five minutes."

Ravi: "Okay, these are parts and parcels. We cannot avoid these things. Anyway, we have to be patient for two to three more days. I will talk to you later."

All the teams were positioned at their respective places. Another three days passed. The Ludhiana team was continuously positioned in the Field Ganj area.

On 18 February, 1998, at approximately 8:15 p.m., an attempt was made on the Pakistani number, but, as instructed, Lakhani did not allow the call to go through. Meanwhile, Inspector Anil Kumar informed me and Rajendra about the call simultaneously. I immediately attempted to contact Rajendra Bhatia, but he did not answer the phone. Then, I contacted Ramesh Sharma right away.

Ravi: "Where are you?"

Ramesh: "Sir, we are on way to the STD booth from where the call was attempted and in a minute, we will be there. Bhatia Sahib is driving the scooter. We will call you later on."

I immediately disconnected the phone and contacted Lakhani again.

Lakhani: "Good evening, sir. He tried two times from the same booth, but as per your instruction, we have disconnected the call...Sir, just hang on. He is trying again from a different booth."

Ravi: "Don't disconnect the call this time; our team must have reached there. Only inform Ramesh Sharma on his mobile number because Bhatia is driving."

Lakhani: "Okay, sir."

Lakhani kept my call on hold and immediately informed Ramesh of the STD phone number.

Lakhani: "Sir, this time the call went through, but no one picked up, and after four or five rings, they themselves cut the phone.:

Ravi: Okay, Lakhani Sahib, we are bothering you too much."

Lakhani: "Not at all, sir; rather, I am enjoying this filmy drama."

Ravi: "Okay; enjoy it. Bye, bye."

After half an hour, Rajendra Bhatia called: "Sorry, sir, we

were almost there at the second booth, but the moment we traced the booth, they had already left about a minute before."

Ravi: "Don't be disheartened; their luck is favouring them. *Bakre ki man kab tak Khair manayegi. Aakhir inki gardan hamare hath mein ayegi. Wow, kya tukbandi hai!*" (Ultimately, their fate will be in our hands.)

Rajendra: "There is no doubt in this, sir. Let us see for how many days this chase will continue. But, sir, the people of the area are getting suspicious about our movements."

Ravi: "Oh, I see. Rajendra, replace the staff immediately."

Rajendra: "Sir, we cannot change the entire staff; we have to keep those who are familiar to the area."

Ravi: "I can understand that. Anyway, interchange the location if possible."

Rajendra: "Okay, sir, I will look into it. *Jai Hind*, sir.

19 February 1998

A list of team members deployed at various booths was provided to SI Rakesh Dixit, who arrived from Lucknow and was stationed at the Ludhiana Telephone Exchange. At about 7:45 p.m., a call was dialled from an STD booth where Head Constable Satyavan was deployed. Dixit called Satyavan as soon as he received the call, but he did not answer. Lakhani, on the other hand, disconnected the call as instructed. Rakesh immediately contacted Rajendra Bhatia, who, along with Ramesh Sharma, rushed to the booth where Satyavan was stationed and from where the call was attempted.

Finally, they recognised Harun and Musa, who made a second attempt at the Pakistan number from the same booth. Ramesh Sharma instantly informed Rakesh Dixit about the situation and advised him not to end the conversation at that time.

On the other hand, when Anil Sharma at VSNL, Delhi noticed Babaji's phone number had been dialled, he immediately informed me.

Anil: "Sir, *abhi phone try hua tha, aur ab dobara ring ja*

rahi hai." (Just now, there was an attempt to make a call and now again its happening.)

Ravi: "Place your telephone in front of the speakers. I would like to listen to this call in real time."

The call went through and the conversation started.

Babaji: "*Salaam walekum, kaun bol rahe hain*." (Peace be upon you, who is speaking?)

Harun: "*Walekum salaam* Babaji, main Harun." (And unto you peace, Babaji, it's Harun.)

Babaji: "*Acchaa accha, Harun kaise mijaj hain aur Musa kaisa hai*?" *Uska khas khyal rakhna hai*." (Okay, okay, Harun, how are you, and how is Musa? Take special care of him.)

Harun: "*Theek hai Babaji. Kya baat hai Babaji, aapka phone hi nahin milta; jab milta hai to koi uthata nahin*." (Alright, Babaji. What's the matter? Your phone is always unreachable and no one picks up when it does get connected.)

Babaji: "*Harun beta, kai dinon se phone aur Fax donon kharab chal rahe hain yahan per kisi ne khudai karte hue cable kat di sare mohalle ke phone kharab pade hain*." (Harun, for several days, both the phone and fax have been out of order here. Someone who was digging, cut the cable and all the phones in the neighbourhood are not working.)

Harun: "*Chalo koi baat nahin, agla hukum batao kya karna hai? Ab to pareshan ho gaye hain*." (Okay, no problem. What's the next command? We are fed up now.)

Babaji: "*Haan, Harun beta, bus ab tumhen kam per lagana hai tum donon agale jumme 34/1 number per pahuncho. Vahan pahunchkar mujhe udhar Anwar wale number per phone karna. Tab tak yahan se ek party tumhari taraf pahunch jayegi. Vahan se tumhen aage jana pad sakta hai aur vah tumhen sab kuchh samjha dega, ki wahan per kaun sa karobar karna hai. Aur usi ke hath mein karobar ke liye faloos bhi bhijwa dunga*." (Yes, Harun, now you just need to focus on work. Both of you reach 34/1(code of some place) next Friday. Upon reaching there, call me at the Anwar's number. By then, a party from here will reach you. They can guide you further as to what business you have to do there and I will also send money for the business via them.)

Harun: *Theek hai Babaji ham pahunch jaenge.*" (Alright, Babaji, we will reach there.)

Babaji: "*Jara Musa se to baat karvana.*" (Let me talk to Musa for a moment.)

Harun gave the telephone to Musa.

Musa: "*Salaam walekum, Babaji.*" (Peace be upon you, Babaji.)

Babaji: "*Walekum salaam. Apna khyal rakhna aur zyada kisi se baat nahin karna.*" (And unto you peace. Take care of yourself and don't talk too much with anyone.)

Musa: *Ji Babaji. Allah Hafiz.*" (Yes, Babaji, *Allah Hafiz.*)

Anil Sharma: "Sir, the phone is disconnected."

Ravi: "Okay, Anil, thank you. Let me talk to Rajendra."

Lakhani also conveyed the details to me regarding that call. Meanwhile, a call was received from Rajendra.

Rajendra: "Sir, both of them have been identified."

Ravi: "Good job, Rajendra. Follow them and locate their hideout. And remember, don't pick them up."

Rajendra: "Okay, sir, I will talk to you later."

To be truthful, Ashok Kumar and Rajendra's movements had been visible to the public for the past two days. The residents of the area alerted the local police, who detained them. Ramesh Sharma contacted the police station's in-charge and revealed their identity. Ramesh Sharma informed the in-charge that they were looking into one cheating case and gathering information on the cheater. The in-charge of the police station then asked Ramesh Sharma to show him the FIR, to which Ramesh Sharma informed the in-charge that no FIR was filed in this matter because it involved a very close cousin of their senior officer and the entire investigation was informal. Ramesh Sharma was able to get Ashok and Rajendra released from the police station after convincing the officer in-charge, without disclosing the real operation.

When the police station in-charge attempted to persuade the residents of the area after revealing the identity and the purpose of the police squad, one of them pointed towards a man lying on a bench and said, *"Sir, ae kedi police hai jedi bhang de pakode khake lumbi paye hai samne."* (Sir, what sort of police is this, enjoying cannabis *pakoras* and lounging with long legs in front of us?)

Ramesh Sharma noted that Head Constable Satyavan was lying on the bench in front of the *pakoda* shop at that point. However, after convincing them all, Ramesh Sharma took Head Constable Satyavan with them.

In fact, when Rajendra Bhatia and his colleague Satyavan were already there at the *pakora* shop, he was starving and unwittingly bought *bhang pakora*. After having one *pakoda*, Bhatia handed over the *pakoda* plate to Satyavan and Bhatia went on to check out the other booths. Satyavan, the Head Constable, was also quite hungry; he inadvertently consumed the entire plate of *pakodas*. He became inebriated and collapsed on the bench. This incident was kept hidden by Bhatia until the operation was finished.

Rajendra Bhatia then tried to find out the further strategy in view of the recent developments. He was conveyed by me that Harun and Musa's travels would be traced and closely monitored until further decision.

20 February, 1998

Karnal Singh at ISC called a meeting early in the morning. Alok Kumar, myself, Dataram, and Subhash Tandon were present in the meeting. A discussion was going on regarding the further course of action to be adopted during the operation.

Inspector Dataram: "Sir, it is high time we pick up Harun and Musa immediately from Ludhiana itself. I think we should not take any further risks."

Ravi: "Dataramji, it would not be a good move to capture them until we identify and catch Kamran. As far as their involvement in the bomb blast is concerned, I can say safely that they are not involved in the blast and this can easily be made out from their conversation with Babaji."

Karnal: "Yes, Dataramji, have you listened to the conversation?"

Subhash: "But sir, there is a risk in prolonging it."

Ravi: "Of course, there is a risk, but what will you do when they are not found involved in any case? Our main motto is 'solve the case first'. It is clear from the latest conversation that they are going to meet some important members of the cadre next Friday. Moreover, the indication given by Babaji to Harun is that they are planning to take some action after meeting someone."

Alok: "Oh no, if they are planning to do so, then we have to catch all of them when they meet."

Karnal: "Yes, Alok, so it is very necessary to identify and arrest the person they are going to meet."

Alok: "Sir, can he be Kamran or Abul Baki?"

Ravi: "He may be anyone and possibly more important than Kamran and Abdul Baki."

Karnal: "Exactly; therefore, we have to strengthen and sensitise all our teams. Let us have patience and track the movements of Harun and Musa until their meeting with their other members of the cadre."

□

19
Emergence of Abdullah

On 23 February, 1998, around 7 p.m. at Delhi, Harbir Singh entered my office.

Harbir: "*Jai Hind*, sir. Today is my son's birthday. If you permit, I'd like to go home for two to three hours."

Ravi: "Congratulations! Okay, you can go, but keep your mobile phone with you."

Harbir: "Thank you, sir. I'll directly reach Sadar Bazar from home by 11:00 p.m."

Ravi: "Right."

Harbir left the office. After half an hour, a call was made to Babaji's Bangladeshi number, but no one picked up the call. All the teams were alerted. Inspector Dataram called Harbir Singh back while he was on his way home. The call was generated from Karol Bagh's TAXT. Ranbir Singh Bhura, who was present at Karol Bagh, traced the phone number from where the call was attempted. It was dialled from an STD booth on Bahadurgarh Road, Sadar Bazar. This booth was different from the one that Kamran often used.

After some time, another call was attempted, but it was from another booth in Kishanganj. This time, the call went through. One Sanaullah picked up the phone.

Sanaullah: "*Salaam walekum. Kaun bol rahe hain?*" (Peace be upon you. Who is speaking?)

Abdullah: "*Walekum saalam, Bhaijaan. Abdulla bol raha hun. Babaji, aa gaye kya?*" (And unto you peace, brother. This is Abdullah speaking. Has Babaji arrived?)

Sanaullah: "*Babaji udhar se kal chalenge. Aap parson phone karen. Abdullah Bhai aap bhi hamari chachaji se sifarish karen ham bhi deen ki khidmat karna chahte hain ab. Yahan bahut din ho gaye hain, aap apne pass bulva lo.*" (Babaji will come from there tomorrow; call day after tomorrow. Abdullah Bhai, you also recommend us to your uncle (Zaki-ur-Rehman). We also want to serve in this religious cause. It's been many days here; please call us over.)

Abdullah: "*Jald hi aapko mauka milega. Chachaji se baat hui thi do din pahle kah rahe the ki kuchh bada business karna hai aur vahan se yani aapki taraf se vah kuchh worker bhijwayenge ho sakta hai vah aapki hi baat kar rahe ho.*" (Soon, you will get an opportunity. I spoke to uncle (Zaki) two days ago; he was saying that there is a big business (planning for action) opportunity and from your side (Pakistan), they might send some workers (terrorists), which might include you.)

Sanaullah: "*Bhai jaan, Allah ki khidmat karne ko bahut dil kar raha hai; jaldi bulva lo.*" (Brother, I am eager to serve in the name of Allah. Please call us soon.)

Abdullah: "*Inshallah, aap mutmain rahiye abaki bar khidmat ka mauka zarur denge. Achcha Allah Hafiz; zyada dair tak baat theek nahin; phone rakhta hun.*" (Inshaallah, you stay content; we will surely provide an opportunity for service next time. Alright, *Allah Hafiz*. I can't talk for too long; I'll hang up now.)

It took roughly ten minutes to locate the booth's address. "At that time, our team could identify the booth but the caller had already left. However, during that time, the house of Kamran and Abdul were secretly checked. It was found that Abdul Baki had not moved from his house since 5:00 p.m., whereas there was no movement at Kamran's house. Subhash Tandon was asked to get the voice identified from the sources, to check whether it was Kamran or someone else. The source checked the voice and it wasn't Kamran. However, Sandeep was asked to analyse the record of both STD booths from where the call originated."

Thanks to the 'Observation on Called Number' feature, a previously overlooked aspect, I want to emphasise that this idea represents a pioneering breakthrough in the history of phone-based communication observation. The sequence has already been covered above. One more name has just emerged through this facility before us to probe further; 'Abdullah, who is he? Why is he attempting to speak with Babaji?' It was concerning that, he was in Delhi.

However, before we (investigators) delve deeper into this individual's history through further investigation, I'd like to furnish my readers with some preliminary background information regarding Abdullah.

Abdullah

Abdullah was born in 1968 in the village of Sadoki, *tehsil* Kamoki, District Gujranwala, Pakistan, and had his primary education at a village school. After that, in the years 1980-81, he started learning to drive and worked as a driver until 1990. After that, he started selling kerosene oil. In the year 1995, one Arshad, Amir of the Sadoke (Kamoki) office of Lashkar-e-Toiba, invited him to listen to the '*taqreer*' at Markaz Muridke. On his invitation, Abdullah stayed in Markaz for two to three months, as Arshad had given him the job of selling *khad* (manure) at the Madina Khad Store in the village. Arshad used to pay him Rs. 2000 per month.

During that time, he got used to listening to *taqreer* regularly, in which appeals were made to go for war (*jihad*) in Kashmir. Having been impressed or provoked by *takreers*, Abdullah also decided to go for training at Muzaffarabad in April 1995. After reaching Muzaffarabad, the subject went to the office of Markaz, where he met Zaki-ur-Rehman Lakhvi, the Amir of Lashkar-e-Toiba, and then filled out the form. Abdullah underwent training – *Daur-e-Aam* and *Daur-e-Khas* – which lasted for more than three months in the hilly area. It was a group of 80 boys. They also took the commando course.

After completing training, he stayed at home for another five to six months. He did nothing during these months except to visit Markaz quite frequently, where Abdul Karim Tunda, Babaji, used to give *taqreer* in Markaz and tell that in Hindustan, Hindus had demolished Babri Masjid, committed a lot of atrocities on the Muslim brothers and killed them openly. They should go to Hindustan and do *jihad*. Babaji taught them how to make a bomb. Abdullah was impressed and convinced. He volunteered himself for committing *jihad* in Hindustan, as per the directions of Babaji.

Abdullah got his passport prepared and in the month of February or March 1996, reached Dhaka by aeroplane; the fare was given by Babaji. Babaji had another hideout in Dhaka besides in Pakistan and also used to live there. In Dhaka, Abdullah met some other Pakistani terrorists of the LeT, including Hussain, Zakaria, Suher, Umar, Sanaullah, Nasrullah and Farid. In the month of May/June 1996, Abdullah, along with Hussain and Zuber, crossed the Bangladesh border from Lal Gola and reached Calcutta, before reaching Delhi by train.

□

20
Identification and Arrest of Module 1

26 February, 1998 (Ludhiana)

At about 6:30 p.m., Harun again contacted Babaji on a Bangladeshi phone number.

Harun: "*Salaam walekum Babaji. Kal party se milane ka waqt diya tha, vahe pakka hai na*?" (Peace be upon you, Babaji. Did you confirm the time to meet the party tomorrow? Is it definite?)

Babaji: "*Walekum salaam, bilkul pakka hai. Kal vahan per pahunch jao.*" (And unto you peace absolutely. Tomorrow reach there.)

Harun: "*Babaji, aapane kuchh number bola tha vah samajh mein nahin aaya. Kahan ka number hai kahan jana hai?*" (Babaji, you mentioned some numbers (34/1 in previous conversation) which I didn't understand. Which place does the number belong to and where should I go?)

Babaji: "*Sanaullah ne aapko code nahin note karvaye the kya?*" (Sanaullah didn't make you note down the code?)

Harun: "*Nahin.*" (No.)

Babaji: "*Chalo koi baat nahin yahan per Fax hai kya? Agar hai to vahan ka number do mujhe main Fax per address bhejta hun. Khayal rahe, patey ko zubani yaad karke Fax phad dena. Is baat ko gaanth bandhlo?*" (Okay, no problem. Do you have a Fax there? If yes, give me the number and I'll send the address via the Fax. Remember, memorise the details and tear off the Fax. Is this clear?)

Harun asked for the Fax number of the STD owner and conveyed it to Babaji.

After some time, Harun received a Fax. The phone disconnected and Harun and Musa went back to the mosque. I listened to the conversation live, of course legally, and immediately contacted Inspector Rajendra Bhatia. He was advised to remain on alert mode because Harun and Musa could leave the station at any time. Bhatia was directed to send advance parties to the railway station and to the Inter State Bus Terminal (ISBT) and he himself had to follow them. Ramesh Sharma arranged for a Maruti car and a scooter through his brother-in-law. They covered all exit points.

At about 9:30 p.m., Harun and Musa came out of the mosque and started walking towards ISBT. After about 1 km., they unexpectedly turned back and started walking towards the railway station. On the way to the railway station, they took a meal at a kiosk and later reached the station. Harun purchased tickets from the ticket-window destined for Delhi. Constable Devender, who was standing behind Harun, also purchased tickets for his party. Constable Devender also conveyed to Bhatia their destination and simultaneously, Bhatia briefed the police teams already summoned at the railway station from different positions. All the teams were asked to board the train in different coaches of the same train in which Harun and Musa would be travelling. Ramesh Sharma and his party were asked to follow Harun and Musa.

In the reservation hall, Harun made an inquiry from a passenger, who, after looking at the time-table, said something. Probably Harun was asking for train timings. After that, both of them reached platform No. 2 and took out and spread their bedsheets on the platform to lie down. Two or three trains going to Delhi passed by, but they did not catch the train.

At about 3 a.m., another train going to Delhi arrived. Harun inquired about that train from one passenger and entered the general coach, which was attached to the train at the end. Constable Devender also entered the same coach. But immediately, Harun and Musa got down from that coach and started running towards the engine. Ramesh Sharma noticed that and signalled Devender not to deboard the coach. Ramesh Sharma immediately alerted the other team members on the platform. No sooner did the train leave the platform, Harun and Musa entered the general coach, which was just behind the engine. Rakesh Dixit and his party also boarded that coach and kept an eye on them. Moreover, the other parties also boarded the train in different coaches, whereas Inspector Rajendra Bhatia and his team travelled in a private vehicle to Delhi.

At about 10:00 a.m. when the train reached Delhi railway station, Harun and Musa deboarded the train; so did the police team. The police team stationed in the Sadar Bazar area, Inspector Dataram and Subhash Tandon, were already alerted. I, along with a small team, reached the Old Delhi station as a backup plan.

After getting off the train, Harun and Musa took some refreshments on the platform. By that time, Rajendra's team in a private vehicle had arrived at the railway station and contacted me. After taking refreshments, Harun and Musa sat on a bench on the platform for about half an hour. After that, they made some inquiries from a Muslim fellow who signalled towards the west side of the railway station. They both took off on the railroad track and after one kilometre, took a left turn to head in the direction of the New Delhi railway station. A mosque was visible next to the railway track. Musa remained outside the mosque while Harun entered. About 10 minutes later, Harun returned.

On reaching the Sadar Bazar railway station, they both offered *namaz* at the station. Following that, they asked something from another Muslim motorcyclist riding a Pulsar. The biker directed them towards Sadar Bazar. They both recommenced their stroll in the direction of Sadar Bazar. I then alerted Subhash and Dataram because it was likely that one of them would head to Paan Mandi Masjid or Kamran's hideout at that moment. Rajendra Bhatia's and my teams, respectively, were pursuing them. Inspector Subhash Tandon was instructed to follow them and keep an eye on their conduct as soon as they arrived in the Teliwara region. They both headed upstairs to Kamran's house in Teliwara, Sadar Bazar, as expected by the police team. Subhash and his team along with a source kept a covert eye on them.

Subhash Tandon quickly got in touch with me and said, "Sir, they both have entered Kamran's house. I think it is high time to catch them."

Ravi: "Subhash, keep your nerves cool. Are you certain Kamaran is inside?"

Subhash replied, "I'm not sure, sir."

I told him to verify it from the informant and after questioning him, Subhash informed me that Kamran was not present in the house.

I instructed Subhash to keep track of everything and relay any pertinent information to either me or Inspectors Rajendra Bhatia and Dataram since he was aware of the location of each team. Until they encountered Kamran, we would watch and follow them. Subhash acknowledged and continued to observe.

After a while, Harun and Musa left the house and retraced their steps along the route they had initially taken to get from the Delhi railway station to Sadar Bazar. They continued walking along the track, making their way back to the Delhi railway station. Having passed through Sadar Bazar railway station in Delhi, they halted briefly to relieve themselves. Harun noticed, possibly recognising Constable Devender, who was standing behind him at the reservation window at Ludhiana railway station, and promptly warned Musa and both started running to escape.

Without any other choice, Subhash shouted, "Catch them right away!" After a brief chase, the squad members surrounded them and captured them. Musa tried to chew off a small pocket diary that he had pulled out of his shirt pocket as soon as they were apprehended. Ramesh Dabas noticed it and forced him to spit it out. Two hand grenades were found during a precautionary examination of their baggage, one from each of them.

Inspector Rajendra Bhatia was asked to initiate legal proceedings against both the accused, Harun and Musa. The other team members began to question each of them independently. Both of them initially attempted to avoid being questioned, but on realising that the diary which Musa had attempted to ingest, was in the police's hands and contained Babaji's phone numbers, Harun broke down. He acknowledged their connection to Babaji @Abdul Karim Tunda @Abdul Kuddus @Anwar. Musa was a hard nut to break but after Harun revealed everything, Musa too followed. Subhash questioned Harun, while Dataram interrogated Musa.

Subhash: "When did you meet Babaji and how did it happen?"

Harun: "Babaji used to come to give lectures at a *madrasa* in Dhaka. I was studying there and that's where I first met him."

I interrupted the questioning: "Subhash, a thorough inquiry is not necessary at this point; instead, we need to learn more about the individual they encountered at Sadar Bazar."

Subhash: "Why did both of you come to meet someone in Sadar Bazar and on whose instructions?" The inquiry surprised Harun but he remained silent.

"Look, Harun, there's no benefit in hiding anything. We are tracing your movements from Lucknow to Ludhiana, and we know about your calls and Faxes in detail. Tell us everything; it's in your best interest," I insisted and tried to convince him.

Harun remained silent once more, but it was clear that he had a message to get across.

Subhash: "Okay, mind your words now and tell us everything. Otherwise you know that the police have all the means to extract everything."

Harun: "I will tell you everything voluntarily and please save me."

Dataram: "Our sir is a very good man; he won't let anything happen to you." The staff member seated behind Harun grinned.

Harun: "Sir, yesterday Babaji gave me Abu Akasa's (this name was given by Zaki-ur-Rehman to Kamran) address through Fax and told me to go there. He said that by visiting Abu Akasha, I would learn about the entire plan."

Subhash: "Where is that Fax?"

Harun: "Babaji said to memorise the address and then tear up and throw away the Fax in the drain. But I remember the address of Abu Akasa's house."

Subhash: "Did you go to this address? Did you meet Abu Akasa there?"

Harun: "No, sir, there was another man there who told me to reveal my location and where I was staying. I gave him the address of Hanifiya Masjid near Sadar Bazar railway line and informed him that we would be there until evening. He then told me to meet at the mosque around 6:00 p.m."

Inspector Dataram, who was interrogating Musa, backed up Harun's account.

At that point, Inspector Rajendra Bhatia had finished the initial stages of the legal process.

I ordered everyone in the team to leave the area right away and find suitable hiding places in order to take strategic positions so that the culprit had no space left to flee. Each member of the team chose a strategic spot and began to wait for Abu Akasa. It was approximately 6:30 at daybreak. Harun then pointed out two boys approaching from the direction of Sadar Bazar.

Harun: "Sir, those two boys coming towards us, the elder one among them is the one I met at Abu Akasa's house."

Subhash: "Alright, I am releasing you. Go and meet him. If any of them is Abu Akasha, give a signal. And if anyone tries to act smart, a bullet will go straight into their backside. Do you understand?"

Harun: "No, sir, nothing like that will happen. If it's Abu Akasa, I will signal to you."

Harun then approached each of them and motioned towards Subhash after talking briefly with them. Subhash quickly sprinted in their direction and yelled to catch them after getting this indication. The crew acted swiftly and briefly, overwhelming both of them. One Webley Scott revolver loaded with six cartridges was found on Abu Akasa, along with 10 additional live cartridges, after a precautionary search. In addition, one briefcase held Rs. 30,000, $1200 US$, a passport, a ration card, an identification card and an empty identity card. Five Urdu-written diaries and some other papers were also recovered. On the other hand, Shakeel alias Hamza was found to have one bag carrying two identical cast-iron cylinders used in bomb blasts, a thermos containing a mixture of potassium chlorate and sugar, rivets, silver foil and one little bottle containing sulphuric acid. They revealed that bombs were to be made by using these items and given to Harun and Musa to plant in a populated area. The team transported all four of them to ISC for additional investigation after completing all necessary legal procedures immediately.

□

21
Interrogation

Karnal Singh and Alok Kumar were informed about their arrests. Both of them reached the ISC.

Karnal: "Excellent job, Ravi. Finally, we caught them. What does he say? Has he admitted to the blasts?"

Ravi: "Thank you, sir; we have just arrived. Kamran is still in shock. First of all, we have to normalise him and after that, we can do the questioning."

Karnal: "Okay, you continue."

Alok: "You have performed a miracle, Ravi."

Ravi: "Thanks, sir."

The interrogation of all the accused persons began independently. Inspector Dataram was asked to interrogate Harun and Musa, while Inspector Subhash Tandon was deputed to question Shakeel @ Hamza, whereas Inspector Rajendra Bhatia and I started questioning Mohammad Amir Khan @ Kamran @ Abu Akasa. Kamran was in a state of shock. He was still not accepting that he had been caught by the police. He had just reached the age of 19. We tried to gain Kamran's confidence at first.

Ravi: "Look, Bhatia Sahib, this poor guy's childhood has just ended. New youth has come and the *jihadis* have put him to work for their *jihadi* agenda. Why didn't Babaji include Arif (son of Babaji) for this task?"

When Kamran heard the names of Babaji and Arif together, he started staring at us surprisingly.

Bhatia: "Absolutely right. They deliberately keep away their own and they brainwash new boys by interpreting false translations of Quranic verses to corrupt their minds and make them *jihadis*."

Ravi: "Consider this – they claim you'll receive 72 angels if you become a *jihadi* and die during *jihad*. They focus on the afterlife without considering the impact on the present, all the while causing harm to innocent lives. Kamran, enlighten me. Is there any mandate in the Quran about killing innocent people?"

Kamran chose to remain silent.

Ravi: "Bhatia Sahib, call Hasrat Ali. He is a Muslim too and see, he is working for our country." (Bhatia called Hasrat Ali who soon entered the room.)

Bhatia: "Hasrat Ali, have you read the Quran?"

Hasrat Ali: "Yes, sir, with the complete and accurate translation, not the one with *jihadi* interpretations."

Ravi: "So, tell me, what he is doing is obligatory in the Quran?"

Hasrat Ali: "Absolutely not. Allah will not forgive him and he will go to hell for this."

Kamran then started debating with Hasrat Ali.

Kamran: "But it is permissible to kill non-believers!"

Hasrat Ali: "Son, is this where your intellect ends? These *jihadi* Maulvis catch innocent kids like you, explain the wrong meanings of the Quran and serve their own motives."

Ravi: "Okay, Kamran, tell me, when did you decide to participate in *jihad*? Were your parents okay with it?"

Kamran: "No, they had forbidden me."

Ravi: "Did you tell them that you were going to become a *jihadi*?"

Kamran: "No, sir."

Ravi: "Well, at least you admitted that you are a *jihadi*. Secondly, it means that if your parents thought it was a noble cause, they would have gladly sent you for *jihad*. Tell me, are you wiser than them? The direct implication is that the philosophy of *jihad* is entirely wrong."

Hasrat Ali: "Those Maulvis must have told you that no matter what happens, do not tell anything to the police. If you do, it will be considered blasphemy against Allah. All these things were drilled into your mind. Now, Allah will forgive you only when you sincerely admit all your sins. Now, openly confess."

Kamran still kept silent.

Rajendra Bhatia: "Son, you can't sustain even for two minutes. It is our boss, who has stopped us, or else we would have finished our work by now."

Ravi: "No problem. Bhatia Sahib, he is just a kid. There is a lot of confusion in his mind. Isn't it, Kamran? Let me tell you one more thing. If today we had caught that Tunda with you, he wouldn't have thought for even a minute and would have spilled the beans in detail. Forget about Allah, faith, everything."

Bhatia: "Sir, you are showing too much compassion to him. You go out for 10/15 minutes and I'll handle him."

Ravi: "Come on, Bhatia Sahib, calm down. He also has to go through this. Let's see; he will understand. He's just a kid. Hasrat Ali, take Bhatia Sahib outside, let me talk to him."

Bhatia went out of the room.

Hasrat Ali: "Sir, it's difficult to stop Bhatia Sahib once he starts. Once he gets started, he doesn't see anything. Last month, you saw what he did to that guy."

Kamran to Hasrat Ali: "Brother, can I talk to a Maulvi? I want to clarify something from him and I want to end the confusion about *jihadi* thoughts in my mind."

Hasrat Ali: "What will the Maulvi do in this?"

Ravi intervened: "Wait, Hasrat Ali, call Harbir. There is a mosque nearby; he will bring the Maulvi."

Hasrat Ali: "Which Maulvi will come at this time? It is midnight, sir."

Ravi: "Just go and call Harbir; he will bring someone."

Hasrat Ali called Harbir into the interrogation room.

Ravi: "Harbir, get the Maulvi from the nearby mosque

and please note - get the Maulvi only, not any random person."

Harbir: "Sir, at this time?"

Ravi: "What is in the time? At least try! We are running out of time since we have to produce him in court in the afternoon and prior to that we have to clear whether he is actually involved in bomb blast cases or not."

Harbir: "Okay sir!"

Ravi: "Okay Hasrat Ali, you give Kamran some food and meanwhile, even we'll have our dinner."

Harbir and I left the interrogation room.

Ravi: "Harbir, bring the Maulvi after briefing him thoroughly. We don't want him to mislead Kamran."

Harbir: "Sir, one of my friends is a Hafiz and he looks like a Maulvi with excellent knowledge of the Quran and Hadith. He also strongly dislikes these *jihadis*."

Ravi: "Are you talking about Rizwan?"

Harbir: "Yes, sir, you've met him too."

Ravi: "He will be perfect."

Harbir: "I'll call him; he will be here in 15-20 minutes. He lives nearby in Paharganj."

Ravi: "That's even better. Quickly call him. Meanwhile, let's have our dinner."

Ravi went to Karnal Singh and informed him about the conversation with Kamran.

Alok: "What will Maulvi be asked?"

Karnal: "*Jihad*."

Ravi: "Who knows what stories these guys spin in their minds. Come on, sir, let's have dinner. Who knows where we might have to go."

All of us finished having dinner. Meanwhile, B.K. Gupta, Additional CP (Crime) arrived. Harbir's friend, Rizwan Ahmed, also arrived. I told Harbir to take him to Kamran and let Kamran remove his doubt about *jihad*. I also briefed Harbir that nobody would be present except Rizwan, Hasrat Ali and Kamran in the room. In this way, there was a possibility of winning Kamran's confidence in Rizwan. But as far as my hunch was concerned, Kamran was trying to emerge from this situation. After some time, Rajendra Bhatia entered.

Bhatia: "Sir, the strategy is successful. He wants to talk to you."

Ravi: "Nice, I am coming."

B.K. Gupta: "What happened, Ravi?"

Karnal: "You proceed, Ravi. I will tell sir the details."

Ravi came to Kamran's room and as soon as he entered, Kamran started to weep. Kamran: "Sir, I have committed many sins under the influence of Zaki Sahib and Babaji. Now, I repent for all those sins and ask Allah for forgiveness. Inshallah, he will forgive my sins. I have written about all the bomb blasts in my diary, which was kept in my briefcase. Apart from this, I have noted down the phone numbers and addresses of people who helped our organisation in sending money, crossing borders and assisting our organisation to stay in Bangladesh after coming from Pakistan. I will show you everything in my diary."

As per my request, Harbir Singh brought his briefcase. Kamran took out the diaries from his bag. Kamran's habit of writing a diary made our task easier to extract information from him regarding the blast committed by him, his mentors, associates, family members and friends, along with the crucial dates that had a purpose for his trip to meet Babaji in Bangladesh. He also recorded the names, addresses and contact information of every person who had ever assisted him while crossing the Indo-Bangladesh border and who all provided refuge during the journey. The diaries also contained the names of sympathisers and *hawala* merchants.

Kamran admitted that from October 1996 to October 1997, he had committed 28 bomb blasts, including planting explosives in busy markets at cracker shops during Diwali, Rani Bagh on the eve of Karwa Chauth, Roshan-di-Kulfi in Karol Bagh, religious processions in Sadar Bazar, moving buses, railway stations, cinema halls and the '*Golden Temple*' train, among others. The details of each incident were mentioned in his diary in Urdu, using code language. This is why, when his briefcase was checked earlier and diaries were found, we could not understand what was written in them. For brevity, I am not going to mention all the incidents but only one to illustrate how he used to describe the incidents and the formula used in making bombs for the knowledge of my readers.

Extracts from Diary

1 October, 1997

"Aaj Imam Sahib, Changez Khan aur Rogan Sahib se Sadar Bazar mein mulakat hui.

Aaj Imam Sahab, Pila Khan aur Rogan Sahib se meri mulakat 'Golden Temple' train main hui."

(Today, I had a meeting with Imam Sahib, Changez Khan and Rogan Sahib in Sadar Bazar. Later, I met Imam Sahib, Pila Khan and Rogan Sahib on the '*Golden Temple*' train.)

Explanation given by Kamran

Kamran and Shakeel prepared six bombs in the Pilakhuva factory two or three days before planting them, using various chemical combinations with code names like Imam Sahib, Pila Khan, Changez Khan and Rogan Sahib. Three bombs were planted in Sadar Bazar, Delhi. The first one below a water cart at 12 Tuti Chowk, the second in a procession tableau and the third in Chandni Chowk.

Later that evening, Kamran planted three bombs in the '*Golden Temple Express*' train, one in the general compartment and the other two in the S-3 coach. These exploded near Sahibabad, UP, in a moving train.

The following names were given by him in accordance with how the bomb was made, using diverse combinations of chemicals. The bomb-making formula was also written in his diary, which I am not going to disclose for security reasons.

- BHURE KHAN
- BADAM ROGAN
- CHANGEZ KHAN
- SULPHURIC SAHIB
- IMAM SAHIB
- PILA KHAN

I informed B.K. Gupta, Karnal Singh and Alok Kumar, who were present in my office and eagerly awaited the outcome of Kamran's interrogation.

B.K. Gupta: "Ah, there you are! We've been waiting for an update. What's the latest?"

Ravi: "Sir, we finally have a breakthrough that has been haunting us for over a year. He has admitted his involvement in as many as 28 blasts."

Karnal: "You mean we finally have with us the person who was responsible? That's incredible news."

Alok: "To the team's unwavering commitment and the successful culmination of this challenging investigation. Cheers!"

B.K. Gupta: "Excellent work, Ravi. This is a major achievement for the team and a great relief for the victims and their families.

Ravi: "It wasn't easy, sir. Initially, the accused was uncooperative, but eventually, he admitted his involvement in the bombings. However, eight are still unsolved. Our hunch was correct: there must be some other group operating in Delhi."

Karnal: "Did the accused provide any valuable information during the interrogation about his network or any clues about the other blasts?"

Ravi: "Definitely, he will tell everything. At present, we have to interrogate him about the operational details on which we have to act immediately. However, he has given some references of the other group that may be involved in other blasts."

B.K. Gupta: "I must commend your dedication and perseverance."

Ravi: "Thank you, sir. But I must give credit to my team. They worked relentlessly, often sacrificing their personal lives and serious family commitments, to solve this intricate puzzle. They deserve all the recognition and appreciation for their unwavering commitment. I'm proud to have led this team."

Dataram: "It was a challenging journey, but seeing the results today makes it all worth it."

Subhash: "Absolutely! This case demanded our best efforts. The trust and support from our superiors kept us motivated throughout the investigation."

Rajendra: "It was a collective effort. We never gave up. I'm glad our hard work paid off."

B.K. Gupta: "Well done, everyone. Your dedication and professionalism are exemplary. I have already sent a message to CP, which I think he has received."

I heard the sound of vehicles entering the office complex.

T.R. Kakkar: "I heard the news! Excellent job, everyone! Your relentless efforts have paid off. I'm incredibly proud of each and every one of you."

B.K. Gupta: "Absolutely. Thanks for their outstanding work."

Karnal: "The city and Delhi Police owe you a debt. This is a significant victory for law enforcement and justice."

T.R. Kakkar: "I must call it the INVESTIGATION OF THE CENTURY. Keep up the excellent work and let this success inspire you to continue making a positive impact in our city."

The investigating team members, along with the senior officers and the chief, shared a sense of accomplishment and relief. The efforts were recognised and applauded by senior officials.

Ravi: "Okay, sir, if you allow us, we may get back to our work."

Karnal: "Okay, you continue, Ravi."

The interrogation of Kamran continued.

Ravi: "Kamran, can you tell us who is behind the remaining blasts?"

Kamran: "Sir, I can't say for sure, but once, when I was going to Sonipat, I met a Pakistani named Hussain on the way and he was associated with the Lashkar-e-Toiba as a *jihadi*. When I asked him what he was doing here, he didn't say much. I suspect he might be behind the remaining blasts. I complained about this to Babaji in Pakistan, expressing concern that Hussain was there on the same route I was working on and I expressly told him to inform Hussain not to go on the same route as it may cause harm to him."

Ravi: "How do you know he was associated with Babaji?"

Kamran: "I met Hussain in Bangladesh at Babaji's hideout, along with other Pakistanis. Once, when I was coming from Bangladesh to India after meeting Babaji, he gave me some money to hand over to Hussain. However, he never came to collect it, so I used that money for myself. I have written this in my diary and you can check it."

Ravi: "Where can we find Hussain now?"

Kamran: "Sir, we neither disclose our whereabouts nor inquire about them. This is a strict directive from our organisation. However, in December, when I went to Pakistan, I saw him going to Paan Mandi Masjid a couple of days earlier."

Ravi to Bhatia: "So, what's special about Pan Mandi?"

Bhatia: "Abdul Baki, sir."

Kamran, hearing Abdul Baki's name, immediately responded: "Yes, yes, sir, Babaji had mentioned this guy too, saying that he had also undergone brief training in India."

Ravi: "Okay, besides Shakil, how many people from your group are present here?"

Kamran: "Sir, apart from Shakil, no one else is with me. Initially, I used to work with Ammar, a Pakistani with whom I carried out blasts in Punjab six months ago. He went to Pakistan nearly six months ago. I met him again when I was in Pakistan in February."

Ravi: "Okay. All these details should be absolutely accurate; no falsehood should be there."

Kamran: "Sir, now that I have decided to confess to all the crimes, you can trust that I won't say anything false."

Ravi: "Where did you find the explosives?"

Kamran: "Sir, initially, Ammar and I went to Bangladesh and brought these from Babaji. Later, after setting up a factory in Pilakuwa, I started buying chemicals from the local market."

Bhatia: "Where did you get the cylinders for making the bombs?"

Kamran: "I had a wooden mould for cylinders prepared by Mehmood Bhai in Pilakhuwa, and subsequently, I personally got the die-casting done of the cylinders from a local factory in Pilakhuwa, which I will show you."

Ravi: "Where have you been all this time?"

Kamran: "I returned from Pakistan just a few days ago and I mostly stay in my factory. Today, I came straight from the factory upon Shakeel's call."

Ravi: "Which factory? Whose factory?"

Kamran: "Sir, on Babaji's instructions, I opened a dyeing and printing factory in Pilakhuwa. Babaji provided the funds for it. He said that two-thirds of people (terrorists) can comfortably adjust there. Additionally, no one would suspect buying chemicals for use in bomb-making, as all the chemicals I use are commonly used in printing and dyeing. I manufacture the bombs there and work with Shakeel on the plant. I have various formulas for making bombs written in my diary. If you'd like, I can take you to the factory and show you."

The recipe for creating 11 different types of explosives and bombs was written in Urdu in another diary of Kamran. Later, Kamran, under police custody, led the police party to the house of Mohammad Sattar, where he was running a dyeing factory and disclosed that the articles for use in the manufacture of bombs were kept in the rear room. Keys to the house of Mohammad Sattar, from where chemicals (in powder and liquid form, weighing approx. 20 kg.) and gadgets and articles used for making bombs were recovered.

The chemicals and components recovered included potassium chlorate, yellow powder and potassium chlorate mixture, magnesium powder, aluminum nitrate, glycerin, potassium permanganate, sulphuric acid, nitric acid and soda, nitrobenzene and potassium chlorate mixture named 'Badamrogan'. There's also a red-coloured powdered chemical named 'Churn Lahoo ika Pushta' and another named 'Marham Dard Josi', as well as a white-powered chemical, a potassium chlorate and sugar mixture named 'Imam Shahib', and powdered sugar named 'CHNP' and 'Bura'.

Solifex adhesive is a rubber-solution, photosynthesis switch used to delay or initialise bombs. Detonators and sensitive chemicals for preparing the detonator are packed in shock-absorbing black, polythene bags. There are 15 crude iron cylinders with threads on both sides, two crude iron cylinders with plates on both sides and 4/4 bolts. The same cylinder was used in the blasts in the train and Roshan-di-Kulfi. Four unfinished cast iron cylinders with two caps each (a total of eight caps), six cylindrical wooden pieces used as specimens for casting the above-mentioned cast iron cylinders, which were used and were to be used in bomb blasts. Iron rivets to be used as a lethal projectile in a bomb, tools for manufacturing bombs and other important articles like beakers, 'chalni', tasley, steel, 'kaddi', and plaster of paris. Also, one kerosene pressure stove used to heat the bomb, manufacturing artifacts and a weighing scale with a capacity of 5 kg. with seven weights (1 kg., 500 gm., 200 gm., 50/50 gm., 20 gm., 10 gm.).

Ravi: "You mentioned that you recently went to Pakistan. Why did you go? When did you go and when did you come back?"

Kamran: "I went on the summons of chachaji."

Bhatia: "Chachaji?"

Kamran: "Zaki Sahib. They call Zaki-ur-Rehman 'chachaji' and Hafiz Saeed is referred to as 'ttayaji'."

Bhatia: "Why were you called?"

Kamran: "They were pleased with my work and wanted to give me more significant responsibilities. When I first met them, they had prepared about 18 boys to settle here in India and they asked me to settle them. For this, they asked me for an address to send Rs. 6.50 lakh through *hawala*. Zaki Sahib had said that this time he would send RDX, C-4 and TNT (highly explosive) concealed in fruit boxes from Kashmir. But I did not want to give them my Delhi address. So, I gave them the address of Mohammad Shamim, Eagle Motor Works, Ph. No. 293806, 52, AJC Bose Road, Pin-700016.

"Babaji told me that I could store any items with him under the name of Anwar (Babaji). I asked Shamim, residing in Kolkata, West Bengal, through Fax to receive the Rs. 6.50 lakh. I introduced myself to Shamim as Amar."

Ravi: "How is the amount of Rs. 6.50 lakh calculated?"

Kamran: "Rs. 3.50-4.00 lakh for the house, 1.50 lakh for Fax, phone and factory and we used the code 'Supari ka dabba' for the boys coming to India. Chachaji also gave me the phone number of a guy named Sulfi (09773121052, given after consulting the diary), who is in Nepal and is an overground worker for Tanjeem."

During interrogation, Kamran also provided the phone numbers of Zaki-ur-Rehman (92342xxxx669, 9242xxxx247) and Hafiz Saeed (9242xxxx106).

These numbers were not in our records. Sub-Inspector Sandeep Malhotra was instructed to take these phones under immediate observation and analyse the records of these phones according to our SOP. Kamran also disclosed other codes used during their conversations, such as '*Kala burka*' (pistol), '*Hari pagri*' (revolver) and '*Landlord*' (police). '*Shahi supari*' (militants), '*Makan kiraye par leliya*' (person arrested), '*Makan malik ke dost*' (intelligence agency).

Briefly, further questioning of Kamran revealed some

hints concerning the remaining seven bombings in Delhi. He admitted that he had travelled to Pakistan when he was 13-years old, in 1989 or 1990. Motivated by Abu Hurrera, he joined the LeT. After completing training at Daur-e-Aam and Daur-e-Khas in Afghanistan, he joined the gang of Abdul Karim (Tunda) and Babaji. Abdul Karim Tunda learned that Kamran was a Delhiite and not a Pakistani, and decided to send him to Delhi for bombings. Kamran received extra training on bomb preparation and Abdul Karim Tunda personally delivered the guidelines at the ISI location. After obtaining Kamran's Pakistani citizenship, Tunda sent him to Bangladesh, using a Pakistani passport and where he met Harun and Musa, among others.

Abdul Karim ordered Kamran to travel across different parts of India before returning to Dhaka. It is likely that Babaji sent Kamran to India to assess his dedication to his job before introducing more associates. Kamran would not have come back if he wasn't being honest. Upon his return to Dhaka from India, Babaji told Kamran that he believed in Allah, saying, *"Ab mujhe poori tasalli hogai ki tum Allah ke kaam ke liye hi bane ho."* (Now I am completely reassured that you are created for Allah's work.) Babaji instructed Kamran to meet Ammar r/o Chechawatni, Pakistan, in Jama Masjid, Delhi. When Kamran met Ammar, he was familiar to Kamran, known by the name Abu-Abbad @ Zabiullah. Ammar knew Kamran by the name of Abu Akasha. They first met in 1995 at Muridke, Lahore, Pakistan. Kamran met several other members of the terrorist organisation during his second trip to Dhaka.

After his third or fourth meeting with Kamran at Matia Mahal Masjid, Ammar gave him Malerkotla's phone number and the address of an STD where he could be contacted. Kamran noted it down in his diary: 'Skyway, STD/PCO, Mohalla Luthra, Moti Bazar, Palviyan Masjid, Malerkotla, Punjab. 0167xxxx997 & 0167xxxx766.' Later, Kamran came into contact with Shakeel and Mehmood at Luharan Masjid in

Pilakhuva through Ammar. They found a suitable location for a printing and dyeing factory in Pilakhuva, UP. Later, Mehmood, Shakeel, Ammar and Kamran travelled to Bangladesh and agreed to launch a printing and dyeing plant with Shakeel and his accomplices. The factory in Pilakhuva was opened and funded through *hawala* transactions. Potassium chlorate and other chemicals were obtained from Tilak Market and Pilakhuva and Kamran and Shakeel Ahmed manufactured the bombs. On a predetermined day, Shakeel would deliver the prepared material (the bomb) in Delhi at a specific location and give it to Kamran.

During his last visit to Pakistan in December 1997 to February 1998, Kamran was given greater responsibility to make contacts in Delhi, Haryana, and UP. Zaki-ur-Rehman, the Amir of Lashkar-e-Toiba, decided to employ him in a more devastating manner after observing his success in the previous year's operation. He was asked to find hiding places. A group of terrorists was under training in Muzaffarabad and 18 of these trained terrorists were scheduled to travel to India at different locations to set off other bombings. They had also conducted surveys in Ludhiana, Lucknow, Mussoorie and Shimla. This time, using their links in Nepal, Kashmir and Bangladesh, they were to get explosive material, including RDX and sophisticated firearms. In order to set up hideouts and plan militant activities, Kamran had to collect Rs. 6.5 lakh through *hawala* from Shamim of Kolkata. The interrogation further reveals that ISI was coordinating with different militant groups and sending Pakistanis and Bangladeshis to India to create internal unrest in different regions of the nation.

Long period of inquiry cut short bombers' 'mission'

Staff Reporter

NEW DELHI: Fifty chosen officials of the city police's crime branch worked for over 112 days to nab the most wanted criminals in the Capital, who have often been described as "phantom bombers or mystery saboteurs," and who have tormented the city police for over a year.

Of the four arrested on Friday — Asif, Shakeel, Haroon and Moosa — Asif, barely 21 years old, alone triggered off around 22 explosions in various parts of the city and north India.

But what led Asif to all this? Police officials say he was sent to the Muzaffrabad area of Pakistan-occupied Kashmir in 1989 and was given extensive training.

He was persuaded to go to Pakistan by an organisation called Markaz-Adawat-Ul-Irshad, which collected funds and instigated people for terrorist activities in India.

"The selected boys were imparted distorted religious training, including fictitious stories of atrocities on people in Kashmir. The training was provided by an organisation called Lashkar-e-Toiba. It was during this training that Abdul Karim Tunda, a known ISI agent, discovered Asif was a Delhiite," an official involved with the probe said.

Tunda got him a Pakistani passport and took him to Dhaka, where Tunda is currently suspected to be based. After training ended, Asif was sent on the special mission of carrying out blasts in Delhi.

The operation to nab the gang behind the blasts was kept a carefully guarded secret and involved some taxing, sometimes fruitless, investigation.

Initially, a police team visited the blast sites in Delhi, Sonepat, Panipat, Jalandhar, Ambala, Bhatinda, and Ludhiana to garner the common points. It so emerged was Tunda was one common thread.

In Delhi, most of the explosions seemed to have some connection to the walled city. So, "records of all the guest houses located near railway stations in Delhi were summoned. With the help of a computer, we narrowed down five persons who used to stay there on the day of the explosions. But their interrogation did not provide any lead," said an official. "We then discovered the gang was using newspapers to wrap the bombs — this included one with a circulation of around 4,000 in Delhi. This, we thought, could provide a clue. It may sound surprising, but we checked all subscribers of this newspaper in Delhi — but again drew a blank," the official said.

The team then focused on the walled city, the "epicentre" of the blasts. "An entire team camped in Sadar Bazaar, Filmistan, and Azad Market and surveyed the entire area," the official said.

Finally, one house was suspected and was kept under surveillance. "A lot of activity was being noticed here. Two persons were repeatedly spotted coming and going from the house," the official said.

They decided to follow them. "On February 27, one of our team nabbed them, but they immediately swallowed two diaries they were carrying — this made us suspicious," the official said. These two turned out to be the Bangladeshi nationals Haroon and Moosa — they gave police the breakthrough.

"We literally made them spit out the diaries and discovered they contained phone numbers in code words," said an official.

"We also recovered two grenades from their bags. After interrogation, it was revealed they had been sent by Abdul Karim Tunda and were supposed to contact the two other members of the gang," the official said.

"They were supposed to meet Asif and Shakeel at the Sadar Bazaar railway station behind the Hanifi masjid. A trap was laid and we managed to nab Asif and Shakeel as well," he said.

He said the code language used by the gang was most interesting. While Tunda was referred to as Baba Sahab, a pistol was referred to as 'kala burka.' The police were referred to as 'makan malik', and the intelligence agents were termed 'makan malik ke dost.'

Their own associates were referred to as 'shahi supari' while the actual blasts would be referred to as a meeting with the 'maulana sahab'. "A meeting with maulana sahab at 5 pm would mean a blast at 5 pm," the official explained.

Kamaljeet Singh

Delhi bomb blast accused being produced in the Tis Hazari courts in Delhi on Saturday.

Four arrested for bomb blasts

Chronology of bomb blast

22
Arrest of Module 2

On 1 March, 1998, Karnal Singh, DCP (Crime) gathered all ISC officers for a meeting to discuss the next steps regarding unsolved cases. Karnal initiated the discussion by seeking independent opinions from each officer, starting with me.

I stated, "Sir, based on Kamran's interrogation, my suspicion falls on Abdul Baki and Hussain, a Pakistani national. I believe we should waste no time and apprehend Abdul Baki and Hussain while also investigating his connection with Babaji. There are references to 'Hussain' and Paan Mandi Masjid in the interrogation reports of other arrested individuals in the Punjab Police case. They were closely associated with Abdul Karim@Tunda@ Babaji. Furthermore, we have been monitoring the movements of Abdul Baki since he dialled Babaji's number from Jain's STD. Sir, my considered opinion is that we should act on this valuable lead without wasting any time."

Karnal expressed his shock, saying, "It's disheartening that neither the Special Cell nor any intelligence agency has pursued this crucial information."

Alok concurred, stating, "Indeed, sir, it's a major failure on their part."

Karnal redirected the focus back to the action plan, saying, "We can discuss their failure later. For now, let's concentrate on our next steps. Alok, what are your views?"

Alok replied, "I agree with Ravi, sir. Rajendra! What is your opinion?"

Bhatia responded, "Sir, we should dispatch a team to West Bengal for further action. We have access to the addresses and phone numbers of most of the individuals involved. To proceed, we should take Kamran with us."

Karnal: "Subhash, what do you think?"

Subhash proposed, "Sir, considering our limited 10-day police custody remand in the current case, it is crucial to prioritise the verification of Kamran's statement. We need to identify the sources from whom he obtained the chemicals and other bomb-making equipment, as well as trace the calls he made to Pakistan."

Karnal: "Dataram, your opinion?"

Dataram added, "Sir, we should take charge of investigating at least two bomb blast cases in which Kamran is involved. This will enable us to interrogate him and cross-examine the other potential suspects who may be arrested in the future, thus validating the authenticity of his statement."

Karnal acknowledged the importance of the suggestion, saying, "Indeed, this is an important point. I agree with you, Dataram. Furthermore, I am concerned about the remaining unsolved cases."

Alok chimed in, echoing my statement, "Abdul Baki's involvement is crucial. We should plan his apprehension immediately."

I added, "Additionally, I believe there may be other modules within India that can only be discovered through technical analysis. I have provided Zaki, Babaji and Hafiz Saeed's Pakistani numbers, along with Ammar's number in Malerkotla, Punjab. Although Ammar is currently in Pakistan, he previously resided in Malerkotla and was involved in a blast in Punjab, with Kamran. He likely has contacts in Malerkotla. Sandeep Malhotra is working on extracting this information from their telephone records, but it will take some time. In the meantime, we should proceed with apprehending Baki."

Karnal summarised the decision, stating, "Alright, I have decided to start with Abdul Baki. Are all of you ready?"

In unison, everyone responded, "Yes, sir."

Karnal concluded, "Great, let's get to work."

After Karnal Singh and Alok left the office, I assumed charge of the meeting and initiated a discussion on the strategy. It was collectively decided during the meeting to apprehend Abdul Baki at a specific location outside the Paan Mandi Mosque. On 4 March, 1998, when Abdul Baki arrived in Inderlok, Delhi, the plan was executed and he was picked up for sustained interrogation. Initially, Abdul Baki denied having any knowledge about Hussain, but when he was confronted with Kamran and the numbers of Babaji and Markaj of Muridke, Lahore written in his pocket diary, he disclosed his association with Babaji, Hussain and one Abdullah, all Pakistanis. He further led the police party to his General Merchant Shop in Sadar Bazar, Delhi, and recovered explosive material, including 26 live cartridges and two magazines of pistols.

The subsequent interrogation of Abdul Baki revealed that he was born in 1976 in Kenya. He received education up to eighth grade at Montessori School in Bara Tooti and Anglo-Arabic School at Ajmeri Gate, Delhi. He came from a family of six brothers and four sisters. For the past three years, he had been running a general store located at Sarai Khalil, Sadar Bazar, Delhi. Most of his relatives were settled in Karachi, Pakistan, which is why he and his family frequently visited Pakistan. He had travelled to Pakistan three times and his last visit occurred in December 1996 to attend the wedding of a relative. It was during this visit that he met Abdul Karim Tunda, alias Babaji, who motivated him to become a member of his terrorist outfit, LeT. Baki agreed to this and filed an affidavit to confirm his allegiance. Since Baki's visa was for a limited period, Babaji gave him a brief training in weapons for two days in Lahore, Pakistan. He returned to India in February 1997.

Bhatia: "When did you meet Hussain and how did it happen?"

Baki: "After returning from Pakistan, Hussain came to our *madrasa* and there he took admission. Around April 1997, he told me that he was also a member of Babaji's organisation."

Ravi: "Really? A Pakistani came to your *madrasa*, took admission and then revealed that he is a member of Babaji's gang? Bhatia, isn't this some movie-like story?"

Bhatia: "Do you think that we all are fools?"

Baki: "No, sir, this is all true."

Ravi: "We'll see if this is true after catching Hussain. Okay, tell me where we can find Hussain?"

Baki: "Hussain is currently living in Govindpuri with Abdullah. Let me show you his room."

Subhash: "Abdullah?"

Subhash whispered to me, "Sir, he is the same person who made a call from Sadar Bazar to Bangladesh about 10 or 12 days ago, wanting to talk to Babaji."

Ravi: "Yes, you are right."

Baki: "Hussain introduced me to Abdullah; he is also a Pakistani. After a few meetings, Abdullah taught me different methods to make bombs. He even showed me how to make a cigarette bomb and provided me with the explosive mixture. Following his instructions, I used it at a Hindu's cloth shop in the cloth market and then escaped."

Baki continued revealing: "Hussain often asked me to collect money sent by Baba from a *hawala* deals in Meena Bazar, Chandni Chowk and he would give me a considerable amount to keep."

Dataram: "Are you his CA?"

Baki: "Sir, now, take it as you want."

Subhash: "Okay, don't stop! Continue with your story."

Baki: "Alright, sir. Once, Hussain gave me a bag to keep it safe as it contained two pistols and cartridges. I placed the bag behind my shop's fridge. After a few days, when Hussain asked me for the bag, one pistol and some cartridges were missing. He got quite angry. I explained that I hadn't removed any pistol from it."

Ravi: "Wait, wait. You're telling a strange story. The bag was in your shop and one of the two pistols went missing. Had some other person stolen the pistol? Why did he not steal both of them? You are great, Baki! You've deceived the Pakistanis."

Baki: "Sir, believe me, it's true. After a month, I found out that my brother Abdul Bari had taken one pistol without telling me, just for fun's sake and fired two rounds."

Subhash: "Whose murder did your brother commit?"

Baki: "Sir, it's not like that. He just took the pistol without telling me, as a playful act and fired two rounds. After that, I informed Abdullah, who asked me to return the pistol. I returned it to Abdullah. Later, Babaji called me on my phone number 75xxx14, which I had given him for sending any messages. He told me to give Abdullah '*ek murgi aur 20 ande*' (one hen and 20 eggs) and share the phone number with a person named Khushi Mohammed. I gave Khushi Mohammed Rs. 20,000, but later Babaji called and said he didn't want the money; he wanted to give one pistol and 20 cartridges. Babaji explained that '*murgi*' meant a pistol and '*ande*' meant cartridges. Later, I called Abdullah to get a pistol and cartridges which he delivered to me in Nehru Place. After that, I called Khushi Mohammed the next day and asked him to meet me at Filmistan Cinema at 9 or 10 in the morning. Instead, a Sikh boy with code number 52 came and took the pistol, after returning Rs. 20,000. Khushi Mohammed is 25- to 30-years old and 6 feet tall."

Bhatia: "Is that all? Tell us how many bombs you have detonated."

Baki: "I have confessed to everything I have done and if I remember anything else, I will surely tell you. I have nothing to hide."

Ravi: "Okay, fine. Now, go and reveal the whereabouts and hideouts of Abdullah and Hussain; only then will we know the truth."

Baki: "Okay, sir, let's go."

We took Abdul Baki to identify Abdullah's hideout in the Govindpuri area, where he specifically pointed out a house. He informed us that Abdullah was residing on the first floor of that house in a rented room. With this crucial information in hand, I decided to send Constable Devender to verify Abdullah's presence in the mentioned room.

To carry out this operation discreetly, Constable Devender cleverly assumed the guise of a municipal corporation employee. Unfortunately, Abdullah was not found in his room at that time. Recognising the importance of maintaining constant vigilance, it was unanimously agreed that a 24/7 surveillance operation was necessary for the identified house. Additionally, the team diligently established covert sources in the area to prevent any inadvertent exposure of their presence near the targeted house.

Over the course of approximately three days, the team exhibited remarkable patience and employed a systematic approach in the Govindpuri area, focusing their efforts near Abdullah's suspected location. Finally, on 8 March, 1998, at about 9:15 p.m., their persistence paid off when they noticed a person acting suspiciously, entering and leaving the house in question. The police team swiftly arrested Abdul Rahman, a resident of Dhora Tanda village (UP), using information from their confidential sources and recovered 4.7 kg. of potassium chlorate and sulphuric acid in his possession. It became evident that Abdul Rahman had acquired this explosive material at Abdullah's request. With this crucial evidence at hand, the team subjected Abdul Rahman to an intense interrogation, unearthing another vital piece of information.

Abdul Rahman revealed that Abdullah may have been hiding himself at Garih, Lajpat Nagar. Capitalising on this new lead, Abdul Rahman guided the police party to a rented room in Lajpat Nagar, where he pointed out a person named Hussain, loitering outside the premises. However, the situation quickly escalated as Hussain drew out his pistol, attempting to fire upon the police party. Undeterred and displaying exceptional bravery, the officers swiftly apprehended Hussain, effectively neutralising the immediate threat. Subsequently, the team entered the room and apprehended yet another individual named Badruddin, who was identified as a Pakistani national. A search of the premises led to the recovery of a huge quantity of explosive material, timing devices and other materials commonly used in the manufacture of bombs.

The combined interrogations of Hussain and Badruddin proved to be highly fruitful. Both individuals provided critical insights into Abdullah's involvement in illicit activities. Armed with this valuable information, the police party wasted no time and promptly proceeded to a house in Devli Khanpur, where they believed Abdullah could be hiding. Their intelligence was accurate as Abdullah was indeed present at the location.

During the search of Abdullah's residence, the police made significant discoveries. They recovered a substantial quantity of explosive material, timing devices and other materials commonly used in the manufacture of bombs. Some of the very sensitive explosives were named 'Lal Khan and Hadtal' by them. Additionally, a sum of $1,000 and Rs. 70,000 was seized from the room, which was rented by a person named Mohammad Shàfiq. This operation marked the team's fastest and most successful outcome throughout the entire mission, underscoring their exceptional skills and dedication to preserving public safety.

Initially, a quick and brief interrogation of the above-accused persons revealed that Abdullah, Hussain Badruddin, residents of Pakistan, and Abdul Rahman, a resident of Village Dora Tanda, UP, were associated with the terrorist organisation Lashkar-e-Toiba. All the accused individuals had undergone extensive terrorist training. Additionally, they had received training in bomb-making from Abdul Karim Tunda, also known as Babaji. Under the guidance of Zaki-ur-Rehman and Babaji, the aforementioned three Pakistani terrorists successfully infiltrated from both Bangladesh and Jammu & Kashmir.

All three individuals with Abdul Rehman played key roles in carrying out the following bomb explosions, in moving buses from December 1996 to December 1997:

- In a Haryana Roadways bus and a jeep at Mukundpur and Mukarba Chowk in Delhi.
- Haryana Roadways bus in Panipat.
- Bomb planted at a vegetable shop in Ballabgarh, Haryana.
- Bomb planted in a bus going to Nangloi, Delhi.
- Bus at Peera Garhi Chowk Delhi.
- Bus near ISBT, Delhi.
- Bus near Sabji Mandi Burfkhana, Delhi.
- Bus at Rampura, Punjabi Bagh, Delhi.

Abdul Rahman, a resident of Dora Tanda, was running an electric shop named Faiz Light House in his village. He was motivated to undergo militant training in Pakistan by Abdul Kalam, who was Imam of Ahale Hadis Masjid, from 1992 to 1994. Abdul Kalam arranged for his passport and visa and sent Abdul Rahman and Abdul Wahid for training in Pakistan. They were taken to Afghanistan at Maskar-e-Toiba camp in Kunar district, where they completed the Daur-e-Aam training course and came back to India.

After a long time, in the year 1996, near Ramzan, Abdul Rahman came in contact with Babaji through one called Rizwan, a confidant of Babaji, who took him to Dhaka, Bangladesh. Abdul Rahman was in Bangladesh for about three weeks, where Babaji taught him how to make different kinds of bombs and sent him back to India after paying him $200 and Rs. 1,000. Babaji asked him to carry out a bomb blast in Kanpur, UP.

Bomb Blast in Kanpur

In May/June 1997, Abdul Rahman and his associates prepared two bombs using stabilisers. The bombs consisted of potassium chlorate, aluminum powder, sulphuric acid and iron balls filled with *masala*. They devised a plan in which one Abdul Khaliq, also known as Maulana, and Rizwan would carry the bombs and detonate them in Kanpur. The following day, Maulana Khaliq, who was running a tent house in his village, also joined them. Rizwan left the village for Kanpur and planted the bombs at Ghantaghar near the railway station, opposite the central *dharamshala*, at 8:15 p.m..

The next day, around 9 or 10 a.m., the police arrived in the village from Kanpur to inquire about the Maulana. They informed the villagers that Maulana had sustained burn injuries due to a bomb explosion and was admitted in a hospital. The people of the village vouched for Maulana's good reputation. Approximately 20 days after the incident, Abdul Rahman visited the hospital to meet Maulana. Maulana revealed that the bomb had exploded in his hand. The police subsequently detained Maulana, whose real name was Abdul Khaliq r/o Vill. Jokhanpura, PS Bareilly.

After two months, Abdullah came to his house with one Shafiq and brought explosives from Bangladesh. He stored these in his shop in the village. However, as a result of Abdul Khaliq's arrest in the bomb blast case, he left the village and followed Babaji's instructions to open a shop in Delhi because it was no longer safe to live there.

The team diligently engaged in a protracted process of interrogating each accused individually, leaving no stone unturned in their pursuit of justice. Simultaneously, the esteemed Central agency, cognisant of the gravity of the situation, undertook their own measures to initiate appropriate actions against the associates and sympathisers affiliated with this nefarious terrorist organisation, scattered across various states. The individuals were presented with a comprehensive compilation of data, encompassing the entirety of the contents in their personal diary; not limited only to phone numbers and addresses but also other pertinent details.

During the months of March and April 1998, a series of meticulously planned operations unfolded, orchestrated by my team of exceptional individuals. Inspector Dataram, Inspector Subhash Tandon and Inspector Rajendra Bhatia embarked on a mission to apprehend the elusive associates of these nefarious terrorists, resulting in the apprehension of Shameem Akhtar, a notorious *hawala* dealer hailing from Kolkata. Humayun Sheikh, Mohammad Umar Ali and Abdul Qasim, all were residents of West Bengal. Furthermore, their efforts led to the arrest of Shafiq-ul Islam, a resident of Bangladesh, while simultaneously recovering a cache of dangerous explosives. During follow-up, we were also able to arrest two more associates, namely Tasleem @ Bannu (34) and Naaimudin @ Mannan (30), both r/o Umri Kalan, Distt. Jyotiba Phule Nagar, UP. They harboured the LeT terrorists like Ammar, etc. and helped them to create a fake identity for obtaining a passport.

In the initial phase of this comprehensive endeavour, the Interstate Cell (Crime Branch) successfully apprehended a total of 14 individuals affiliated with the Lashkar-e-Toiba terrorist organisation. Among those detained were three Pakistani, three Bangladeshi and eight Indian nationals. With the apprehension of the culprits, a staggering tally of 39 bomb blast/planting incidents that had plagued the regions of Delhi, Uttar Pradesh and Haryana were successfully unravelled, bringing a sense of relief and pleasure to the affected communities.

In possession was a sum totalling $2,200 and Rs. 1,00,000 in cash, accompanied by a weighty cache of 50 kg. of explosives. From their possession, a formidable array of weaponry was unearthed, comprising two hand grenades, a single revolver and a pistol along with corresponding cartridges. Furthermore, among their cache were cast-iron cylinders, acids and detonators, all serving as ominous reminders of the potential devastation that lay within their grasp.

The Police Commissioner swiftly discerned the invaluable contributions rendered by the team collectively, promptly bestowing well-deserved out-of-turn promotions upon 29 members within his purview of authority. A proposal was submitted to the esteemed Lieutenant Governor of Delhi, advocating for out-of-turn promotion to myself (ACP, Ravi Shankar) to the rank of Additional DCP, alongside Inspectors

Dataram, Subhash Tandon and Rajendra Bhatia, who were to be elevated to the rank of ACP. Regrettably, the proposal was met with a wave of discontent from envious colleagues, ultimately in vain. Nevertheless, the team's morale remained unscathed in the face of these obstacles. They pursued the leads to their inevitable conclusions. Dear reader, I must assure you that this tale is far from reaching its conclusion. Having concluded the initial legal formalities against the accused individual, the diligent Crime Branch team swiftly resumed their pursuit.

THE TIMES OF INDIA

New Delhi, Tuesday, March 10, 1998

Three Pakistanis among 5 held for Delhi blasts

At least two gangs still active; Kakkar refuses to rule out more explosions

5 more arrested for blasts

City policemen bringing in men involved in blasts in Delhi to Tis Hazari courts on Monday.

THE PIONEER

...nd Lucknow http://www.the-pioneer.com New Delhi, Tuesday March 10, 1998 Late City Vol. 8

Six explosion cases solved

3 Pakistanis among 5 held; ITO, Chandni Chowk blasts still unsolved

Staff Reporter
New Delhi

THE DELHI Police on Monday claimed to have solved six more cases of bomb blasts which rocked the Capital last year.

Five persons, including three Pak nationals, have been arrested in this connection, Police Commissioner T R Kakkar told reporters at a Press conference.

The Pakistani nationals, identified as Abdullah, Mohd Hussain and Badruddin, along with their Indian accomplices Abdul Baki and Abdul Rahman were arrested from different parts of the Capital, Mr Kakkar said.

While Baki was arrested on March 4, his interrogation led to the arrest of Rahman on March 8 following which the Pakistanis, including their leader Abdullah, Hussain and Badruddin, were arrested from Lajpat Nagar and Kalkaji areas of South Delhi on Sunday, the police said.

Forty-five kgs of explosive material, two hand grenades, one revolver, one pistol, 43 live cartridges and articles of making bombs like cast iron cylinders, sulphuric acid, batteries, detonators and watches, besides 2,200 American dollars and Rs 70,000 have been recovered from their possession, Mr Kakkar said.

"With these arrests, all bomb blast cases, except the ones at Chandni chowk in North Delhi and opposite Police Headquarters in the ITO area, have been worked out," Deputy Commissioner of Police (Crime) Karnal Singh said, adding that with these arrests blasts in Sonepat and Kanpur have also been solved.

Answering a question, Mr Kakkar said the five members belong to one of the several groups of the notorious Abdul Karim Tunda gang, which was also responsible for the serial blasts at Mumbai. Tunda, the brain behind the blasts, is a hardcore militant who has been actively sponsoring militant activities in India and is wanted by various investigating agencies for several crimes in the country. Tunda is reportedly hiding in Bangladesh.

In past few years Tunda has turned out to be one of the most active Inter-Services Intelligence (of Pakistan) sponsored militant. Delhi Police has requested the Home Ministry for a country-to-country contact for his extradition, Mr Kakkar said.

Among the arrested militants, Abdul Baki is a shop-owner from Gali Chulhe Wali in Walled City and Abdullah alias Abdul Rehman is a resident of Dhora Tanda in Bareilley district of Uttar Pradesh. The other three are Pak nationals.

Delhi Police is also on the look-out for two more groups of the Tunda gang. "We have identified at least one more group to be directly involved in the Chandni Chowk and ITO blasts," Mr Kakkar said. The Commissioner added that most of these groups consists of Pak nationals.

Answering another query, Mr Kakkar said there was nodal person of the organisation in India and the orders came directly from across the borders. "We are in the know of their modus operandi but we would not disclose the details now," he said.

The Commissioner added that on gaining entry through the porous borders with Bangladesh these terrorists often went to mosques run by Ahl-e-Hadis and were met by their contacts there. Mr Kakkar has not ruled out further blasts in the Capital. "With a foreign Government backing these groups nothing could be ruled out," he said.

Meanwhile, the four terrorists arrested on Sunday were sent to the police custody by Metropolitan Magistrate Rakesh Garg till March 18. The four accused were produced in the court at about 2.15 pm with muffled face under tight police security.

Three Pak nationals, accused in series of bomb blasts, being produced at Tis Hazari Court in the Capital on Monday *Pioneer*

Phase II

Meeting with Shri L.K. Advani, Home Minister of India

During that time, Shri L.K. Advani, who held the position of Home Minister of India, thoughtfully organised a meeting to express his congratulations to us and thoroughly review the investigation we had conducted. Present at this meeting were not only myself and senior officials from the Intelligence Bureau, but also the Commissioner of Police, T.R. Kakkar, B.K. Gupta, Additional Commissioner (Crime), Karnal Singh, DCP and Alok Kumar, Additional DCP.

In the course of our in-depth discussion, we revisited the extensive investigation we had previously conducted, unveiling the clandestine networks behind the establishment of the LeT bases in Delhi and the orchestration of bomb blasts in Delhi, Haryana, Punjab and Uttar Pradesh. We also presented him with a detailed outline of our entire operation and the prospective strategy we intended to implement.

Shri L.K. Advani was effusive in his praise for the remarkable work carried out by our dedicated investigative team. He commended us by saying, "I am deeply impressed by the diligence, dedication and professionalism displayed by this team in unravelling these complex networks and ensuring the safety of our citizens. Your efforts have not only safeguarded our nation but have also set an exemplary standard in intelligence and law enforcement. Your work reflects the highest degree of commitment to the security of our country and for that, I extend my heartfelt gratitude to each one of you."

□

23

Hyderabad Module Unveiled

There was a significant setback for this organisation with the detention of two different modules based in Delhi – one led by Kamran and the other led by Hussain and Abdullah, based in Delhi. There was a break in their communication network for nearly a month. The majority of information that emerged after these arrests regarding the presence of other modules or infiltrated terrorists from Pakistan was quite ambiguous and general in nature. Because these two modules were indirectly handled by LeT leadership through Abdul Karim Tunda @ Babaji, the arrested accused did not have a fair amount of knowledge about the presence of other modules that were being handled directly by the leadership. Therefore, it necessitated extensive background research at the pan-India level. The material would further surface during the monitoring of the entire Indian network of LeT terrorist organisations and their handlers based in Pakistan. Furthermore, the team's attention was drawn to several significant clues pertaining to the additional module present in India. But some clues required immediate attention and follow-up.

Therefore, to get the STD record of the phone number linked to one of the LeT terrorists, Abu Umes@Raju and his other associates, Abu Darda, Yasir, whose phone numbers were found mentioned in Kamran's diary, we decided to send a team to Mumbai. In fact, Azam Cheema called Abu Umesh and

Abu Darda from Pakistan on that number while Kamran was present. Kamran remembered that number and later noted it down that in his diary. In the first week of April 1998, one team was dispatched to Mumbai to collect the records of the aforementioned booth. Another team was sent to Malerkotla to find and collect the records of the STD booth where Ammar was purportedly employed. The staff was given the explicit directive that, while no open inquiries would be conducted in that area, discreet inquiries could be undertaken, if at all possible. Regarding Ammar's presence, Kamran revealed that he was in Pakistan when he returned to India in February 1998.

The team returned with the records from Punjab and Mumbai. The record was analysed. The analysis revealed two numbers: one being 009262xxxx069, which was from Pakistan, and another was a Mobile Number 9849xxxx04, from Hyderabad. I asked Sandeep Malhotra to promptly gather the call information for the Hyderabad mobile number and to take Pakistan's phone number under observation in VSNL immediately. Further analysis of the Pakistan number turned out to be that of Azam Cheema, the launching commander of LeT.

When the call information for the Hyderabad mobile number was received, it was examined. The subscriber had made a sizeable number of calls to Pakistani numbers, which were already under observation at VSNL, but oddly enough, we weren't receiving any corresponding communication in Delhi.

Ravi: "Sandeep! How is it possible? Give me the specifics. It is quite odd. Are you sure these numbers are still being observed at VSNL in Delhi?"

Sandeep: "Yes, sir. These highlighted numbers are the ones that we have been monitoring from the beginning."

Ravi: "Yes, I know! Okay, let me ask Mr. Bansal about this first. I believe we are lacking something."

He immediately reached out to Mr. Bansal at VSNL.

Ravi: "Good morning, Bansal Sahib."

Bansal: "Good day, Raviji. What's up? You likely felt some relief at this point."

Ravi: "Yes, to some extent. There is still a long way to go, sir. I need some monitoring-related clarity, Bansalji. In actuality, there are some international call interceptions that we are missing. I simply want to let you know that we have the call records of that mobile number of Hyderabad. According to our findings, that mobile number from Hyderabad had called those Pakistani numbers multiple times, which are under surveillance at VSNL. However, we never received a corresponding communication regarding those calls. Would you kindly explain how it is possible?"

Bansal: "Sure, could you please send us the call details for that number?"

Ravi: "Just hang on." He then asked Sandeep to take out a duplicate copy of the mobile details.

Ravi: "Bansal Sahib, I am coming to see you if you are not occupied with any other assignment."

Mr. Bansal: "I am, in fact, present. Kindly come. You're welcome!"

I reached the VSNL conference room and had a friendly discussion with a VSNL engineer about the situation.

Engineer: "Sir, Hyderabad is where these calls came from. Therefore, either the Chennai gateway or the Mumbai gateway of VSNL was used to send these calls directly to Pakistan. There are actually four gates of VSNL for international calls, and calls can be forwarded through any open gateway."

International calls originated in southern India would typically be forwarded to that country through the Chennai gateway. Like that, international calls from eastern India are routed through the Kolkata gateway. Western and Central India usually send these calls through the Mumbai gateway. Northern India usually sends these calls through the New Delhi gateway.

Though all calls are routed through their dedicated gateways, it could adopt the routes of any other gateway when its dedicated gateway is busy and another gateway does not have traffic.

Ravi: "What is the cure then? Listening to all the calls to these numbers in Pakistan can help uncover their entire network, which is really important."

"There is just one exit," the engineer said. "I just wanted to let you know that we're looking to redirect all calls to Pakistan originating from any state in India through the Delhi gateway, instead of their dedicated gateways. However, we need to get permission from higher management first. We needed senior management's approval in order to redirect all calls to Pakistan through the Delhi gateway."

Ravi: "You will get these instructions as soon as possible. Okay, thanks. I will now take your leave."

The matter was discussed with Karnal Singh, who immediately fixed a meeting with Nikhil Kumar in at the Ministry of Home Affairs (MHA), which had sent the instructions to the Ministry of Communication for further necessary action. They assured me that everything would be completed by the next evening.

All calls originated from India on Pakistan numbers were diverted through New Delhi gateway.

Finally, the system started working in the third week of April. As a result, the team enthusiastically began working day after day. Despite that, our main concern was that the system wasn't showing the calling number when any call was made to a Pakistani number from India. They only provide TAXT details with each call. Obtaining a calling number from TAXT further involved several feeder exchanges.

After locating that exchange, we were only able to find out the calling number, which would ultimately turn out to be an STD number. This process was time-consuming and took a lot of effort to trace the calling numbers. When making these calls, the callers used different phone booths and during the conversation, they spoke in a cautious manner without revealing where they were. In addition, they would often choose to Fax important conversations or messages instead of using the telephone to communicate. Most of the time, when a caller from India contacts someone in Pakistan, they usually provide the STD booth number without mentioning the area code. This is because the person in Pakistan is already aware of the area code. Now he would make a call to an Indian number from Pakistan so that the call couldn't be intercepted. This modus operandi further added to our woes.

We wanted to gather as much information as possible about the modules in India by using technical analysis and interactive communication. This process took quite a bit of time and required a significant amount of work in the field. After an exciting one-and-a-half months of fieldwork and technical exercises, we were able to gather some valuable and actionable information.

Here's what we found:

Some calls to Pakistan on LeT numbers were routed through:

1. Agra TAXT came from various STD booths in Aligarh, Uttar Pradesh.
2. Patiala TAXT calls were made from the STD booths in Malerkotla, Punjab.
3. Moreover, some calls to those numbers were traced to STD booths in Asansol, West Bengal, Jodhpur, Rajasthan and Mumbai. Previously, we were missing the interceptions of these phone numbers of Pakistan because they were sent directly to Pakistan from the dedicated gateways, i.e. Chennai, Mumbai and Kolkata. In order to trace the origins of the calls, Sandeep Malhotra was put on the job.

A joint team of ISC and IB was sent to Malerkotla, Punjab. However, as decided at Deputy. Prime Minister's meeting, the Intelligence Bureau was enlisted in all upcoming operations in the light of pan-India implications. A joint team of IB and

ISC was sent to Melerkotla, in the state of Punjab. However, the IB deployed its own sources in Bombay, West Bengal and Jodhpur, in the state of Rajasthan.

Our meetings with Intelligence Bureau and Delhi Police took place in the latter two weeks of June 1998. After conducting a comprehensive rundown at each team's location, we tasked them with to conduct additional research on the hiding places of individuals suspected of being terrorists. As there were multiple TAXT's involved in Pan-India network, it took us a bit longer to identify the STD booths from which these calls originated. But when all the calls originated from any place in India were diverted through New Delhi TAXT, it gave us very enthusiastic results. We started receiving the intercepts from different parts of India, which I would be discussing module by module at relevant places in the book.

□

24
Module 3—Arrest of Junaid

Junaid, a Pakistani LeT Operative in Hyderabad

Analysis of previous records of the calls routed through Chennai TAXT made from Hyderabad were traced to the mobile number in question in Hyderabad.

Moreover, we started receiving the interceptions of Junaid, who was talking to Azam Cheema and Zaki-ur-Rehman in Pakistan. Those intercepts revealed that Junaid relocated to Hyderabad around two years ago from Pakistan. He married an Indian woman in Hyderabad and was recently blessed with a second child. He had been handling or providing the logistics for each module as and when needed. He was in the process of strengthening the base by purchasing a farmhouse and vehicles, i.e. trucks and Jeeps, after transferring the in-hand vehicles to Gujarat- and Punjab-based LeT operatives. He was also going to build underground bunkers. Junaid also repeatedly demanded explosives and weapons, as well as money from them. During that particular time, Zaki sent two terrorists to Junaid, but Junaid asked Zaki to send seven or eight more with at least 16 short-barrel AK rifles, two for each. Besides, Junaid once attempted to persuade Zaki-ur-Rehman to inspire Maldivian students studying in Pakistan to practice *jihad*, they are Muslims by religion. Since there were good relations and communication between India and the Maldives then, it was easy to infiltrate their men and smuggle explosives from Pakistan into India if they were successful in inspiring those students.

Zaki was also trying to know the details about the arrests of Abu Akasa@ Kamran and the other Pakistanis. He wanted Junaid to explore whether he could be of some help to get him released, but Junaid showed his inability, at least until Kamran was in police custody remand. However, Zaki cautioned him to remain vigilant.

The calls are mentioned below and are self-explanatory:

Call 1: Abdullah Faruq to Junaid

Abdullah Faruq: "*Salaam walekum.*" (Peace be upon you.)

Junaid: *Walekum salaam. ALhamdulillah. Cheema Sahib hain?* And upon you be peace. Is Cheema Sahib there?)

Abdullah Faruq: *Nahin vah to nahin hai. Aap kaun*?" (No, he is not here. Who are you?)

Junaid: *Main Junaid India se. Cheema Sahib, ghar per honge kya? 621 per*?) (I am Junaid from India. Is Cheema Sahib at home? At 621? (Three digits of Cheema's phone number.)

Abdullah Faruq: "*Nahin vah bahut dur hai jahan unka ilaka hai vahi hai.*" (No, he is quite far. He is in his area.)

Junaid: *Theek hai. Cheema Sahib aaye to bolna ki Junaid ko phone kar lenge.*" (Okay, if Cheema Sahib comes, tell him to call Junaid.)

Abdullah Faruq: "*Aap chacha se baat karenge?*" (Will you talk to uncle?)

Junaid: *Kya yahi aaspaas hain*?" (Is he around?)

Abdullah Faruq: *Han yahi hain.*" (Yes, he is here.)

Junaid: "*To fir baat karao.*" (Then connect me with him.)

Zaki: *Salaam walekum. Rahmatullah Sahib theek thak*?" (Peace be upon you and the mercy of Allah. Is everything fine?)

Junaid: *Bilkul theek. Aap kaise hain Zaki Sahib*?" (Absolutely fine. How are you, Zaki Sahib?)

Zaki: "*Allah ka fazal hai.*" (By the grace of Allah.)

Junaid: "*Bacche aapko salaam kar rahe hain.*" (The kids are sending their greetings.)

Zaki: "*Kya naam hai inke*?" (What are their names?)

Junaid: *Nahi Zaki Sahib mein apne dusre ladke ki baat kar*

rha hun... Ladka hua hai. Fahad naam rakha hai uska." (Zaki Sahib, I am talking about my second son who was recently born. I've named him Fahad.)

Zaki: *Mashallah! Mashallah! O bhale aadmi kabhi ghar per bhi baat kar liya karo. Vahan markaz per phone karke bol dena vah aapke abbu ko bula denge."* (*Mashallah! Mashallah*! Oh, good man, talk to your family at home sometimes. Call on the landline of *markaz* (Pakistan) and tell them, they will call your father.)

Junaid: *Maine kara tha kisi ne phone nahin uthaya. Ye dono bacche bhi jo aapne abhi bheje hai aapko salaam bol rahe hai."* (I called, but no one picked up. These two boys (terrorists) that you had sent are sending their greetings.)

Zaki: "*Walekum salaam Rehmatullah. Achcha yah batao kya aap abu Akasa (Kamran) ke liye kuchh kar sakte ho?"* (Peace be upon you and the mercy of Allah. Okay, tell me, can you do something for Abu Akasa,(Kamran)?)

Junaid: "*Vah aisa hui abhi hamen kuchh nahin karna chahie jab tak wo scientist ke saath hai. Iss se masla ban sakta hai."* (He is in such a situation that we shouldn't do anything for now as long as he is with the scientists {code for police}. It can create issues.)

Zaki: "*Kya uske sath koi Pakistani bhi pakde gaye hain?"* (Have any Pakistanis been caught with him?)

Junaid: "*Han kafi naam hain, maine cutting Cheema Sahib ko bhijwa di thi ek mahina ho gaya. Abhi naam to mujhe jabani yad nahin hai."* (Yes, there are quite a few names. I sent the news cuttings to Cheema Sahib about a month ago. I don't remember the names now.)

Zaki: *Chalo dekhna agar ham kuchh kar sakte hain to, achcha tum Dakhal Sahib se baat karo."* (Okay, let's see if we can do something. Alright, you talk to Dakhal Sahib.)

Dakhal: "*Salaam walekum, kabhi idhar bhi chakkar laga liya karo."* (Peace be upon you, also visit here sometime (Pakistan).)

Junaid: *Han, han main aaunga, tumhari badi yaad aati hai.*

Abhi maine ek delivery leni thee jo le li hai, aur meri jimmewari khatam ho gayi. Ab main yah gadi Punjab bhejunga aur ek dusri gadi lekar Gujarat bhejunga uske bad mein aaunga lekin main Iran wale raste se aaunga main passport per Pakistan ki stamp nahin lagwana chahta, usse masla ban sakta hai." (Yes, yes, I will come. In fact I had to take a delivery,(weapon and explosives) which I have taken. My responsibility is over. Now, I will send this vehicle (truck) to Punjab and send another vehicle (truck) to Gujarat, after that I will come. But I will come via the route of Iran. I don't want to get a Pakistan stamp (visa) on my passport; it can create issues.)

Dakhal: "*Theek! Theek! Aur apna dyan rakhna koyi tere hi magar na pada hoe? Achcha Zaki sahib se baat karlo.*" (Okay, okay. Take care, and make sure no one recognises you. Alright, talk to Zaki Sahib.)

Zaki: "*Rehmatullah*!" (Peace be upon you.)

Junaid: "*Zaki Sahib aap Cheema Sahib ko bataiye na yahan per bahut problem a rahi hai jald se jald paise bhejne ka intejaam karen.*" (Zaki Sahib, please tell Cheema Sahib that there are a lot of problems here, arrange to send money as soon as possible.)

Zaki: "*Theek hai main karta hun. Inshallah, ho jaega fikra na karen.*" (Okay, I will do it. *Inshallah*, it will be done. Don't worry.)

Junaid: "*Achcha Allah hafiz.*" (Okay, *Allah Hafiz.*)

Call 2: Abdullah Faruq to Junaid

Abdullah Faruq: "*Salaam walekum*!" (Peace be upon you.)

Junaid: "*Walekum salaam. Alhamdulillah ! Zaki Sahib hai kya*?" (And upon you be peace. Is Zaki Sahib there?)

Abdullah Faruq: "*Aap kaun* (Who are you?)

Junaid: "*Main Junaid, India se.*" (I am Junaid from India.)

Abdullah Faruq: "*Lijiye baat kijiye.*" (Okay, talk.)

Zaki: "*Salaam walekum.*" (Peace be upon you.)

Junaid: *Alhamdulillah Zaki Sahib. Main Cheema Sahib ko bahut rafta karne ki koshish kar raha hun lekin unka phone kai din se mil hi nahin raha aap unko mera ek message pahuncha dain ki yah jo do bacche aaye hain vaise hi 7/8 bacche aur bhijwa den bilkul waisehi. Aur unke sath vah chhoti nali wali, samajh gaye na ek to AK hi hoti hai aur ek usse chhoti vah bhijwa de."* (Peace be upon you, Zaki Sahib. I am trying to contact Cheema Sahib, but his phone is not connecting for the last few days. Please deliver my message to him that unlike two kids (terrorists) sent earlier by him, send 7/8 more kids (terrorists) to him, alongwith the small barrel rifles. Do you understand? Right?)

Zakil: "*Kitne? 2 bhijwani hai?*" (How many should I send? Two?)

Junaid: "*Nahi aath bacche hai to 16 bijwaey. Kyunki abhi aman hai, jitna bhi bhej sakte ho saman bhijwa do. Aur sath mein paise bhi bhijvao bina paise masala banaa hua hai.*" (No, there are eight children, so send 16. Since it is a peace-time, send whatever supplies you can. Also, send money without delay, as there's already a problem due to lack of funds.)

Zaki: "*Main bol doonga.*" (I will inform them.)

Junaid: "*Zaki Sahib, yahan ek farm kharidna hai, ek Jeep kharidni hai, ek gadi kharidni hai, aur ek tahkhana banvana hai. Iss baat ko aap bilkul bhi najar andaaz mat karen.*" (Zaki Sahib, we need to buy a farm, a jeep, a car, and build an underground here. Don't ignore this matter at all.)

Zaki: "*Theek hai, main Cheema Sahib ko bol dunga aap, befikar rahe. Allah Hafiz.*" (Alright, I will inform Cheema Sahib. Don't worry. *Allah Hafiz.*)

Call 3: A. Faruq to Junaid (with Zaki on the call)

Abdullah Faruq: "*Salaam walekum*!" (Peace be upon you!)

Junaid: "*Walekum salaam*! *Main Junaid, India se. Zaki Sahib se baat karvao.*" (And upon you be peace! I want to talk to Zaki Sahib. I am Junaid from India.)

Zaki: "*Alhamdulillah! Rehmatullah*! *Main bol raha hoon.*" (Peace and Allah's mercy be upon you! I am here.)

Junaid: *Zaki Sahib, paise nahin pahunchate hain masala*

bana hua hai. Aap Cheema Sahib ko kaho na wah is taraf gaur karen." (Zaki Sahib, the funds aren't reaching and the issue is becoming critical. Please ask Cheema Sahib to pay attention to this matter.) Junaid continues: "*Achcha dusri baat yah hai Zaki Sahib, maine aapko phone isliye kiya hai ki tumhari taraf Maldives ke bacche padh rahe hain. Agar aap unse rafta kayam karke unko mutmain (convince) kar sakain to karen; yah bahut achcha hoga.*" (Another thing, Zaki Sahib, I called you because the children from the Maldives are studying there (Pakistan). If you can convince them and establish a connection, it would be very good.)

Zaki: "*Kisliye?*" (Why?)

Junaid: "*Kyunki Maldives se India ke tallukat bahut acche hain. Agar hamara koi adda wahan per khul jata hai aur kisi jahaz vagaira ka intezaam ho jaaye to hum saman aur bacche Maldives ke jarie bhijwain to bahut aasani bhi hogi kyunki passport visa ka koi chakkar nahin hai. Aur hame yah sasta bhi padega.*" (Because the connections between the Maldives and India are very good, if we can establish a base there and arrange for a ship or other means, it would be very easy for us to send supplies and children via the Maldives, without the hassle of passports and visas. And it would be cost-effective for us.)

Zaki: "Hmmmmm."

Junaid: *Ye, mera apna andaza hai. Aaap is per study karvakar aage ke liye soch sakte hain. Aur Zaki Sahib, maine Cheema Sahib ko saman bhejne ke liye bhi kaha tha, uska kya raha aur unse paison ke liye bhi bolna. Jald se jald bhijwain. Theek hai. Allah Hafiz.*" (This is just my estimation; you can think about it for the future by studying it. And Zaki Sahib, I had also asked Cheema Sahib about sending supplies and funds. What's the status on that? Let me know. Alright then. *Allah Hafiz.*)

Zaki: "*Allah Hafiz.*" (*Allah Hafiz.*)

There were several attempts by Junaid to locate Azam Cheema, but he could not get him through. Finally, he confronted him and demanded money, weapons and explosives from him. Cheema assured him that he would be sending money as early as possible, as he had to arrange the amount from different sources because the amount was large. Therefore, he forbade Junaid to sell trucks in hand because he was in the process of sending a consignment of explosives and weapons when the phase of full moon night got over and the phase of dark nights started. Junaid was also in the process of settling the two Pakistani-trained terrorists in Hyderabad and arranging some employment for them. Junaid also discussed about sending one Ismail with some boys from Hyderabad for training in Pakistan because they were very desperate for undergoing training. Cheema asked Junaid to send them through Imran, a Burmese guide settled in Pakistan and who used to facilitate the terrorists and smuggling of arms and explosives into India through the Indo-Pakistan border illegally. Imran at that time was present in India. But Junaid showed the inability to send them illegally; he therefore asked Cheema to arrange visas for them.

Relevant conversations intercepted are given below:

Call 1

Cheema: "*Salaam walekum.*" (Peace be upon you.)

Junaid: "*Cheema Sahib bol rahe hain*?" (Is this Cheema Sahib?)

Cheema: "*Han, han kaise hain, aap*?" (Yes, yes, how are you?)

Junaid: "*Eid ke chand ho gaye hain aap; aapka phone hi nahin lagta. Aisa karen aap, ek badhiya sa mobile le jiski range bahut door tak ho. Jaisa Syed Sahib (Dubaiwale) ne liya hai aur apne pass rakhen taki rafta karne mein koi masala na rahe. Bahut pareshani hoti hai, Cheema Sahib.*" (It's been a while since Eid. Your phone is not reachable. Please get yourself a good mobile phone with an extensive range like Syed Sahib (Dubaiwale) has. Keep it with you so that there are no issues in communication. It gets quite troublesome, Cheema Sahib.)

Cheema: "*Vah aisa hai na main abhi kafi din se fansa hua tha bujurgon ke kam per laga hua tha to kabhi idhar kabhi udhar. Bahut zyada masrufiat thee isiliye aapse koi baat nahin ho pai. Achcha, kya Syed Sahib ka phone aaya tha? Paise bhijwaye thay kya?*" (Yes, it's true. I was caught up in the work of the elders and was busy here and there. That's why I couldn't talk to you. By the way, did Syed Sahib's call come regarding sending money?)

Junaid: "*Nahin paise to nahin bhijwaye mujhe! Baat karni thi kya? Main janbujhkar unse baat nahin karta kyunki vah yah sochenge ki ham paison ke liye kam karte hain.*" (No, he didn't send money. Did you want that I should talk to him? I intentionally didn't talk to him because he might think that we work for money.)

Cheema: "*Nahin, nahin, achcha kiya! Main karvata hoon aur jald se jald bhijwata hoon.*" (No, no. It's alright. I'll arrange for it and send it as soon as possible.)

Junaid: "*Cheema Sahib, saman bhi bhijvao na.*" (Cheema Sahib, please send the supplies as well.)

Cheema: "*Vah aajkal chand poora hai. Kuchh din ke bad bhijwata hun.*"

(Sure, the moon is full these days. I'll send it after a few days during the dark nights.)

Junaid: "*Theek hai. Allah Hafiz.*" (Alright then, *Allah Hafiz.*)

Call 2: Cheema to Junaid

Cheema: "*Salaam walekum.*" (Peace be upon you.)

Junaid: "*Walekum salaam! Alhamdulillah! Cheema Sahib, yah Ismaile (resident of Hyderabad) vagaira udhar aane ke liye bahoot zor de rahe hain. Mera to inse kal kafi jhagada bhi ho gaya hai. Aapko to inki tareekh ka pata hi hai. Tipu Sultan wali akad hai in logon mein.*" (And upon you be peace! Cheema Sahib, Ismaile and others from Hyderabad are insisting on coming there. I had a heated argument with them yesterday. You know their attitude is like Tipu Sultan's.)

Cheema: "*Achcha theek hai Imran udhar hi hai. Main usko bolata hun ki vah inko lekar aa jaaye.*" (Alright, fine. Imran is there in India. I'll tell him to bring them along." (Imran used to assist the infiltration of terrorists into India from Pakistan and vice versa besides smuggling explosives and weapons from Pakistan into India.)

Junaid: "*Nahi, nahi. Cheema Sahib, yah iss raste se nahin chal kar a sakte.*" (No, no, Cheema Sahib, they can't come through this route.)

Cheema: "*To fir inke passport banva dain. Visa ke liye main baat kar lunga.*" (Then let's get their passports made. I'll talk about the visa.)

Junaid: "*Theek hai, main karta hun aur aapko batata hun. Achcha yah gadi bilkul kharab ho gai hai. Main isko bech raha hun. Aap paise bhijwaye, main nai gadi lunga.*" (Alright, I'll do that and let me tell you, the truck is not useable now. I am selling it. Please send the money and I'll get a new one.)

Cheema: "*Abhi kuchh din rukiye aap. Pahle main jo aapko saman bhejunga, vahan se lekar aana. Uske bad hi bechna. Tab tak main paise bhej dunga. Theek hai, main panch-chhai din mein. Tab tak, andheri raatain ho jayegi, saman bhijwata hoon aur paise bhi bhijwata hoon.*" (Please wait for a few days. First, let me send the supplies. You bring them from there (border). SubsequentlyI'll send the money. Okay, I'll send both the supplies and the money in five to six days. By then, the nights will get darker.)

Junaid: "*Aisa karte, karte, kafi din ho gaye.*" (It's been quite a few days doing this.)

Cheema: "*Aisa hai na, paisa bhi bahoot zyada hai na. Intzam karne me time to lagta hai.*" (Yes, it's true. It's not only a matter of a lot of money, but it also takes time to arrange it.)

Junaid: "*Achcha maine ek ladke (Pakistani) ko to autoriksha dilva di hai aur dusre (Pakistani) ko bhi main kahin per kaam par lagwa raha hoon.*" (Alright, I've arranged an autorickshaw for one guy (Pakistani) and I'm trying to find work for another (Pakistani).)

Cheema: "*Theek hai, theek hai. Bahut badhiya. Chalo ab rakhta hun. Allah Hafiz.* (Alright, alright. Very good. I am disconnecting. *Allah Hafiz.*)

Team's Arrival in Hyderabad

Given that we were monitoring the conversation of Pakistan number that originated from the personal mobile number of Junaid, who was located in Hyderabad, it was agreed that we would make it a top priority to track him down and detain him. In the last week of June 1998 after discussing in detail with V.N. Singh, Commissioner of Police, I went to Hyderabad with my team and a team of officers from the Intelligence Bureau.

We reached Hyderabad in the evening. IB requested the service provider to put the Mobile number of Junaid under observation with parallel listening facility, which would be started from next morning. Meanwhile, the call record was also analysed to find out the probable residence and workplace of Junaid.

Ravi: "Rajendra I believe you have seen that after examining the call details, we are readily able to make out that Junaid's mobile position remains in the Tolly Chowki Area during the daytime, but that during the night, he is present in the Mallapalli Area. This is something that we can easily figure out."

Rajendra: "Yes, sir, this indicates that Toli Chowki is his place of business and Mallepally is his home."

Ravi: "Alright, first we need to check the coverage of a specific Cell ID (Identification no. of cell through which mobile call is transmitted to subscriber from service provider switch) at both locations; after that, only we will be able to conduct the raid."

Rajendra: "Absolutely, sir."

Throughout the course of the night, we made a note of the radial area of the cell ID in both locations with the help of a software which was installed in our cellphone.

Ravi: "Now it is time to investigate and evaluate the specifics of the call while keeping the following hypothesis in mind:

1. Any landline number installed in the Mallepally area received calls most frequently from the Toly Chowki area or from anywhere else besides the Mallapalli area, from Junaid's mobile number.
2. Any land line number installed in the Toly Chowki area received calls frequently from any location except the Tolly Chowki area from Junaid's mobile."

There were a few things that ASI Ashok wanted to know about the premise that we were basing our data analysis on.

ASI: "Sir, can I ask you something?"

Ravi: "Of course, ask away, my child."

ASI: "Sir, the logic you are applying, enlighten me about it."

Ravi: "How many days have you been with us? Haven't you understood this yet?"

ASI: "Sir, as you've always placed us on the field operation and you yourself handle the technical matters – we are prone to it."

Ravi: "Alright, now you've become ASI; I'll have to explain because you also need to investigate these type of matter in future. Let me ask you a straightforward question, answer it, and everything will become clear to you. It's a very simple matter."

ASI: "Sir, go ahead and ask."

Ravi: "During the day, you are in the office. There's no landline available in the office, and if you make a call on your home landline from your mobile phone, where will the Cell ID of your mobile be registered?"

Immediately, ASI responded: "Understood, sir. I understand. But there's another thing; if there's no landline phone at home, then what do we do, sir?"

Ravi: "That's a good question too. Then we'll check if any other landline phone is being used in the neighbourhood."

ASI: "If there isn't anyone nearby, then?"

Ravi: "Then we'll check the mobile phone record of the suspect to see if there's any mobile in that particular Cell ID radius, who frequently make or receive call to and from suspects mobile number."

ASI: "Sir, even if there's no mobile."

In a humorous tone, Ravi responded, "I will break your head now. Alright, it's 4 a.m. now. Take a little rest, then get up quickly and get to work."

After conducting a comprehensive investigation of mobile phone records and intercepting the conversation the next day, we were able to zero in on two landline numbers: one in the name of Abdul Rahim, installed in his home in Tolly Chowki, who was running a shop selling tailoring materials. This number was used as PP number by Junaid and his associate Ismail, whose electric shop was adjacent to Abdul Rahim's shop, and Junaid oftenly used to sit there during daytime.

Another number was installed in the name of Junaid's in-laws in Battery Lane in Mallepally area, from where Junaid's wife used to call him.

The identification of Junaid was to be done discreetly. Therefore, deployment was made in the Tolly Chowki area near Ismail's shop. It was very difficult to raise the surveillance at the residential location in Battery Lane due to the community that inhabited that area and the difficult topography of the area, as there were opportunities for the police team to be exposed.

Junaid, along with two Pakistani terrorists of LeT, was arrested.

The following day the team was able to identify Junaid and Ismail sitting at the electricity shop. Immediately, one team in the Tolly Chowki area at the probable route of Junaid to his residence, and another team close to the Mallepally Battery Lane, which was considered to be a potential access site, were deployed. It was determined to intercept and take him into custody on the way to his residence because that operation carried the least amount of risk or any other possibility.

In a well-coordinated operation, Junaid was stopped and taken into custody. Based on a speedy and concise line of questioning, important information was elicited and conveyed to the Hyderabad Police. A team comprised of police officers from Delhi Police, IB, and Hyderabad Police worked together to make three arrests: one Ismail, who was providing logistics to Junaid, and two Pakistani nationals, Mansoor and Shakeel, sent by Azam Cheema in the later half of 1997.

On further questioning, Junaid disclosed that previously Azam Cheema gave Junaid the directive to meet Mansoor and Shakeel at a mosque in Bhuj, Gujarat as they had brought with them two firearms, ammo, around 20-25 kgs. of RDX, remote control devices and detonators. The artificial hollow created in the diesel tank of the vehicle was used to carry the items from Bhuj to Hyderabad. Both of them were accommodated by Junaid at Abdul Rauf's farmhouse as night guards. Their arrest resulted in the recovery of 15 kgs. of RDX, a complex detonating device, an electronic circuit for the fabrication of a car bomb, four nine-millimetre handguns, ammo and magazines, three wireless sets and other items. They had planted a bomb on the Garhkeshar railway line in district Rangareddy, Andhra Pradesh, according to revelations made by Junaid and his accomplice Mohammad Ismail of 'Electric Point'. Moreover, they were preparing to carry out a series of explosions during the time of Ganesh Chaturthi (26 August, 1998) in Hyderabad, using the available RDX, in order to incite communal violence and to draw a wedge between Hindus and Muslims.

After Junaid's arrest, he was subsequently taken to Delhi, where he was subjected to a prolonged and thorough interrogation. His questioning led to the discovery of nefarious activities, a vast network and the terrorist organisation Laskar-e-Toiba's future plans. The following is a concise account regarding his profile and disclosure:

"Junaid, 27, r/o Kala Gujran district of Jhelum, Punjab, Pakistan, was motivated and brainwashed by Maulvi Abdul Sattar to do *jihad* against *kafir*. So Junaid contacted one Zafar Hayat Aamir of Lashkar-e-Toiba at his office in Jhelum. In June 1992, he was moved to the Maskar-e-Toiba training camp, located in the Kunnad district of Afghanistan, where he completed his training Daur-e-Aam in Maskar-e-Toiba and Daur-e-Khas in the camp of Maskar-e-Akasha. After that, he was given the job of running the garment store until January 1994 in the Muzaffarabad training camp. During that time he met Babaji at Muzaffarabad.

In 1994, he and a few other terrorists made an unsuccessful attempt to be launched into India by Azam Cheema with the help of Pak Rangers from Aath Mukam and Kotli Mirpur. After that, they entered Jammu & Kashmir through Sialkot with a guide by the name of Baba Kashmiri, who was 56-years old and from the Doda area of Jammu province. After crossing the border through Sialkot, they walked for perhaps eight or nine hours before arriving at a site close to Jammu city in the early morning hours of the next day. Prior to that, they acted swiftly and buried all their weapons, including AK-47s and magazines, in the ground. These were scheduled to be picked up by Baba Kashmiri at a later time.

They then travelled to Nizamuddin, Delhi. Zaki gave them the location of Ahle Hadis Madarsa in Paan Mandi, Sadar Bazar. Junaid met Abdul Majid and Abdul Wahid, father and grandfather of Abdul Baki (since arrested), and stayed there for two days. After that, he also journeyed to Bangladesh, where he was given Rs. 50,000 by Babaji who also taught Junaid how to assemble low-intensity IEDs out of common chemicals. Junaid complied with the directives of LeT leaders and proceeded to Hyderabad. In Hyderabad, Junaid got in touch with Abdul Rauf, who operated a chicken farm and a feed plant on Maheshran Road at Ranga Reddy in the city of Hyderabad. He was a Jamait-e-Islami member. After meeting with Abdul Rauf, Junaid briefed him on his organisation's mission. In Hyderabad, Junaid came in close contact with Ismail, who ran an electrical store in Tolly Chowki. Junaid tied the knot with a native woman and then moved into the house of his father-in-law. Junaid started the business relating to automobile components for a cover. He had gotten himself a Canter automobile as well as a three-wheeler and a two-wheeler. Finding Muslim men in the surrounding areas, sending them to Pakistan for training and finally resettling them in and around Hyderabad were his primary responsibilities. He was, in essence, attempting to establish a sizable network of LeT members in Hyderabad and other regions of India. During this period, he reached out to local leaders affiliated with SIMI, JEI, and Ahle Hadis to inquire about the opportunities for sending Muslim boys to Pakistan for training.

In June 1996, Junaid went to Dehradun, where he met someone named Hassan Fauzi (an ex-armyman) whose brother was a sympathiser of the cadre. He remained for a week with Hassan Fauzi and instigated for *jihad*. After that, they travelled to Nepal and met Maulvi Tahir (0097xxxx1180) to receive the money. Tahir introduced Junaid to other members of the outfit, including professors from JNU who were already familiar with Babaji. Junaid also met Abu Bakar and two other Pakistan-trained terrorists who were supervising the functioning of the LeT in Nepal.

Junaid further revealed that in July 1997, he and his associates again visited Hassan Fauzi in Dehradun with explosives in a briefcase. They made preparations to place a bomb inside a briefcase. The remaining explosives were buried close to the bank of the Aasan river. They placed the briefcase inside the suitcase and then, after taking Hassan's Hero Honda motorcycle with the number plate UP-07-3603, they arrived at the Dehradun railway station, at approximately 6:30 in the evening. They parked the motorcycle in the parking lot and entered a nearby street. Junaid placed the batteries and the timepiece, activated the bomb and planted the same in a military compartment of the *'Doon Express'* train. They started the day by reading the *Rashtriya Shahara* newspaper, in which they found the information about the explosion that had occurred when armymen noticed smoke billowing out of the suitcase and threw away the suitcase near Buxar out of the compartment. The suitcase blew up.

In April 1997, Azam Cheema sent a consignment of 15 jackets (pistols) and instructed Junaid to get in touch with Syed Sahib and Babu Bhai based in Dubai and follow his instructions to receive the delivery. Cheema provided their mobile numbers. As per the instructions received, Junaid reached at the Ahle Hadis Masjid near Beed, Naka Bhuj, Gujarat, a week after the Bari Eid with his Canter vehicle.

Two people arrived at the predetermined date and time with the consignment and asked Junaid in code as 'EID KAB HAI', Junaid replied 'AAP QURBANI KA SAMMAN LAYE HO'. After confirmation of the code, they delivered the package to Junaid. After that, they contacted a transport service outside Bhid Gate, Bhuj, Kutch, Gujarat, and loaded the truck with consumer goods and brought the consignment containing pistols to Hyderabad. After some time, an individual named Saleem, who was Syed Sahib's companion, took the consignment (15 pistols) from Junaid.

2 July, 1998

After completing the legal formalities and obtaining police custody remand for accused Junaid, a press conference was organised by the Commissioner of Police, V.N. Singh in Delhi. Thereafter, my team and I went to Interstate Cell, Chanakyapuri, Delhi and had some refreshments.

While I was sitting with my team, Inspector Rajendra Bhatia requested, "Sir, it has been more than two weeks since none of the members of my team who had gone to Hyderabad, including you, were able to pay a visit to our families. We would be really appreciative if you could let us know whether or not it is okay to depart for the night?"

I responded, "Rajendra, you have stolen my heart. Of course, we should have done it earlier! But, anyway, in any case, show up at 9:30 in the morning and adjust your schedule accordingly."

Rajendra replied, "No worries, sir; but, after we successfully finish this operation, the entire team is going to take a very lengthy break."

Dataram added, "The staff is interested in visiting Vaishno Devi as well as the other *devis* that can be seen in Himachal Pradesh."

I said, "Okay, I will be in charge of putting up this tour programme. Don't worry."

Subhash asked, "Sir, what happened to the Rs. 5 lakh prize that the CM of Delhi announced?"

I assured, "Don't be concerned; you will receive it by the end of the week. CP has forwarded the file to LG in order to get the permission."

Subhash expressed gratitude, "Thank you, sir."

I concluded, "Okay, guys, let us move. Anyway, who is going to stay tonight in the office?"

Dataram: "Subash and I will stay; you need not worry."

After that, I called the team members assigned to night duty and briefed them. Then, I proceeded to leave the office and drive home.

My daughters ran out on to the balcony as soon as they heard the sound of my car approaching. They then ran back inside the flat, yelling, "Papa" to open the door. As I approached the front entrance, my wife and daughters, who had been waiting outside, ran up to give me a bear hug. My wife passed my two-year-old son from her arms to mine.

Sushma: "Today it's raining for this reason."

Priyanka: "Dad, we saw you on TV."

Iteeh: "And Dad, your name was also in the newspaper."

Ravi: "It will come again tomorrow! Come inside now. How is Maa?"

Sushma: "Go, talk to her yourself. She thinks about you every day. She checks the newspaper daily and asks the kids if your name has come in the newspaper."

I entered my mother's room and touched her feet. She took me in her arms and became sentimental, "Are you okay, son? I was so worried, thinking you might get hurt by those dangerous people."

Ravi: "Maa, when your blessings are with me, nothing can go wrong."

My mother noticed that my wife and children were sitting by my side. In fact, they were so happy to see me after a long time that they forgot to even offer water.

Maa: "Girls, at least bring a glass of water for your father."

My wife realised her mistake and asked me, "Should I order something from the market with tea?"

Ravi: "Order it."

Sushma: "What should I order?"

Ravi: "You already know, right?"

Sushma: "*Panipuri*?"

Ravi: "Everyone knows that."

At the same time, my *bhabhi* rang up Sushma, who picked up the phone. Sushma broke the news to her about my arrival. My elder brother, also residing in the same sector, was going to come to see me. The opportunity presented itself, so Sushma took advantage of it by requesting them to buy *golgappas* from the market. After waiting for a while, my brother and his family eventually arrived, carrying *golgappas* and *tikkis*. The *golgappa* celebration and the ensuing dinner were quite enjoyable for all of us. That evening, we made the most of our time together by celebrating to the utmost extent until midnight. However, my mother intervened during the discussion that was going on among the family members: "*Eb isne son bhi deoge*" (et him sleep). Everyone left. My wife and my son came to our bedroom, but my son was not ready to sleep.

Sushma: "*Yah abhi tak confused hai. Yah aadami kaun hai kabhi-kabhi aata hai.*" (He is still confused on seeing you as you are rarely home.)

Ravi: "*Le lo maje, le lo.*"He switched off the light.

The Statesman

DELHI, SATURDAY, 4 JULY 1998

Blast plans thwarted, four ISI agents held

STATESMAN NEWS SERVICE

NEW DELHI, July 3. - A plan to execute a series of bomb blasts in Hyderabad like those in Coimbatore on the occasion of Ganesh Chaturthi, 26 August, has been thwarted with the arrest of four Inter-Services Intelligence agents in Hyderabad in a joint operation of Delhi Police and Hyderabad Police. All of them were members of Lashkare-Taiba - an outfit of ISI.

Police said, in a hurridly convened Press conference today, that they had assembled 15 kilograms of RDX, several detonating devices and an electronic circuit for fabricating a car bomb for the planned blasts. Also recovered from them were four 9 mm pistols, ammunition and magazines and three wireless sets. This included device which was capable of detonating a bomb at five separate places, simultaneously.

So far their involvement in any of the bomb blasts have not been ascertained but have been arrested for "waging war" against the nation.

The agent arrested on 1 July on whose instance the other three were arrested was, Mohammad Saleem Junaid alias Mohammad Ishtayaq, 27, a resident of Jhelum, Punjab of Pakistan.

He was arrested by a Delhi Police Crime Branch team led by Assistant Commissioner of Police, Mr Ravi Shankar. The other three - Mohammad Ismail, an electronic shop owner in Toli Chowk in Hyderabad and Shakeel and Mansur, residents of Pakisthan, who had arrived in India four months ago - were arrested today by Hyderabad Police.

The Deputy Commissioner of Police, Crime Branch, Mr Karnail Singh said, Junaid came to Delhi via Jammu and Kashmir in 1993 and resided in Okhla under the name of Ramzan. He, however, left Delhi in mid-1996, for Hyderabad as he was unable to find a safe shelter.

There he was appointed as resident agent of ISI for Andhra Pradesh. He married a local there and fathered two children. He bought a canter, AP-13 U 7622 and started living in the guise of a transporter. He had even constructed a cavity in the vehicle in which the RDX brought from Pakistan was smuggled from Buch, Gujarat to Hyderabad some time back.

Mr Singh added that he received arms training from Abdul Tunda in Muzzafarabad, Pakistan, who also helped him to infiltrate into India. After that Zakir-ur-Rehman assisted him in establishing him in India.

The Commissioner of Police, Mr V N Singh, said that Tunda was in Bangladesh but so far there was no progress in the request made to the Ministry of External Affairs for his extradition. Junaid had reportedly met him in 1995 in Bangladesh.

Police, however, ruled out his involvement in any of the blasts in Delhi, including one in Greater Kailash-II, last week, but suspected his role in the Mumbai blasts after the Babari Masjid demolition. The role they played in those blasts could have been smuggling RDX into India, Mr Karnail Singh, said.

Junaid tried to influence the young Muslims in Hyderabad using his contacts in fundamentalist organisations like Jameet-e-Islam and others. His main task was to recruit young people from India whoh could be sent to Pakistan to be trained and sent back with their minds washed.

Four months ago, two Pakistani ISI agents Shakeel and Mansur were sent to Hyderabad to assist Junaid. With the help of Ismail, the local, they were employed as security guards in a farmhouse and from there continued their activities with his help.

Both of them had received 21 days extensive training in weapons before being sent to India, a Press communique from Hyderabad Police, stated.

Mr Karnail Singh added their involvement in recent communal riots in Hyderabad was being investigated.

They were arrested at the instance of Ismail and RDX and arms were recovered from them. Mr V N Singh said that one of them was an expert in dealing with high power bombs.

Junaid, who was brought to Delhi yesterday, has been remanded in judicial custody till 13th of this month. The other arrested could be brought to Delhi for further investigation, Mr V N Singh said.

The ISI agent, Mohammad Junaid, who was arrested in Hyderabad on 1 July 1998 by Delhi Police, at a Press conference in the Capital, on Friday evening. - The Statesman.

Coimbatore-like strike plan in Hyderabad foiled

Key ISI agent arrested

Staff Reporter

New Delhi

Blasts foiled

RDX, VHF sets seized from ISI agents

By Our Staff Reporter

Blasts averted, say Delhi police

By Our Staff Reporter

25
Modules 4 and 5

3 July, 1998 to 10 July, 1998

From 3 July, 1998 onwards, the interrogation continued with sustained and methodical cross-examination. Upon confronting the suspect with the telephone diary that he attempted to dispose of during his arrest, further important facts and clues regarding other modules based in different states were revealed. He provided support to these modules during his stay in Hyderabad, arranging for their temporary accommodation, logistics and money until they could find permanent hideouts in other states. This was carried out while they were actively searching for such hideouts. Additionally, he supplied them with firearms, ammunition, explosives and the components necessary for bomb construction, all originating from Pakistan and sent by Azam Cheema.

Module 4 (Dehradun): Arrest of Junaid's Associate, Resolution of Train Blast in Military Compartment and Recovery of RDX

Following Junaid's earlier disclosures, a team was dispatched to Dehradun to locate Mohammad Hassan. On 8 July, 1998, Mohammad Hassan's house in the village of Bhuddi, Dehradun, was raided, based on Junaid's information. An investigation at Mohammad Hassan's residence revealed that his parents had provided false information, claiming their son had gone to Saudi Arabia. However, a credible source indicated that Hassan was present an hour before the raid, thinking a sudden raid would be more successful upon his return. The police party, appearing to believe the false information, left the premises. A secret source was deployed to trace Hassan's movements.

In the meantime, Junaid guided the police team to a bridge on the Assan river near the village of Borowala, where he had buried the remaining RDX and detonators after the train blast. Based on this information, Mohammad Saleem Junaid led the recovery of one kilogram of RDX and 30 live detonators from the Assan river bridge village in Barowala.

On 10 July, 1998, after receiving information from a secret source that Mohammad Hassan was spotted in Doiwala, Dehradun, a police party promptly headed to Doiwala. With the assistance of the station officer of police station, Doiwala, Dehradun, they successfully apprehended Mohammad Hassan from a railway crossing in Teliwara.

Module 5 (Malerkotla, Punjab)

It may be recalled that the intercept of Azam Cheema's Pakistani number had been going on for more than two months. The various conversations intercepted revealed that Mehmood, another Pakistani terrorist sent by LeT, had arrived in India in early 1998 and was staying there in Malerkotla, Punjab. Azam Cheema had sent money to him and instructed him to conduct a survey in Punjab, provide a list of potential targets and places to establish suitable hideouts and Fax the same to Azam Cheema. Mehmood wanted to establish himself in Malerkotla, Punjab; therefore, he was requesting for more money from Azam Cheema through *hawala*. A conversation between Mehmood, Azam Cheema, Abdullah Faruq and Ahmed Hussain, a Bangladeshi guide who used to facilitate the terrorists in crossing the Indo-Pak border and also smuggle explosives, arms and ammunition from Rajasthan to India, revealed that in the coming four to five days Ahmed Hussain would be coming to India with a consignment of explosives for Mehmood. Mehmood also requested Ahmed Hussain to bring a lady's watch and some clothes for Halima, the sister of Noman with whom he had developed intimacy. During the conversation, the names of one Ismail and one Walid also emerged.

Mehmood used to communicate with Azam Cheema and Zaki-ur-Rehman through the Malerkotla STD booths.

The intercepted calls were, as under:

Call 1: Mehmood to Azam Cheema

Mehmood: "*Salaam walekum*!" (Peace be upon you.)

Azam Cheema: "*Walekum salaam! Kaun bol raha hai*?" (And upon you be peace. Who is speaking?)

Mehmood: "*Main Mehmood! Nanaji bol rahe hain*?" (It's Mehmood! Is this (Nanaji?)

Azam Cheema: "*Han. Kaise ho? Paise mil gaye the*?" (Yes, how are you? Did you receive the money?)

Mehmood: "*Han mil gaye the, Nanaji*." (Yes, Cheema Sahib, I received that.)

Azam Cheema: "*Achcha ek kam karna aapke ilake mein jo bhi aisi jagah ho jahan ham apna karobar badha sakte hain, uski ek list bhej dena*." (Alright, do one thing. Send me a list of the places in your area where we can expand our business.)

Mehmood: "*Nanaji, aapko to pata hi hai likhane ke bare mein*." (Nanaji you know about my writing skill.)

Azam Cheema: *Achcha, aisa karna aapka koi sathi vahan per ho usse likhva kar bhej dena*." (Alright, ask one of your associates to write it and send it to me.)

Mehmood: "*Theek hai, Nanaji. Achcha vah aapko saman ke bare mein kaha tha, uska kya hua*?" (Okay, Nanaji. By the way, what about the supplies he was talking about?)

Azam Cheema: "*Inshallah, vah bhi jald se jald pahunch jaega. Aur Halima biwi ka kya hal hai? Shaadi hui ki nahin hui*?" (God willing, it will also reach soon. And how is Halima, your girlfriend? Has she agreed to the marriage?)

Mehmood: *Uske Baba aur Ammi to taiyar hain lekin vah abhi nahin man rahi.*" (Her parents are ready, but she is not agreeing yet.)

Azam Cheema: *Inshallah, man jayegi, fikar na karo.*" (Inshallah, she will agree. Don't worry.)

Mehmood: "*Achcha nanaji, main kal sham ko phone karunga. Ahmed Hussain ko bulakar rakhna.*" (Okay, Nanaji, I'll call Ahmed Hussain tomorrow evening. Make him available.)

Azam Cheema: "*Theek hai. Allah Hafiz. Duvaon mein yaad rakhna.*" (Alright, *Allah Hafiz.* Remember me in your prayers.)

Call 2: Mehmood to Ahmed Hussain

Ahmed Hussain: "*Salaam walekum.*" (Peace be upon you)

Mehmood: "*Walekum salaam! Kaun bol rahe hain*?" (And upon you be peace. Who is speaking?)

Ahmed Hussain: "*Main Ahmed Husain.*" (It's Ahmed Husain)

Mehmood: "*Arey tune achcha badnaam kiya mujhe.*" (Hey, you've tarnished my reputation!)

In fact Ahmed Hussain had spread the news about the relationship between Halima and Mehmood.

Ahmed Hussain: "*Mai ne kuchh nahin kiya; Cheema Sahib ne bataya sabko.*" (I haven't done anything; Cheema Sahib told everyone.)

Mehmood: "*Achcha chalo, tum kab tak aaoge*?" (Okay, when will you be coming?)

Ahmed Hussain: "*Main ek hafte mein aa raha hun; 5 tarikh tak pahunch jaoonga.*" (I'll be coming in a week; by 5th of May, I should reach.)

Mehmood: "*Achcha, aisa karna ki ek lady's watch lekar aana.*" (Alright, make sure to bring a lady's watch as a gift.)

Ahmed Hussain: "*Halima ke liye*?" (For Halima? Ha, ha!)

Mehmood: *Han, han, aur vah jo ladies ke kuchh kapde hote hain vah bhi dekh kar le aana. Uske baba aur ammi ka visa lag gaya hai aur abhi Noman aur Halima biwi yahin hain.*" (Yes, yes and bring some clothes for the ladies as well. Her parents' visas have been approved and currently, only Noman and Halima are here.)

Ahmed Hussain: "*Han vah to tere liye hai na*?" (Yes, she is for you only, isn't it? Ha, ha!)

Mehmood: "*Kya walid se baat ho sakti hai*?" (Can I talk to father?)

Ahmed Hussain: "*Vah to tumhari taraf hi hai India mein, Junaid ki taraf.*" (He is on your side, with Junaid in India.)

Mehmood: "*Achcha lo, Ismail se baat karlo.*" (Phone given to Ismail). (Okay, talk to Ismail.)

Ismail: "*Salaam walekum. Tum kab tak aa rahe ho? Tumhari yaad aati hai*?" (Peace be upon you. When will you be coming? I miss you.)

Ahmed Hussain: "*Aaj 26 tarikh hai. Main 5 tarikh tak pahunch jaunga.*" (Today is the 26. I'll reach by the 5th.)

Ismail: "*Theek hai. Allah Hafiz. Duaon mein yaad rakhna.*" (Alright, *Allah Hafiz*. Remember me in your prayers.)

Further conversations indicated that Ahmed Hussain was sent with explosives and other items but failed to arrive at his intended location, i.e. Malerkotla. However, the chat intercepted between Abdullah Faruq and one other terrorist, namely Raju, who was also based in India, to make enquiries about Ahmed Hussain furthered the idea that two Bengali nationals connected to terrorist outfits had been detained by the Border Security Force with explosives at the Jaisalmer border. In fact, Raju came to know about the detention of two Bengali nationals through a newspaper, shared the details with Abdullah Faruq and suspected that Ahmed Hussain could be one of them. Therefore, Raju requested to give the information to Azam Cheema for quick action. In response to that information, Abullah Faruq shared a message from Azam Cheema to Mehmood to be cautious, implying the need for discretion. As a result, it was easy to assume that Ahmed Hussain was detained on the Rajasthan's border town of Jaisalmer. This fact was already communicated by IB to us. Thus a joint team was already stationed at Malerkotla but whereabouts of Mehmood couldn't be ascertained since he had already left the place after the arrest of Ahmed Hussain.

Conversation intercepted between Raju and Abdullah Faruq:

Faruq: "Salaam walekum." (Peace be upon you.)

Raju, another operative of LeT, earlier based in Mumbai and after committing blasts in Mumbai, had shifted to Jodhpur in Rajasthan. He replied, "*Walekum salaam. Cheema Sahib hain*?" (And upon you be peace. Is Cheema Sahib available?)

A. Faruq: "*Vah to nahin hai.*" (No, he is not.)

Raju: "*Abdulla Faruq? Main Raju.*" (Abdullah Faruq? I am Raju.)

A. Faruq: "*Pahchan gaya.*" (Yes, I recognise you.)

Raju: "*Sorry yaar, uss din main pahchan nahin paya.*" (Sorry, buddy, I didn't recognise you that day.)

A. Faruq: "*Itni narazgi acchi nahin hoti.*" (There's no need to be upset.)

Raju: "*Sorry yaar. Ahmed ka kuchh pata chala.*" (Sorry, buddy. Did you get any information about Ahmed Hussain?)

A. Faruq: "*Uska koi pata nahin.*" (No, there is no information about him.)

Raju: *Achcha maine vah uss din aapko phone kar ke bataya tha na ki yahan per Jaisalmer mein do Bengali pakde gaye hain jo Lashkar ke liye kam karte hain aur border se saman vagaira aur aatankion ko border par karate hain. Lekin paper me koi naam nahin tha aur ab to mujhe date bhi nahin maloom jo mai cutting bhej doon. Aisa to nahin ki wohi log hon? Ahmed ke saath koi aur bhi tha kya?"* (By the way, I informed you that day that two Bengalis were caught here in Jaisalmer who work for the ISI and smuggle goods and terrorists across the border. But there were no names in the paper and now, I don't even know the date to send you the news cutting. Is it possible that they were the same people? Was there anyone else with Ahmed?)

A. Faruq: "*Nahin, akela hi tha.*" (No, he was alone.)

Raju: "*Abdullah! Cheema Sahib ko bolna ki Raju ka phone*

aaya tha. Unko bolna wo kaam jaldi karwadenge; mai bahut pareshan hoon." (Abdullah! Tell Cheema Sahib that Raju called. Ask him to expedite the work; I am very worried.)

A. Faruq: "*Theek hai, main ittila kar dunga.*" (Alright, I will informhim.)

Raju: "*Sorry yaar! Allah Hafiz? Duaon mein yad rakhna.*" (Sorry, buddy! *Allah Hafiz*! Remember me in your prayers.)

Abdullah Faruq: *Salaam walekum*!" (Peace be upon you.)

Mehmood: "*Walekum salaam*! Abdullah Faruq?" (And upon you be peace! Abdullah Faruq?)

A. Faruq: "*Ji, ji.*" (Yes, brother.)

Mehmood: "*Ahmed Hussain ka kuchh pata chala*?" (Did you find out anything about Ahmed Hussain?)

A. Faruq: "*Abhi tak nahin pahuncha vahan*?" (Hasn't he reached there yet?)

Mehmood: "*Nahin, abhi tak to nahin pahuncha.*" (No, he hasn't reached yet.)

A. Faruq: "*Achcha, theek hai. Suno, Cheema Sahib kah rahe the aap zara etihat rakhna; samajh gaye na*?" (Alright, listen, Cheema Sahib was saying that you should be careful. Understood?)

Mehmood: "*Theek hai! Nanaji ko bata dena ki Halima ke baba aur Ammi vahan pahunch gaye hain aur Halima ke visa ke bare mein bhi koshish karna. Vah yahan roti rahti hai.*" (Okay! Tell Cheema Sahib that Halima's parents have reached there (Pakistan) and try to arrange for Halima's visa. She keeps on crying.)

A. Faruq: *Theek hai, Mehmood Bhai, main bol dunga.*" (Okay, Mehmood Bhai, I will inform him.)

Mehmood: *Achcha, Allah Hafiz. Duaon mein yad rakhna.*" (Alright, *Allah Hafiz*. Remember me in your prayers.)

Mehmood's Arrest

On 6 July, 1998, in the evening, Inspector Anil Kumar informed me about a call intercepted at VSNL. Mehmood placed the call to Azam Cheema in Pakistan from Saharanpur.

Intercept revealed that Mehmood and Ahmed Hussain were planning to meet in Subhash Park, Jama Masjid, the following afternoon. This represented a very significant turn of events because Mehmood was untraceable since Ahmed Hussain was arrested at Jaisalmer. However, this intercept really confused us because as per the information received from IB, Ahmed Hussain had been arrested at Jaisalmer the previous month. In order to confirm whether IB was conducting some covert operation through Ahmed Hussain, I contacted them. But their reply was in the negative. Presuming that he might be a different fellow bearing an identical name, we planned out everything in minute detail to apprehend those scumbags.

After receiving the call, a source from Malerkotla was also brought to Delhi, to identify Mehmood. Around 11:30 in the morning, I provided the team with an in-depth briefing. They were given orders to take up positions at the location where the meeting was supposed to take place. The staff deployed at VSNL was also instructed to stay vigilant. After that, the team proceeded to Subhash Park, Jama Masjid. On reaching the spot, they took up strategic positions; later, I also joined them. Meanwhile, one young man came to Subhash Park in the afternoon and sat down on a bench. About 40 minutes later, a short-statured youngster arrived at the scene and met Ahmed Hussain (name revealed after arrest). After obtaining confirmation from the source that he was, in fact, Mehmood, the police squad, upon receiving the signal, moved quickly and detained both of them; discovering RDX and detonators in their possession.

Mehmood, aged about 20 years, disclosed that he was born in Idgah, Cox Bazar (Chattogram), Bangladesh. His mother was Burmese and his father was a Pakistani. They shifted to Pakistan in 1980-1981 and settled permanently at Karachi. The religious leader's speeches on *jihad* during the time when he used to offer namaz at the mosque, deeply touched him. He contacted the local LeT office and completed Daur-e-Aam's 21-day training. His father was against his participating in the *jihad* and had warned him repeatedly, but he ignored him. Later on, he went to Muzaffarabad for three months of specialised training (Daur-e-Khas). After training as per the directions of Azam Cheema, Mehmood crossed into India through the Rajasthan border along with one guide, Ahmed Hussain (detained at Jaisalmer). But they were apprehended by the BSF personnel when they entered India. They pretended to be Bangladeshis; therefore, the BSF deported them to Bangladesh by train. He remained behind in Bangladesh with Ahmed Hussain at his relative's place. After some time, Mehmood crossed the India-Bangladesh border through Chandpur along with Ahmed Hussain and his family members, before reaching Saharanpur. Thereafter, Mehmood and Ahmed Hussain reached Malerkotla where they stayed with Noman, r/o Katika Mohalla, a contact of Ahmed Hussain. Meanwhile, Mehmood visited Delhi to collect money from Abdullah through *hawala*, which was sent by Azam Cheema from Pakistan. The subject developed intimacy with Halima, sister of Noman, and gave her Rs. 34,000. The subject had acquired this money to start some business and develop a cover.

After staying for a week, Ahmed Hussain left for Pakistan alone, leaving behind Mehmood in Malerkotla, Punjab. Subsequently, Mehmood made frequent telephonic contacts with Azam Cheema to obtain sufficient arms, ammunition and explosive material to cause bomb blasts at pre-determined targets in Ludhiana, Amritsar, Patiala, Ambala and Chandigarh. Azam Cheema sent Ahmed Hussain back to India with a consignment of explosives meant to be delivered to Mehmood. But he was arrested at the Jaisalmer border by the BSF.

In fact, Ahmed Hussain, resident of Dinajpur, West Bengal (this man shared an identical name with the Ahmed Hussain, who was arrested in Jaisalmer, Rajasthan), also used to facilitate the terrorists to cross the border from the Ganganagar side and carry explosives from Pakistan into India. In Delhi, Ahmed Hussain was awaiting the arrival of two boys, Akram and Farooq, who were wanted in the Mumbai bomb blast cases in February 1998. They were to be taken to Pakistan to be trained. Meanwhile, Azam Cheema directed Mehmood and Ahmed Hussain to meet and discuss further plans. Therefore, on the day they met at Subhash Park, Jama Masjid, Delhi, both of them were arrested.

□

26
Module 6—Abu Saeed

10 July, 1998

Junaid, who was in police custody at the time, was being questioned in connection with his relationship with Abu Saeed. Valid information was uncovered through Junaid's interrogation as he stated that Abu Saeed had crossed the border into India in April 1997. Abu Saeed called up Zaki-ur-Rehman when he was unable to find a secure place to stay. Zaki-ur-Rehman advised Abu Saeed to travel to Hyderabad and provided him with Junaid's mobile number, which was 09849xxxx04. Abu Saeed then called Junaid, his fellow trainee.

In May 1997, Abu Saeed visited Junaid in Hyderabad. After spending the first 15 days at Azizaya Lodge, Junaid arranged for him to move to an Ahle Hadis Madarsa. Eventually, he found accommodation at Abdul Rauf's farmhouse. Abu Saeed began his screen printing training at a screen printing factory, located within Char Minar. Through Junaid, he also met Ismail of Tolly Chowki in Hyderabad. Abu Saeed suggested to Junaid that they could transport explosives, arms and ammunition through Bhuj, Gujarat, as Abu Saeed was familiar with the smuggling routes across the Indo-Pak border in Bhuj, Gujarat. They then submitted a list to Cheema in Pakistan by Fax at the phone No. 0092621xxxx69, requesting supplies of four TT pistols (Tula Tokarev, a Russian Pistol), 60 detonators, two rolls of wire, a timer and a 10/12 PTD (Programmable Time

Delay) switch, with the request that Cheema should provide these supplies by July 10.

Azam Cheema informed Junaid that Yunus, the guide, would deliver the items to one Abdul Wahid later that evening. To reach Ahmedabad, both Saeed and Junaid travelled by rail and then proceeded to Bhuj, where they stayed in the Ahle Hadis Masjid, adjacent to the railway station, with Kari Ahmed as its Imam. When Junaid learned that the consignment would arrive late, he decided to go to Hyderabad instead of waiting and left Abu Saeed behind.

After two days, Abdul Wahid informed Abu Saeed that the shipment would arrive at his place in the evening. Two Pakistanis, Abu Darda and Yasir, along with Abdul Wahid, brought a briefcase containing black RDX, four pistols, a switch and a time device. They buried the package near two electric poles to conceal the location. Abu Saeed and Abu Darda then travelled to Hyderabad. Abu Darda informed Saeed that he needed to stay with Raju in Mumbai, as per Azam Cheema's instructions. After a few days, Raju arrived in Hyderabad and took Abu Darda to Mumbai. In January 1998, Abu Saeed was directed by the higher cadre of LeT to leave Hyderabad to establish the LeT base in western UP.

During the operation in Punjab and Hyderabad, we intercepted calls at the VSNL. Abu Saeed contacted Azam Cheema, Zaki-ur-Rehman and other LeT cadres in Pakistan via STD booths in Aligarh. It was revealed that Azam Cheema instructed Abu Saeed to determine suitable cities or places for hiding and thereby inform him through Fax. Abu Saeed was also pressuring Cheema to send explosives and other contraband at the earliest. Azam Cheem asked Abu Saeed from where he could easily pick the consignment of explosives. Saeed replied that he did not have any vehicle to receive the consignment from any other place but Abu Saeed insisted on sending the same to his place only. Abu Saeed transmitted the list through the Fax. Conversation further revealed that two other Pakistani terrorists named Faisal and Shoaib were also associated with Abu Saeed and were residing at a different place as per his knowledge.

The following reproduced intercepts are pertinent: Cheema: "*Salaam walekum.*" (Peace be upon you.)

Saeed: "*Walekum salaam.*" (And upon you be peace.)

Cheema: "*Achcha, aapko maloom ho gaya hoga ki Fax lag gaya hai yahan. To aap aisa karen jo maine aapko jagah batai thi, ilaqa bataya tha! Samajh gaye na! Aap vahan per jakar ek list banakar bhej dena jahan per ham apna karobar kar sakte hain! Aap samajh rahe honge na main kya kahna chah raha hun.*" (Alright, you must be aware that the Fax has been installed here (Pakistan's LeT office). So, what you need to do is to go to the places I had mentioned! Understand? Go there, make a list and send it to me, indicating where we can establish our business (hideout)! You understand what I'm saying? Right?)

Saeed: "*Han, han, main samajh gaya.*" (Yes, yes, I understand.)

Cheema: "*Aap dekhen koi aisi jagah ham apna karobar aaram se kar sake. Yeh list banakar mujhe jald bhijwana.*" (You see, find a place where we can easily conduct our business. Chalk out a list and send it to me soon.)

Saeed: "*Salaam walekum.*" (Peace be upon you.)

Unknown person: "*Walekum salaam! Kaun*?" (And upon you be peace. Who is this?)

Saeed: "*Main Saeed, India se. Aap kaun*?" (I am Saeed from India. Who are you?)

Hammad: "Hammad." (I am Hammad.)

Saeed: "*Cheema Sahib hain*?" (Is Cheema Sahib available?)

Hammad: "*Nahin vah to nahin hain.*" (No, he is not.)

Saeed: "*Achcha, main Fax kar raha hun aur Cheema Sahib ko bol dena ki yah saman ek mahine ke andar bhijwayen. Aap Fax* on *karen.*" (Okay, I am Faxing now and tell Cheema Sahib that this shipment needs to be sent within a month. Please turn on the Fax.)

Hammad confirmed that the FAX had been received. This

Fax was related to the consignment of explosives, arms and ammunition.

A. Faruq: *Salaam walekum.*" (Peace be upon you.)

Saeed: "*Walekum! Cheema Sahib hain? Saeed bol raha hun, India se.*" (And upon you be peace. This is Saeed speaking from India.)

A. Faruq: *Han hai! Cheema Sahib! Saeed!*" (Yes, Cheema Sahib is here! Saeed!)

Cheema: *Salaam walekum.*" (Peace be upon you.)

Saeed: *Walekum salaam, Cheema Sahib. Vah hamare dusre saman ka kya hua*?" (And upon you be peace, Cheema Sahib. What happened to our other shipment?)

Cheema: "*Usmein abhi time lag jaega; kareeb 20/25 din.*" (It will take some time; around 20-25 days.)

Saeed: "*Achcha theek hai. Zarur bhejvana. Aisa hai na ek hi chakkar lage to theek hai.*" (Okay, send it, without fail. It would be better if we could collect in one go.)

Cheema: "*Theek hai, theek hai! Achcha, ye batao ki saman kahan se le sakte ho? Idhar ki udhar se utha sakte ho?"* (Alright, alright! Tell me, from where can you collect the consignment? Can you pick that up from nearby or from elsewhere?)

Saeed: "*Yahin se hamare pass se hi. Hamare pass gadi wagairah ka intzam nahi hai.*" (Yes, we don't have arrangements for vehicles. Send it to my place.)

Cheema: "*Theek hai. Mai fir aapko batata hoon.*" (Alright, I'll guide you on this.)

Saeed: "*Shoaib Bhai, aaj aap se baat karenge.*" (Shoaib Bhai will talk to you today.)

Cheema: "*Dono karenge*?" (Both will talk?)

Saeed: *Nahi. Faisal abhi doosri jagah hai.*" (No, Faisal is at another place.)

Cheema: "*Theek hai, main ek baje tak yahi par hoon. Us se pehle pehle baat karlen.*" (Okay, I'll be here until one. Talk to me before that.)

Saeed: *Theek hai. Allah Hafiz.*" (Okay. *Allah Hafiz.*)

After the second round of interrogation, I was left with

some doubts and uncertainty in my mind about whether or not Junaid and Saeed had communicated with each other since January 1998 or not, when Saeed left Hyderabad. This confusion and uncertainty stemmed from the fact that I was unsure whether or not Saeed had revisited Hyderabad and contacted Junaid during that period, as per the communication overheard between Azam Cheema and Junaid in which Saeed informed Cheema that he had spoken to Junaid regarding the address in Delhi to collect some items. Junaid, however, suggested that Saeed should speak directly to Cheema and mentioned that if Cheema approved, he would provide the address. Cheema agreed to talk to Junaid and handle the matter.

Saeed then requested Cheema to share some addresses in Delhi from where he could collect the items. Cheema mentioned that he currently did not have Junaid's number but would provide it to him later.

The call intercepted was as under:

Call 1

Cheema: "*Salaam walekum.*" (Peace be upon you.)

Saeed: "*Walekum salaam*! *Cheema Sahib, meri Junaid se baat hui thi. Uss se maine Delhi ke Address per mange thay saman lene ke liye. Lekin usne aap se baat karne ke liye kaha. Bola agar wo bolenge to de doonga.*" (And upon you be peace! I spoke to Junaid. I asked him for the addresses in Delhi to pick up the goods. But he said to talk to you. He mentioned that if you agreed, he would provide the address.)

Cheema: "*Theek hai, main karta hun. Abhi mere pass se uska number idhar-udhar ho gaya hai. Main baad mein aapko batata hun.*" (Okay, I will do it. Right now, his number is not available with me. I'll let you know later.)

Saeed: "*Chalo theek hai. Allah Hafiz.*" (Okay, that's fine. *Allah Hafiz.*)

Before confronting Junaid with the above intercepted call, I preferred to carry out another round of interrogation of Junaid.

Ravi: "Do you still talk to your Abu Saeed?"

Junaid: "He went to Hyderabad in January 1998 and about two months ago, I got a call from Abu Saeed on my mobile. He was asking for the address of a *hawala* dealer in Delhi and I told him to talk to Azam Cheema. If Cheema agrees, I'll give him the address. After that, I didn't receive any call from him."

Junaid's statement corroborated the intercepts of the above-mentioned call. Nevertheless, I was interested in learning more about him to glean any information, some of which may not have been relevant to Junaid but may be important to us as we continued our investigation. When Junaid provided a crucial piece of information concerning Abu Saeed, my suspicions got justified.

Ravi to Junaid: "But I can't believe that you don't know anything about Saeed. The way you were talking to Azam Cheema suggests that you're involved in handling the organisation's activities in India."

Rajendra Bhatia: "Hey, no need to act too smart! People here talk like big parrots, but we haven't been harsh with you yet. Don't force us to be."

Junaid: "No, sir, I'm not hiding anything from you. Honestly, I don't know the exact location, but I heard that Abu Saeed was talking about working with pottery dealer somewhere around Aligarh. I don't know where he is now."

Ravi: "Okay, fine. Besides, provide Inspector Sahib with complete details of the phone numbers written in your diary. If anything important comes to your mind, I'll talk to you again tomorrow."

Follow-up on Leads Emerged during Interrogation of Junaid

While Karnal Singh was on his way to my workplace, I requested Inspector Sanjay Singh to take him into custody and place him in solitary confinement. After some time, Karnal Singh arrived and I saluted him, recognising my greeting, "*Jai Hind*, Ravi. Did he provide any fresh information in his talk?"

Ravi: "Not specific, but we can continue investigating those clues. According to Junaid, Abu Saeed had contacted him on his cell phone from an STD booth in Uttar Pradesh, about two months ago. So, we need to investigate his mobile number to find out Saeed's contacts. Additionally, we had sent a request to obtain STD booth records in Aligarh, from where Abu Saeed previously contacted Azam Cheema."

Karnal: "Have you received the information regarding STD booths?"

Ravi: "Permit me to verify with Sandeep, please. Could you please come?"

Sandeep entered the room. Sandeep: "*Jai Hind*, sir."

Karnal: "*Jai Hind*, Sandeep! Have you received the call records of all the STD booths in Aligarh?"

Sandeep: "Yes, sir, we have received everything that was sent to us until the 15th of June. I have previously examined the specifics but nothing of significance has emerged from my findings."

Karnal: "Analyse the mobile details of Junaid. Find out if any common number for Aligarh or nearby exists in STD records and mobile records."

Sandeep: "Sir, during the time when Ravi sir was in Hyderabad, I had already completed this exercise. Results are nil, sir. On the other hand, the records of booths from Aligarh upto June 30 would be delivered to us within three to four days. Let us keep our fingers crossed that we will receive something."

Ravi: "*Aameen*. ...Oh, I'm sorry, sir, I just realised that I forgot to inform you of one more significant piece of information."

Karnal: "What is that all about?"

Ravi: "Sir, I will be dispatching a group to Khurja to gather more information about the pottery industry there. In fact, Junaid disclosed to us that Abu Saeed was attempting to acquire ownership of a pottery plant located in the state of Uttar Pradesh. The fact that Abu Saeed is making calls from Aligarh leads us to believe that Abu Saeed lives in or around Aligarh, in some small town or village. To the best of my knowledge, the centre of the pottery industry is located in Khurja."

Karnal: "You have a good point. Because I went to that place quite a few times, I am aware of this fact."

Ravi: "I am aware of that. As per the intercepted conversation, Abu Saeed had received Rs. 1,50,000/- from Azam Cheema so that he could buy a factory. Please listen to that interception."

Call 1

A. Faruq: "*Salaam walekum.*" (Peace be upon you.)

Saeed: "*Walekum salaam. Cheema Sahib hain*?" (And upon you be peace. Is Cheema Sahib there?)

A. Faruq: "*Haan hai, baat karo.*" (Yes, he's here, talk to him.)

Saeed: "*Achcha Cheema Sahib, humne jo 150 (Rs. 1,50,000) wali baat kari thi, wo karkhana hum le rahe hain. Uska bayana humne de diya hai, to jald se jald paise bhejwane ki koshish karen.*" (Alright, Cheema Sahib, regarding the discussion we had about the 150 (Rs. 1,50,000), we are acquiring the factory and we have provided the details. So, please try to send the money as soon as possible.)

Cheema: "*Theek hai, main karvata hun jald se jald.*" (Alright, I will arrange for it as soon as possible)

Saeed: "*Aur baki samaan bhi bhejwaye. Allah Hafiz.*" (And send the remaining goods as well. *Allah Hafiz.*)

A. Faruq: "*Salaam walekum.*" (Peace be upon you.)

Saeed: "*Walekum salaam! Cheema Sahib hai? Main Saeed, India se.*" (And upon you be peace. Is Cheema Sahib there? I am Saeed from India.)

A. Faruq: "*Vah to nahin hain.*" (No, he's not here.)

Saeed: "*Zaki Sahib hain*?" (Is Zaki Sahib there?)

A. Faruq: *Nahin, vah bhi nahin hain. Cheema Sahib aur Zaki Sahib, donon kal Muridke meeting mein jaenge, vahan unse baat kar lena.*" (No, Zaki Sahib is also not here. Both Cheema Sahib and Zaki Sahib will go to the Muridke meeting tomorrow; you can talk to them there.)

Saeed: "*Achcha, aisa hai, agar Cheema Sahib aayen to unko bol dena ki humne unko khali karne ke liye bol diya hai, to jald se jald paise bhijwayen.*" (Alright, if Cheema Sahib comes, tell him that we have asked the factory owner to give possession, so please send the money as soon as possible.)

A. Faruq: *Han, han, theek hai. Cheema Sahib keh rahe thay ki paise 7-8 din mein bhijwa denge.*" (Yes, yes, alright. Cheema Sahib was saying that he will send the money in seven to eight days.)

Saeed: *Chalo, theek hai. Allah Hafiz.*" (Okay, that's fine. *Allah Hafiz.*)

Call 2

Cheema: *Salaam walekum.*" (Peace be upon you.)

Saeed: *Walekum salaam.*" (And upon you be peace.)

Cheema: "*Kaise ho Saeed Bhai? Paise mil gaye? Maine parson bhijwa diye hain, aap vasool kar lein.*" (How are you, Saeed Bhai? The money has been sent; I dispatched it day before yesterday; you can collect it.)

Saeed: "*Theek hai, kal vasool kar lunga. Allah Hafiz.*" (Alright, I wlll collect it tomorrow. *Allah Hafiz.*)

Ravi continued: "More than that, Abu Saeed once gave Abdullah Faruq a five-digit number, 41890; that probably belongs to a suburban town near Aligarh because in Aligarh only six-digit phone numbers exist. But when the telephone attendant in Pakistan tried to get the city code, Abu Saeed avoided that by saying that Azam Cheema was aware of the code. The conversation suggests that the number is at least his PP number for a suburban area."

Karnal: "Do you have that intercept? I also want to hear that."

Ravi: "Sure, sir. I just listened to that conversation two or three times when Junaid disclosed about the pottery factory. It is readily available."

He played the tape and the conversation started:

A. Faruq: "*Salaam walekum.*" (Peace be upon you.)

Saeed: "*Walekum salaam, Cheema Sahib hain? Main Saeed*

bol raha hun India se." (And upon you be peace. Is Cheema Sahib there? This is Saeed calling from India.)

A. Faruq: "*Pehchaan liya! Vah to nahin hai.*" (I recognised! He's not here.)

Saeed: "*Achcha, aap ek number note karen, 41890. Cheema Sahib ko bolna, vah iss number per phone karenge.*" (Alright, please note down a number, 41890. Tell Cheema Sahib to call on this number.)

A. Faruq: "*Code kya hai, 0571?*" (What's the area code, 0571?)

Saeed: "*Nahi, vah sab unko maloom hai. Unko bolna ki is phone per message kar denge, ki Saeed ko bolo ki vah Cheema Sahib se baat kar le. Theek hai? Yad karke bolna.*" (No, they know about it. Tell them to send a message for Saeed on this phone, asking him to talk to Cheema Sahib. Okay? Remember and convey this.)

A. Faruq: "*Theek hai, bol dunga.*" (Alright, I will tell them.)

Saeed: *Achcha, Allah Hafiz.*" (Okay, *Allah Hafiz.*)

Karnal: "Yes, this is important. Let us probe it further."

Ravi: "I have already briefed my team to make sure the number is set up in Khurja. If what we suspect is true, then the scope of our study would be significantly reduced."

Karnal: "If that's the case, we can focus on that telephone number while also learning about the most recent sale/ purchase or of a factory that's been opened. Good job, Ravi."

12 July, 1998

Karnal Singh and I were seated at ISC, Chanakyapuri, talking about further measures that could be implemented. The severity of the situation was reflected in the fact that the table was covered with scattered maps, files, call information for international and domestic numbers and the transcripts of interrogations of all terrorists who had been detained throughout the operation.

Ravi: "Sir, even though we have come a long way in the past 10 months, we cannot afford to let our guard down at this point in time."

Karnal: "Agreed. In our approach, we need to maintain

vigilance and be as comprehensive as possible. Can you provide me with a high-level summary of the information we have gathered so far about the other terrorists?"

Ravi: "Sir, based on the interrogation of terrorists who have been captured, intercepted communications and the reports of informants, we estimate there are four likely places of operation for these remaining three modules – Abu Saeed in Aligarh and Khurja (Uttar Pradesh), Aamir's in Burhanpur, West Bengal. Raju@ Abu Umes in Jodhpur, Rajasthan and Mumbai, Maharashtra. We have reason to think that these modules have retreated underground as a result of the recent arrests."

Karnal: "That is a large region that needs to be covered, but we can make it more manageable by giving higher priority to locations with the potential for the greatest impact."

Ravi: "Absolutely, sir. Regarding West Bengal, Mumbai, Maharashtra and Rajasthan, the information that we have is extremely premature. But there is a good possibility that we will be able to track down the module's current location in Khurja and Aligarh, Uttar Pradesh, where I have already sent a team last week, after discussing the specifics with you. We need to focus our efforts in Khurja and Aligarh and ask the Intelligence Bureau to develop more information and take appropriate action in the other states. They have already questioned all the people who were arrested and we have already given them the information that we have with us at this time."

Karnal: "Excellent point. Collaboration is essential in this regard. We need to establish that combining our resources and sharing the information we have will increase our chances of being successful."

Ravi: "Sir! We have begun conducting covert operations in the area of Khurja and we are concentrating on collecting human intelligence."

With a solid plan in place, Karnal Singh left ISC. We were ready to execute the strategy and bring the remaining underground terrorist modules to justice. The road ahead was treacherous, but our resolve was unwavering.

RDX, TNT seized

Five ultras nabbed

GTB staff on hunger-strike

मुम्बई में विस्फोट करने वाला उग्रवादी दिल्ली में पकड़ा

Breakthrough in 6 more Delhi blasts

3 Pakistanis among five held

•Always first with the news

DELHI MID DAY

Plot to strike at army targets in Delhi Cantonment

Burmese in five ISI agents held with RDX

दैनिक जागरण

नई दिल्ली, शनिवार 1 अगस्त 1998

दिल्ली में सैन्य ठिकानों को बम से उड़ाने की साजिश

27
Hideout of Abu Saeed Traced

Hideout of Abu Saeed in Khurja; 13 July, 1998 to Last Week of July 1998

The following morning, Subhash Tandon and I posed as prospective customers for wholesale ceramics as we made our way to Khurja. In order to gather intelligence and secure confidential sources covertly in Khurja, I sent Harbir Singh and Dabas to investigate and uncover the fact that the telephone Abu Saeed had provided to Azam Cheema for communication had been installed in Khurja.

Dabas informed me that a person named Sadiq, residing in Khurja, had recently purchased a factory called Paras Pottery from B.K. Lal, advocate, around four months ago. There were rumours that Sadiq's cousin, a recent resident of Khurja from Hyderabad, had purchased this pottery factory. The ongoing inquiry was validated by the gathered data. Despite this, I decided to speak with B.K. Lal to obtain additional details. Together with Subhash Tandon, I preferred to meet him. We were open and honest, providing a comprehensive account of the reason for our visit. When they learned the specifics, they hesitated to reveal the information. However, after reassurance on their safety, they agreed to sell their pottery factory to Sadiq's cousin for Rs. 150,000/- around four months prior, through Sadiq. They showed the duplicate copies of the signed documents. Mr. Lal believed that Sadiq's cousin had arrived in Khurja either in December 1997 or January 1998.

After gaining Mr. Lal's trust, I instructed him not to divulge any information about the investigation to anyone, even his well-wishers. Following his guarantee, we chose to leave the town while Harbir and Dabas remained in Khurja to gather more information concerning Sadiq and his cousin, who happened to be none other than Abu Saeed.

The next day, Inspector Subhash Tandon, supervising the operations in Khurja, informed me that secret sources from Khurja had disclosed that one brother of Sadiq resided in Bhawalpur, Pakistan. Sadiq had visited Pakistan two or three times to meet his brother. This information was crucial as Azam Cheema also had an office in Bhawalpur. The inspector further informed that the two boys (Pakistani) living with Abu Saeed in the pottery factory had gone to Kolkata the previous month, and Abu Saeed was not seen in Khurja for 10 to 12 days. This fact was corroborated through an intercepted call.

Saeed: "*Salaam Walekum.*" (Peace be upon you.)

A. Faruq: "*Walekum salaam" Abdullah bol raha hun.*" (And upon you be peace. This is Abdullah speaking.)

Saeed: "*Pehchan gaya. Achcha vah saman ka kya hua*?" (I recognised you. Alright, what happened to the consignment?)

A. Faruq: "*Vah to bhijwa diya, 4/5 din ho gaye.*" (It has been sent, about four to five days ago.)

Saeed: "*Kaun aa raha hai*?" (Who is coming?)

A. Faruq: "*Vahi hai, Ahmed. Achcha, vah Cheema Sahib se baat hui thi, vah keh rahe the ki unko wapas hi bulwa len.*" (It's Ahmed. Alright, I spoke to Cheema Sahib and he wanted to call them (Shoaib and Imran) back to Pakistan.)

Saeed: "*Han, aap dekho na, yahan yeh itna bada shahar hai lekin vah kapde kharidne rajdhani mein gaya, rukta hi nahin hai. Kahin na kahin nuksan karva dega, to unko (Shoaib and Imran) bulana hi theek hai. Unka kuchh jaldi se jald karo.*" (Yes, you see, this city is so big, but he goes to buy clothes in the capital. He does not restrain himself and roams here and there. He might cause some loss somewhere to the outfit, so calling them back is the right thing to do. Do it as soon as possible for them.)

A. Faruq: "*Theek hai. Allah Hafiz.*" (Alright. *Allah Hafiz.*)

The below-mentioned call was intercepted after Junaid was arrested and Shoaib and Imran were en route to Pakistan via Bangladesh. Saeed inquired if there had been any communication with Imran. Abdullah Faruq informed him that there hadn't been any communication yet. Saeed instructed Abdullah Faruq to maintain contact with Imran once he called from Bangladesh. Saeed also informed Abdullah Faruq that he had informed Cheema Sahib about his intention to visit Pak for a few days and suggested discussing it further when Cheema Sahib arrived.

A. Faruq: "*Salaam walekum.*" (Peace be upon you.)

Saeed: "*Walekum salaam! Abdullah Bhai, Imran ka koi phone aaya*?" (And upon you be peace! Abdullah Bhai, did you receive any massage or call from Imran?)

A. Faruq: "*Nahin, abhi to koi rafta nahin hua.*" (No, not yet,)

Saeed: "*Vah, aapko BD se phone karenge. Aap unse rafta rakhna. Aur mai ne bhi Cheema Sahib ko kaha tha ki main bhi kuchh din ke liye aana chahta hun.*" (Alright, they will call you from Bangladesh. You keep in touch with them and I also asked Cheema Sahib to permit me to come there (Pakistan) for a few days.)

A. Faruq: "*Theek hai, Cheema Sahib aaye, tab baat kar lena.*" (Alright, when Cheema Sahib arrives, talk to him.)

Saeed: "*Allah Hafiz.*" (*Allah Hafiz.*)

27 July, 1998

I convened a meeting of the officers of ISC to discuss a further action plan because there were neither the suspects in Khurja nor any communication from anywhere. In the light of these facts, I wanted to ensure we had a solid game plan. Additionally, the officers stationed in Khurja were present for the conference.

Ravi: "Tell me more about Sadiq's movements, please."

Subhash: "The only time he had moved was to make some purchases at the market. He has not gone anywhere else."

Ravi: "Hmm, it seems there is nothing we can find out about Abu Saeed."

Harbir: "We don't know anything about him!"

Ravi: "What do you say, Dataramji? Subhash, Bhatia Sahib?"

Bhatia: "Sir, I am confident that they have made their escape from this location after learning that Junaid was in custody."

Dataram: "Sir, the only other option is to take Sadiq in for questioning since it is necessary at this time."

Subhash: "This is also the viewpoint that I hold. The fact that he had gone to see his brother in Bhawalpur, Pakistan, on multiple occasions makes me believe that his interrogation would yield some useful information."

Ravi: "The office of Azam Cheema is also located in the city of Bhawalpur. I have no doubt that he is associated with Azam Cheema in some capacity. Let us go and question him."

Dabas: "*Janab, na naqad, na tera udhar, aur ganda pado khet te bahar.*" (Do the work as soon as possible.)

Ravi: "Okay, let me talk to DCP Sahib. This afternoon, I will get in touch with you."

After that, I went to the office of the DCP, and we had a detailed discussion about the circumstances as well as our choice to interrogate Sadiq. It was clear that he was satisfied. On the other hand, it was decided that Sadiq would be questioned first thing in the morning on 29 July, 1998.

29 July, 1998

After receiving information that Sadiq was at home, a small team raided his residence in the morning. We let Sadiq know that we were from the Department of Taxation and wanted to ask about the purchase of a pottery firm.

Ravi: "Sadiq! We have come to know that you recently bought a factory and used fake documents for it?"

Sadiq: "Yes, sir, my cousin Saeed purchased it but it is wrong to say that we have used fake documents."

Ravi: "Where does your cousin Saeed live? We need to talk to him."

Sadiq: "Sir, he belongs to Hyderabad and has been staying with me for the past six to seven months."

Ravi: "Alright, tell Saeed we need to talk to him."

Sadiq: "Sir, he went to Hyderabad about 20-25 days ago."

Subhash: "When will he be back? Can you give us an address or phone number where we can contact him?"

Sadiq: "Sir, I'll check and let you know. In the meantime, I'll make tea for you."

Harbir: "Yes, yes, go ahead. This is necessary and it would be great if you could manage it."

This act by Harbir was deliberate to convey to suspect Sadiq our casual attitude. Luck always favours those who believe in *karma*. During the investigation, one of our sources communicated with Inspector Subhash Tandon and informed him that he had extremely relevant information regarding the guys who had travelled to Kolkota. He informed Subhash that both guys would be travelling to Delhi from Kolkata on the '*Poorva Express*' the following day, which was July 30. The informant conveyed that they had already boarded the train. Inspector Subhash Tandon immediately provided me with the information. We decided to halt the investigation right away and after taking tea, I instructed Sadiq to bring his cousin brother to the SDM office next week on his arrival, to show Sadiq that it was a casual inquiry.

In fact, it was a tactful retreat from Sadiq's residence, but we were uncertain whether or not he believed our account of events. It was expected that surveillance would continue through covert sources and communication would be intercepted. Since the suspects had already boarded the train, there was less possibility of them contacting anyone in Khurja, particularly Sadiq, while they were travelling because they would not use mobile phones. On the other hand, it was likely that they would get in touch with Sadiq after they deboarded the train in Delhi. Therefore, it was decided to catch them upon arriving at the Delhi railway station. However, identifying the suspects remained the primary challenge; as a result, I requested that Subhash Tandon bring at least one or two individuals who were in a position to recognise the suspects to the railway station.

30 July, 1998

Abu Saeed and Companions Carried RDX; Arrested

The police force split into two sections upon arrival at New Delhi railway station around 7 in the morning. The first section further divided into groups, monitored by Subhash Tandon, Dataram and Rajendra Bhatia; while the second section was placed under the supervision of Inspectors Anil Sharma and Rakesh Dixit, along with others. The '*Purva Express*' was already running behind schedule and falling even further behind.

Around 12:30 in the afternoon, it was reported that the '*Purva Express*' would arrive on platform No. 7. Instantaneously, both police parties assumed predetermined positions at the bridge approaching from platform No. 7. One group positioned on the Paharganj side of the bridge and the other towards Connaught Place. The '*Poorva Express*' arrived at the station around 1 p.m. and the passengers disembarked on platform No. 7 through the connecting bridge.

After 10-15 minutes, the informer with Inspector Subhash Tandon and the party spotted and pointed out three boys – one carried a green attaché case, while the other two held bags. Another individual accompanied them, whom the informer couldn't identify. The police easily overcame all the four individuals. Upon questioning, they initially admitted to using fictitious identities and residing in Khurja.

Inspection of their suitcases led to the recovery of 2 kgs. of RDX, 1 kg. of PETN and other items, including 30 detonators. Finally, their true names were revealed: 1. Abu

Saeed (20) @ Abdul Sattar, resident of Faislabad, Pakistan; 2. Abu Waleed (19) @ Mohd Faizal Hussain @ Imran, resident of Karachi, Pakistan; 3. Abu Shoaib (19) @ Mohd Sanaulla @ Soeb Alam, resident of Muzaffargarh, Pakistan; and 4. Alam (19) @ Imran, resident of Burma but presently staying in Bhawalpur, Pakistan. They were all taken into custody. After their disclosure, Mohammad Sadiq (40), resident of Khurja, who had been harbouring them, was also taken into custody.

During the interrogation of these accused persons, it came to light that Abu Saeed had entered India from the Bhuj sector of Gujarat in April 1997 after completing his training at Daur-e-Aam and Daur-e-Khas in the use of various types of weapons and warfare tactics. Under the direction of Azam Cheema, he came to Hyderabad and stayed with Junaid until February 1998. After receiving instructions from Azam Cheema in December 1997, he met Mohammad Sadiq in Khurja, Uttar Pradesh, to establish their base and engage in subversive activities in Delhi and the surrounding areas. Mohammad Umar, the brother of Mohammad Saddiq, residing in Bhawalpur, Pakistan and a close friend of Azam Cheema, provided financial support to the terrorist organisation. Mohammad Umar also instructed his brother, Mohammad Saddiq, to provide Abu Saeed with cover while he carried out his actions.

Mohammad Sadiq offered Abu Saeed a safe haven in Khurja. After Abu Saeed established himself in Khurja, he called on two other Pak-trained terrorists from LeT, specifically Abu Soeb and Abu Waleed, to assist him. Both had successfully completed their Daur-e-Aaam and Daur-e-Khas courses. In February 1998, Azam Cheema launched both of them from the Rajasthan border with the help of Pakistani Rangers and Bangladeshi guide, Ahmed Hussain.

Abu Saeed successfully obtained a fake birth certificate listing his parentage and Mohammad Sadiq's residence. He intended to apply for an Indian passport, using this record as the foundation for his application. Additionally, he purchased a pottery factory named Paras Industries in Khurja, Uttar Pradesh. Azam Cheema managed the financial arrangements for the purchase through *hawala*, providing Rs. 150,000/-. He planned to carry out an attack in Delhi, specifically in the Cantonment area and on Army vehicles parked in civic places, such as bus terminals and railway stations, to destabilise the crucial infrastructure in and around Delhi.

To facilitate these subversive activities, he contacted Azam Cheema, requesting for 200 kgs. of RDX, or other high explosive material, hand grenades, AK-series rifles, pistols, remote control devices and wireless sets. These items were to be received by Mohammad Saleem Junaid in Hyderabad. Abu Saeed constructed a bunker within his pottery to hide the consignment expected from Azam Cheema, Bhawalpur, Pakistan. However, due to Mohammad Saleem Junaid's detention by the Crime Branch in Delhi, the shipment was not dispatched by Azam Cheema.

Upon learning of Mohammad Saleem Junaid's apprehension, Abu Saeed immediately escaped to Bangladesh and met up with Abu Soeb and Abu Waleed at Abdul Karim Tunda's hideout, where they were waiting for documents, i.e. fake passports, etc., to escape into Pakistan, as ordered by Azam Cheema on Abu Saeed's complaint. Alam, a Burmese national and confidant of Azam Cheema, facilitated the infiltration of LeT terrorists via the Indo-Bangla border and the Indo-Pakistan border. He was also present in Bangladesh at that time. After spending approximately 20 days at Abdul Karim @ Tunda's base in Yatrabari, Dhaka, Bangladesh and being unable to arrange their return to Pakistan, they were instructed to return to India with Alam's assistance before entering Pakistan through the Rajasthan border. However, they were arrested.

□

28

Module 7—Bombay-Jodhpur-Ahmedabad

When it comes to probe into the other two modules, the first one was establishing a base of operations in or near Asansol, West Bengal, and the second one started off from Bombay before moving to Jodhpur, Rajasthan and in the midst of it, their activities started expanding in Ahmedabad, Gujarat. Both these modules were under investigation.

During the second phase of the operation, Junaid and Mohammad Farooq were apprehended, while their interrogation information with respect to movement of Raju (@Usmam @AbuUmes @Hassan @Babloo) and his associates was disclosed.

You might recall that on 23 July, 1998, Mohammad Farooq was taken into police custody based on information from a confidential source while our team was focused on tracking Abu Saeed in UP. Subsequent investigations revealed that Farooq operated a temporary stall on the pavement, selling various items. He frequented Jama Masjid in Santa Cruz for prayers due to its convenient location. Since 1988, he began preaching the Quran at Chaupati near the Laudal building on Tuesdays and Fridays, and with friends on Sunday afternoons at Chaupati.

At the beginning of 1997, he was put in contact with a Pakistani named Raju by a man named Zafar Bhai, who was originally from Santa Cruz (East), Bombay. They were delighted when Raju admitted to them that he was a member of the LeT, which is a Pakistani extremist group. He had previously participated in militant training, also known as Daur-e-Aam and Daur-e-Khas. He made it clear that one of his goals was to visit India and provide support to the local Muslim population. Raju gave Farooq the *taqrir* and then asked him to read some Hadis and *aayat*." He stated that Muslims in India were being harassed and tortured and that the future of Muslims in India was uncertain.

Raju strongly encouraged Farooq to travel to Pakistan in order to receive and acquire militant training to better defend their community and participate in *jihad* against *kafirs*. One night, Raju stayed at Farooq's house, delivering speeches on *jihad*, or *taqrir*, throughout the night. Responding to Raju's request, Farooq arranged for Raju to meet 9-10 close friends of his. Influenced by Raju's impassioned speeches and his emphasis on reading Hadis and *aayats*, they became motivated and prepared to undergo militant training in Pakistan. In June 1997, Raju went to Kutch, Gujarat, with three-fourth of Farooq's acquaintances in order to move to Pakistan with him. However, their journey was thwarted due to regional instability and the designated guide's failure to show up at the meeting point. Consequently, they had to return to Bombay on their own.

In the past, Raju used to make regular trips to Farooq's, Aftab's and Zafar Bhai' homes in order to instruct them on the process of creating explosives out of a variety of chemicals. During this period, a Pakistani-trained terrorist of LeT, by the name of Abu Darda sent by Azam Cheema, joined them and remained with them.

In September 1997, Raju, Abu Darda, Farooq Aftab and their associates devised a scheme to disrupt Mumbai's Ganpati holy procession by distributing packets of poisonous fruit juice. Their intent was to cause significant casualties, sparking widespread community unrest. However, their plan was thwarted by the pouring rain on that day and over the following days, rendering the execution of their plot impossible. Consequently, on the evening of 31 December, 1997, Raju, Farooq, Akram and several associates plotted to poison beer and distribute it to young people in Mumbai. They placed the poisoned beer bottles in a taxi, but unexpectedly, the poison began to react, causing the beer to leak from the bottles. Witnessing this, they were forced to make a rapid retreat, resulting in the failure of their scheme.

In February 1998, Raju orchestrated a plan to explode multiple bombs across Bombay. Assigning Abu Darda to retrieve the RDX/PETN explosives from Junaid, it was Abu Darda who delivered the shipment. Raju, Aftab, Yakub, Akram, Farooq and others planted the bombs at various locations in Mumbai, including Jama Masjid, Crawford Market, railway lines in Kurla and Kandiwali, Golibar, railway station in Kandiwali and Virar, resulting in six separate explosions. Raju and Aftab suffered significant burn injuries from the blasts and received discreet medical assistance in the seclusion of Aftab's house in order to avoid public attention.

In the event of their associates' arrests by Mumbai Police, Raju relocated from India to Pakistan. Subsequently, Farooq and Akram went into hiding, dispersing to various locations on the outskirts of Mumbai and seeking refuge with their families, friends, and well-wishers. They also sought shelter in Ahle Hadis Masjid and *madrasas* to evade detection.

Finally, Akram reached out to Azam Cheema, expressing the desire to travel to Pakistan for training. Azam Cheema directed them to contact Junaid. Upon meeting Junaid, he assured them of being sent to Pakistan in the coming days for further training. However, Junaid was later apprehended by us. They again contacted Azam Cheema, who advised them to go to Bangladesh. At this point, Akram opted out of the training, while Farooq was arrested by the police in Delhi, while en route to Bangladesh.

We closely monitored several phone numbers linked to the LeT group through VSNL, earning valuable insights and allowing us to uncover their multiple modules. Whenever any arrests occurred, the cadre would quickly halt communication, opting to either hide or cross the border and flee to Pakistan. This was done with the intention to evaluate the response and subsequent actions of the security personnel.

Junaid, during his investigation, said that Raju crossed the border after the arrest of the accused's in the February 1998 Bombay blast. However, approximatey two months later, in April 1998, the intercepted chats at VSNL revealed that Raju again came to India and frequently travelled between Mumbai and Jodhpur to collect money sent by Azam Cheema. During these conversations, Raju sought references or addresses for accommodation in Rajasthan from Azam Cheema. On one occasion, he requested Azam Cheema's permission to assassinate a three-star level individual (likely a police officer), but permission was denied. Raju also insisted on obtaining explosive weapons and ammunition for the next action plan.

At this Abdullah Faruq agreed to discuss the matter with Cheema.

A. Faruq: *"Salaam walekum!"* (Hello, peace be upon you.)

Raju: "*Walekum salaam, Abdullah. Cheema Sahib kahan hai? (Abdullah! Where is Cheema sir?)*

A. Faruq: "*Vah to nahin hai.*" (He is not here.)

Raju: *"Achcha aisa hai, yahan per ek three-starwala shifta hai, uska kam kar dun kya?"* (Okay, there is a three-star officer here; should I kill him?)

A. Faruq: *"Kya bol rahe ho? Kya hai, samajh nahi aaya."* (What are you saying? I am unable to understand.)

Raju: *Teen-stars-wala shifta samjho na yaar; kar dun kya uska kam. Lekin fir koi address dena padega aur yahan se ekadam nikalna padega.*" (Understand, buddy, three-star officer; should I kill him? But then I'll need to be given an address; I have to get out of here aa soon as possible.)

A. Faruq: *"Theek hai, main Cheema Sahib se baat karke batlata hun."* (Alright, I'll talk to Mr. Cheema and let you know.)

Subsequently, Raju inquired about the update on the topic he had discussed earlier.

A. Faruq: *Salaam walekum."* (Hello, peace be upon you.)

Raju: "*Walekum salaam, Abdullah. Cheema Sahib kahan hai?* (*Walekum salaam*, Abdullah. Where is Cheema Sahib?)

A. Faruq: "*Vah to nahin hai yahan, bahar hain."* (He is not here; he is outside.)

Raju: "*Kya hua mere kam ka?"* (What happened about my work?)

A. Faruq: *"Vah jo aapne bola tha? Nahin abhi kuchh nahin karna hai. Cheema Sahib ne bola hai.*" (The one you mentioned? Nothing needs to be done for now; Cheema Sahib said so).

Raju: *Arey chhodo usko. Main nukud (money) ki baat kar raha hun*?" (Forget that; I'm talking about the money.)

A. Faruq: *Cheema Sahib ne bola hai do-teen din mein karvata hun.* (Cheema Sahib had said that it will be done in two to three days.)

Raju: "*Kya khak karvayenge. Pata hai tumhen main kitna pareshan ho raha hun yahan per*?" (What will he get done? Do you know how troubled I am here?)

A. Faruq: *"Theek hai, main bol dunga.*" (Alright, I will convey your message.)

In the unfolding narrative, Raju, after contacting Talha, sought to convey a message to Abdullah.

Talha: "*Salaam walekum!*" (Hello, peace be upon you.)

Raju: "*Walekum salaam! Main Raju bol raha hun India se. Abdullah hai kya*?" (Peace be upon you. This is Raju speaking from India. Is Abdulla there?)

Talha: "*Nahin, vah nahin hai.*" (No, he is not here.)

Raju: "*Achcha aisa hai, Abdullah ko bolna ki vah Abu Shahid (Junaid) ko phone karen aur uski khairiyat puche. Uska phone nahin lage to Abu Saeed se uska koi dusra number lekar uss per rafta karen aur uski khairiyat puche.*" (Okay, tell Abdullah to call Abu Shahid (Junaid) and inquire about his well-being. If he can't reach him, he should contact Abu Saeed (based in

Khurja) and get Abu Shahid (Junaid)'s alternate number, and check on him.)

Talha: *"Kya baat hai? Sab theek to hai?"* (What's the matter? Is everything okay?)

Raju: *"Nahin, mujhe kuchh gadbad lagti hai. Tum Abdullah ko yah bol dena. Allah Hafiz."* (No, I feel something is not right. Tell Abdullah about this! Goodbye.)

Thereafter Raju again contacted Abdullah Faruq, expressing his concern after seeing someone resembling Abu Shahid (Junaid) on TV and noticing the soap pieces, i.e. explosives that they had used earlier in Mumbai blast cases. Abdullah Faruq reassured Raju, explaining that Cheema Sahib has assured there was nothing wrong but advised him to remain vigilant. Raju again instructed Abdullah Faruq to prompt Cheema to expedite the dispatch of goods and concluded with a farewell.

A. Faruq: *Salaam walekum* (Hello, peace be upon you.)

Raju: *"Walekum salaam! Abdullah yaar kya hua Abu Shahid (Junaid) ka? Maine TV mein dekha Abu Shahid (Junaid) jaisa hi laga aur sabun ke 7/8 pieces bhi TV mein dekhe the jo humne vahan istemal kiye thay.* (Hello Abdullah! What happened to Abu Shahid (Junaid)? I saw someone with his resemblance on TV and he looked just like him. I also saw the soap (RDX), about seven to eight pieces, which were used by us earlier.)

A. Faruq: *"Achcha Cheema Sahib ne kaha hai aisa kuchh nahin hai lekin aapko bolane ko kaha hai ki tum dhyan se rehna*." (Okay, Cheema Sahib said there's nothing like that, but he has asked me to tell you to be careful.)

Raju: *"Theek hai, Abdullah. Cheema Sahib ko bolkar saman jaldi se jaldi bhejo. Allah Hafiz."* (Alright, Abdullah, tell Cheema Sahib to send the goods quickly. *Allah Hafiz*.)

In the first week of July 1998, upon learning about Junaid's detention on TV, Raju promptly informed Abdullah through Talha in Pakistan. Abdullah Faruq and Raju were engaged in a conversation when Raju informed Abdullah Faruq that he had confirmed about Junaid's arrest just two hours earlier from another source. When Abdullah Faruq acknowledged the accuracy of the information, Raju expressed frustration at Abdullah, who worked as the telephone attendant in the LeT office. Raju was upset that Abdullah had not confirmed the news of Junaid's arrest despite having informed him as soon as he learned it from the news broadcast. Raju viewed their behaviour negatively as it put him at risk due to Junaid's knowledge of his contact details because previously, Azam Cheema had shared Raju's phone number (0291 xxxxx 194 in Jodhpur) with Junaid, who attempted to contact Raju in June.

A. Faruq: "*Salaam walekum*!" (Hello, peace be upon you.)

Raju: "*Walekum salaam, Abdullah! Meri baat sacchi hui na abhi do ghante pahle maine pata kiya hai Abu Shahid ke bare mein*." (Hello Abdullah! My information about Abu Shahid turned out to be true! I found out about it just two hours ago.)

A. Faruq: "*Han, han vah to baat sach hai.* (Yes, yes, that's true.)

Raju: *To yaar mai ne tumhen bataya tha, lekin tumne mujhe nahin bataya bus kahate rahe ki aisa kuchh nahin hai, aisa kuchh nahin hai. Tumhen pata hai uske pass mera adress hai. Agar vah idhar lekar aa jaata mehmanon ko to kitna nuksan ho sakta tha*." (So, buddy, I told you so, but you kept saying that nothing like that was happening. You know, he had my address; if he had brought trouble (police) here, how much damage could have been done?)

A. Faruq: "*Accha, usey pata tha tumhare address ka*?" (Oh, did he know about your address?)

Raju: "*Haan yaar! Accha rakhta hoon. Allah Hafiz*." (Yes, buddy! I have to be careful. Goodbye.)

After this episode, Raju immediately contacted Abdul Karim Tunda@Babaji in Bangladesh in the name of Hashim. Babaji mentioned the apprehension of his associates in Delhi and Junaid in Hyderabad during the conversation. He cautioned Raju about the sensitivity of phone conversations and advised adoption of brevity. Raju acknowledged the advice and Babaji concluded by encouraging Raju to stay vigilant and focus on the operations while keeping in touch.

Babaji: "Salaam walekum." (Hello, peace be upon you.)

Raju: *"Walekum salaam. Babaji, main Umesh hun."* (Hello, peace be upon you. Babaji, it's me, Umesh.)

Babaji: *Pehchana nahin."* (Didn't recognise you.)

Raju: "*Hashim, Raju*!" (Hashim, Raju!)

Babaji: *"Kya hal chal hai tumhara? Wo tumhe oata chala Jehlumwale (Junaid) ka?"* (How are you doing? Did you hear about Jehlumwale (Junaid)?)

Raju: "*Haan! Pata chala*." (Yes, I heard.)

Babaji: *"20/25 din ho gaye, kafi ladke pakde gaye hain. Mere bhi kafi ladke the; Delhi mein pakde gaye hain. Apna khyal rakhna. Telephone per bhi zyada mat baat karna. Abhi kahan se bol rahe ho*?" (It's been 20/25 days; many boys have been caught. Quite a few of our boys have been caught in Delhi. Take care and don't talk too much on the phone. Where are you calling from right now?)

Raju: "*Vah tumhen to pata hi hai. Chalo chhodo. Bahut dur se bol raha hun, Babaji*." (You already know. Let it go. I'm speaking from a very distant place, Babaji.)

Babaji: "*Theek hai, kam karte raho aur mujhe bhi phone karte raha karo. Allah Hafiz*." (Alright, keep working and keep calling me too. *Allah Hafiz*.)

Keeping in view the arrest of LeT terrorists, especially of Junaid and Abu Saeed, Azam Cheema, however, issued Raju strong instructions not to contact them on Pakistan's phone numbers for at least two months. If a message was scheduled for Azam Cheema or Zaki-ur-Rehman, Cheema instructed him to get in touch with Syed or Mustafa in Dubai right away. The telephone number 28xxx3588 of Syed Bhai and 62xxx65736 mobile number of Mustafa's Dubai contacts were given to Raju by Cheema. After that, they could contact him independently through a reliable channel of communication. Relevant conversations are reproduced below:

A. Faruq: "*Salaam walekum*." (Hello, peace be upon you.)

Raju: "*Walekum salaam. Kya yaar Abdullah, mai ne phone number diya aapko, aapka abhi tak phone nahin aaya?* (Hello, peace be upon you. Abdullah, I gave you my phone number; you haven't made any call yet?)

A. Faruq: "*Main idhar se mila raha hun, lekin India ka circuit busy aa raha hai. Achcha aisa hai, Cheema Sahib ne kaha hai ki do-teen mahine is phone per koi phone nahin karna tumhen. Jo bhi paigam dena hai, vah phone number likho, uss per dena.*" (I've been trying, but the Indian circuit seems busy. Well, Cheema Sahib has said not to make any calls on this phone for the next two to three months. Write down the phone number for any messages you may want to convey.)

Raju: "*Likhvao.*" (Sure, go ahead.)

A. Faruq: "*28xxx3588 yah Syed Bhai ka number hai dusra number 62xxx65736. Yah mobile Mustafa ka hai; Dubai ka number hai yah. Asal mein to pahle number per aapki baat ho jayegi, lekin agar nain hoti to doosre mobile per Mustafa Bhai se baat kar lena aur yah sirf paigam dene ke liye hai. Aur kisi cheez ke liye nahin hai.*" (28xxx3588 is Syed Bhai's number and the second number, 62xxx65736, is Mustafa Bhai's mobile in Dubai. Ideally, your call should go through on the first number, but if it doesn't, talk to Mustafa Bhai on the second mobile. And this is only for passing on messages, not for anything else.)

When Raju tried to contact these numbers of Dubai, he did not receive a positive response from Mustafa. At this, Raju again contacted Abdullah Faruq and expressed his disappointment. Abdullah Faruq informed Raju that they had received a Fax message from Mustafa in which he had apologised for not responding to his call. Abdullah Faruq advised Raju to contact again, assuring that Mustafa would respond this time

A. Faruq: "*Salaam walekum.*" (Hello, peace be upon you.)

Raju: *Walekum salaam. Addullah yaar, wo Mustafa koi baat nahi karta.*" (Hello, peace be upon you, Abdullah. Mustafa doesn't talk.)

A. Faruq: "*Achcha, tumhari vahan Dubai baat nahin hui?*" (Really? You didn't talk to him in Dubai?)

Raju: *Han, mai ne ki thi, usne kaha mere pass koi paigam nahin hai. Bolata hai, aayela hai, jayeela hai, Bambaiya bhasha mein.* (Yes, I spoke to him. He said he doesn't have any messages and he said in Mumbai's slang, '*aayela hai, jayeela hai.*')

A. Faruq: "*Achcha nahin tum dobara baat karo, vah baat karega. uska Fax aaya tha, maafi mang raha tha. Kah raha tha mujhe paigam nahi aaya tha. Ab karlena.*" (Well, call him again; he will talk. He sent a Fax apologising, that the was sorry because he didn't receive any message from us. Call him now.)

Besides the above, the following chats went on to indicate that Raju was attempting to purchase a house some place on the Jodhpur side and that he demanded Rs. 2 lakhs from Azam Cheema as down payment for the property. In addition, Raju was complaining to someone named Salahuddin about the youngsters (terrorists), whom Azam Cheema had sent from Pakistan at this crucial time when Raju and his companions, Shafiq and Saleem, were themselves underground and having trouble finding a suitable refuge. In order to help them feel more at home, Raju asked Azam Cheema to provide an address where they could remain until they were able to find a more permanent location after buying a property in Jodhpur or the surrounding area of Rajasthan. Raju inquired whether Cheema had granted approval for the purchase of the Rs. 2 lakh worth house. Abdullah Farooq confirmed that Cheema had indeed given his approval for the transaction. In addition to this, Raju asked them multiple times to provide explosives, weapons and ammunition. However, their handlers in Pakistan were doing nothing at all. Abdullah Faruq again stressed and conveyed Cheema's message, emphasising that Raju should refrain from directly discussing sensitive matters on a Pakistani phone.

Call 1

A. Faruq: "*Salaam walekum.*" *(Hello, peace be upon you.)*

Raju: "*Walekum salaam. Achcha Shafiq ne Rafta kiya? Mai ne unko bola tha Shafiq aur Salim donon saath hain aur mere se thoda alag hain.*" (Hello, peace be upon you. Has Shafiq made any contact with you? I told them to contact you, since Shafiq and Salim are together and a bit separate from me.)

A. Faruq: "*Abhi to koi rafta nahin hua.*" (No contact has been made yet.)

Raju: "*Wo rafta karenge aap se. Achcha mai ne Cheema Sahib se poochha tha ki makan le loon ke nahi? Do lakh ka aaega. To kya kaha unhone?:* (They'll contact you. By the way, I asked Cheema Sahib if I should buy the house or not worth Rs. 2 lakhs? What did he say about that?)

A. Faruq: "*Unhone kaha, le le.*" (He said, 'Buy it.')

Raju: "*Do ka aaega.*" (It will cost 200,000.)

A. Faruq: "*Han, han, theek hai, le le.*" (Yes, yes, that's fine; take it.)

Raju: "*Theek hai, main vahin per lunga, Shafiq ki taraf.*" (Okay, I'll take it there near Shafiq's house.)

A. Faruq: "*Achcha buzurgon ne doobara hidayat di hai ki is phone per bilkul baat na karen. Do teen mahine jo baat karni ho, aap Mustafa Bhai ki taraf se karen. Jo paigam dena ho, udhar se hi den. Chalo theek hai. aap ehtiat se rahen.*" (Okay, the elders have once again given strong instructions not to talk at all on this phone for two to three months. Whatever communication has to be made, do it through Mustafa Bhai. Alright, stay cautious.)

Call 2

Unknown: "*Salaam walekum.*" (Hello, peace be upon you.)

Raju: "*Walekum salaam! Kaun*?" (Hello, peace be upon you. Who is this?)

Unknown: "*Lo Sallauddin Bhai se kar lo baat.*" (Here, talk to Sallahuddin.)

Raju: "*Salaam walekum, Salahuddin Bhai. Bahut dinon mein baat hui hai aapse.*" (Hello, peace be upon you, Sallahuddin Bhai. It's been a long time since we spoke.)

Salahuddin: "*Khairiyat se hain aap. Aap idhar baat hi nahi karte.*" (Are you well? You hardly talk here.)

Raju: "Kya Salahuddin Bhai sab gadbad ho raha hai aur ab dekhona inhone bhi julm kar diya; chote, chote bacche bhej diye." (Salahuddin Bbhai, things are going wrong and now they have sent novices.)

Salahuddin: "*Kaun kaun hai?*" (Who all are there?)

Raju: "*Tanvir, Shoaib vagaira aur idhar sab gadbad hua pada hai. Na hi inke liye koi address dete hain; bahut pareshan hun. Ham khud rooh-posh hain. inko kahan rakhoon.*" (Tanvir, Shoaib, and others and everything's in trouble. They don't even provide an address for them. I'm very worried. We ourselves are in a difficult situation. Where should I keep them?)

Raju: "Aur hame yahan aaye teen mahine ho gaye saman vagaira kuch bhi nahi bhej rahe hain. Kya karun main. Phir bolte hain koi kaam nahi kar raha, nikamma hai, kya karoon?" (And it's been three months since we came here; they're not sending anything (explosives, etc.). What should I do? Then they say, no work is being done; what can I do?)

Salahuddin: "*Ab kya kar sakte hai? Chalo theek hai, aap khyal rakhna apna.*" (What can be done now? Alright, take care.)

There was very little communication between them following Junaid's detention, but following Abu Saeed's arrest after July 1998, there was no communication at all about the numbers that were under observation. I want to emphasise that throughout the entire operation, it was seen that the handler and the operative either preferred an inward call from Pakistan to India on any STD booth where the Indian operative would be present and had provided the Pakistan handler with the phone number, or else they communicated via Fax. We had a lot of trouble tracing and arresting the different modules as a result of this modus operandi. They had not suspended contact between them previously, but this time they have done so after suffering significant setbacks due to the arrest of their highly placed operatives in various states. However, shortly before cutting off their line of communication, Raju gave Azam Cheema a mobile number – 9820xx x840 and that call was overheard at VSNL. In the following conversation, Raju made a call to Pakistan inquiring about Abu Ahmad. The caller directed Raju to speak with Cheema Sahib. When Cheema answered, Raju greeted him and requested for a swift arrangement of funds. Cheema assured that he would arrange the funds in four to five days and advised Raju to instruct the other associates also not to talk directly to Mustafa in Dubai. Instead, Raju should handle evey communication and make them understand. Raju informed Cheema that he had conveyed his new mobile number to Mustafa in Dubai in order to forward the same to him. Raju asked Cheema if Mustafa had given that number to him? Even after confirmation, Raju again gave his mobile number 9820xxx840 to Cheema.

Unknown: *Salaam walekum*!" (Hello, peace be upon you.)

RAJU:" *Walekum salaam! Abu Ahmad hai?* (Hello, peace be upon you. Is Abu Ahmad there?)

Unknown: Vah to nahin. Aap Cheema Sahib se baat kar lo." (No, he's not here. Talk to Cheema Sahib.)

Cheema: "*Salaam walekum*!" (Hello, peace be upon you.)

Raju: "*Walekum salaam! Cheema Sahib, paison ka jaldi se jaldi intezaam karvayen.*" (Hello, peace be upon you! Cheema Sahib, please arrange for the money as soon as possible.)

Cheema: "*Theek hai, main chaar-paanch din mein karvata hun aur aisa hai, aap in bacchon ko bole ki vah Mustafa se direct baat na karen. Jo bhi baat karni ho, aap hi karen, unko samjha den.*" (Alright, I'll arrange it in four-five days. And tell these kids not to talk directly to Mustafa. Whatever they need to say, you should convey it to him.)

Raju: "*Theek hai Cheema Sahib. Mustfa ne aapko mera number de diya*?" (Okay, Cheema Sahib. Mustafa gave you my number?)

Cheema: "*Han, han de diya hai.*" (Yes, he has given it.)

Raju: "*Theek hai, fir bhi aap likh lo.*" (Okay, write it down just in case.)

Cheema: "*Likhayen.*" (Write it down.)

Raju: "*982 0xx x840 mobile hai*?" (Is it the mobile number 9820xxxx840?)

Cheema: "*Iss per to yahan se baat nahin hogi.*" (You won't be able to talk to him on this number from here.)

Raju: "*Ho jayegi. Aap try karenge to international hai. Theek hai, rakhta hoon. Allah Hafiz.*" (It can happen; you can try since it's an international number. Alright, I'll end here. *Allah Hafiz.*)

The mobile records were gathered and thoroughly examined, revealing a minimal number of calls, with the only connections being to or from an STD on that mobile phone. Further investigation revealed that Raju had terminated that mobile number too.

On the other hand, despite extensive efforts by the Intelligence Bureau, no breakthrough emerged from Asansol regarding Abu Abdullah@Aamir and from Mumbai or Jodhpur, about Raju. The agencies in these locations were tasked with essential work while legal procedures for the arrested individuals were underway, but unfortunately, no significant progress was reported from these areas.

Besides, in the last quarter of September 1998, the Intelligence Bureau received information about the movement of an ex-LeT terrorist named Suhail, a resident of UP. He had recently shifted his loyalty to another terrorist outfit, Harkat-ul-Ansar, headed by Maulana Fazlur Rahman. Umar Saeed Shaikh, released in the IC-814 hijacking case and involved in the abduction of two British nationals from Delhi, was a member of this organisation. Suhail was appointed as chief of Harkat-ul-Ansar in UP and had previously been arrested by the UP Police for planning to abduct the son of Mulayam Singh Yadav, former Chief Minister of Uttar Pradesh.

The information received by the IB was developed further and on September 24, we laid a trap on secret information near Nizammuddin flyover, and arrested Suhail @ Izhar Hussain r/o Muzaffarnagar, UP and Abdul Gafoor of Kupwara, J&K. Nearly 2 kgs. of RDX was recovered from their possession. They had come here to hand over the RDX to the operational group Harkat-ul-Ansar. The had to hand over to Raja and Nasir, both Pakistani trained terrorists, but who failed to turn up.

At their instance, a raid was conducted at the hideout of one Taslim, r/o Janshat, Muzaffarnagar, UP, in the Zaffarabad area of Seelampur, Delhi. Two kgs. of PETN and pencil timers were recovered from him. The arrested terrorists were affiliated with Harkat-ul-Ansar. The activities in Delhi and UP were organised through Taslim's brother Salim Kari of Janshat, Muzaffarnagar, UP. Salim Kari, a blind man, was involved in terrorist activities while preaching in a mosque in Srinagar.

In 1996, a bomb explosion occurred in a bus at Modinagar, resulting in the death of 16 people. Taslim's brother Salim Kari was involved in that explosion. Salim Kari, along with Abdul Gafoor, had gone from Srinagar to Pakistan through Bangladesh, where they met Abu Saeed Khalil, an associate of Umar Saeed Sheikh, who was wanted in the case of kidnapping two British nationals from Delhi (later released by the Indian government during the IC814 hijacking case).

Salim Kari frequently visited Delhi and had taken eight boys, particularly from Muzaffarnagar, for training in Pakistan. He was an expert in bomb manufacturing. He had lost one finger in an explosion while preparing a bomb in his village with the help of his brother Taslim.

Upon interrogation of these terrorists, it was revealed that Pakistani terrorists who were supposed to receive explosives from Suhail had successfully created Indian identities using fake names, like Raja and Nasir. The above-mentioned terrorists provided logistical support. Raja and Nasir were trained terrorists of the Harkat-ul-Ansar terrorist outfit and both of them took up residence at Bombay.

Sohail, Taslim and Gafoor provided some information about them. They also gave us the Pakistani phone number of Fazlu Rehman, chief of Harkat-ul-Ansar, which they used to contact, as well as the mobile numbers used while staying with them in UP. After a thorough analysis of the numbers, a team of the Intelligence Bureau and Delhi Police, led by Inspector Rakesh Dixit, was sent to Bombay. The team put all the relevant phone numbers on observation and started listening to their conversations.

Mobile Intrument of Raju Activated Seizing the opportunity, we placed Raju's (Abu Umesh's) mobile phone number, which he had provided to Cheema before suspending communication, under surveillance. Additionally, the instrument number (IMEI) was also put on observation. Our strategy worked, and after two or three days, Raju's IMEI number became active with another SIM card (982xxxx403). The conversation was intercepted and the voice was identified. Raju was speaking to a *hawala* dealer to fetch money sent from Saudi Arabia. As soon as this call was received, Rakesh Dixit immediately contacted me and conveyed the new mobile number of Raju. I promptly asked Sandeep Malhotra to remain in contact with the Nodal Officer of that service provider and find out the location of the mobile.

Tracking down Raju's mobile proved to be a time-consuming task. Malhotra shared with me that the mobile-owner was heading towards Surat. Without hesitation, I instructed Sandeep Malhotra to reach out to the Nodal Officer in Gujarat to obtain the real-time location of the mobile phone. Much to my satisfaction, he had already taken that initiative. The following day, we successfully traced the mobile's location in Ahmedabad.

The telephone was put on observation and in the evening, a call was intercepted. Raju and one Qasim were talking wherein Raju informed Qasim that he had reached Ahmedabad. Raju inquired about some other members of their group and their locations. Qasim informed him that they were at the same place where they were left by Raju. Raju directed Qasim to inform them that they had to leave Ahmedabad as soon as the direction was received from Pakistan.

In the subsequent days, additional conversations unfolded between Raju and Qasim, shedding light on Qasim's occupation as a mason working on an under-construction house. With their limited conversation, which was in coded language and their frequent movement, we found it very difficult to catch them and locate their hideout. The name 'Qasim' kept popping up in my mind, prompting me to search through the interceptions to trace where I had heard it. After revisiting them, I eventually stumbled upon the context and conversation related to Qasim@Ajmal who was sent by Azam Cheema from Pakistan to India. However, at that time, Junaid was arrested. Therefore Abu Saeed, who was based in Khurja, made a call to Pakistan in order to warn Qasim not to attend any call made by Junaid. It was further revealed during that conversation that Qasim was trying to get in touch with Aamir who was based in West Bengal. But neither Qasim nor the Pakistan headquarters of LeT were successful in their endeavours. Due to this, the higher cadre of LeT was very upset with Aamir. This was made clear in the below-mentioned conversations intercepted at VSNL between Abu Saeed, who was located in India, and Abdullah Faruq, who was located in Pakistan, prior to our arresting Abu Saeed.

A. Faruq: "*Salaam walekum.*" (Hello, peace be upon you.)

Saeed: "*Walekum salaam! Abdullah Bhai, Qasim Ajmal ka koi phone aaya*?" (Hello, peace be upon you! Abdullah Bhai! Did Qasim Ajmal make any call?)

A. Faruq: "*Nahin koi phone nahin aaya.*" (No, there hasn't been any call.)

Saeed: "*Abhi kahan par hain, wo?*" (Where is he right now?)

A. Faruq: "*Aamir ki taraf hai, lekin uska phone hi nahi mil raha; jahan milta hai wo bula nahi rahe. Cheema Sahib bhi Aamir par bahut naraz ho rahe thay.*" (He's near Aamir's place (Asansol, West Bengal), but his phone is not reachable and wherever else we tried to contact Aamir, those people would not call him to attend to the call. Cheema Sahib is also quite angry with Aamir.)

Saeed: "*Achcha, Qasim ka phone agar aaye to bol dena ki agar uske pass Junaid ka phone aaye, to koi baat na kare. samajh gaye na*?" (Okay, if Qasim's call comes through, tell him that if he receive Junaid's call, he should not respond. Do you understand?)

A. Faruq: "*Saeed Bhai, yahi hidayat mujhe mili hai. upar se unhone bhi yahi paigam diya hai.*" (Saeed Bhai, the same instructions I have received from above.)

Saeed: "*Theek hai, dhyan se. Allah Hafiz.*" (Alright, be careful. *Allah Hafiz*.)

However the conversations of Raju and Qasim also suggested that they were planning something in the future. Finally, a decision was taken to involve ATS Ahmedabad and a strategy was devised. According to that, ATS Ahmedabad would remain in the field and conduct field inquiries. After a careful study of Raju's mobile, we narrowed down to the area of movement where ATS Ahmedabad was deployed in plain clothes. They also deployed their sources in that area to trace the hideouts and movements of Raju and Qasim. During the second week of October 1998, a conversation between Azam Cheema and Raju was intercepted at VSNL, revealing that Qasim had been apprehended.

Cheema: "*Salaam walekum.*" (Peace be upon you.)

Raju: "*Walekum salaam! Cheema Sahib, lagta hai Qasim mehman ho gaya.*" (Peace be upon you too! Cheema Sahib, it seems Qasim has been arrested.)

Cheema: "*Kahan se bol rahe ho aap? Maine kaha hua hai ki iss number per phone mat kara karo.*" (Where are you calling from? I've already told you not to call on this number.)

Raju: "*Main kya karun Cheema Sahib baat hi itni zaruri thi. Aisa hai main sari detail bad mein Fax karunga. Abhi main yahan se nikal raha hun aur Babaji ki taraf ja raha hun. Lekin yah shukar hua ki mai ne baki logon ko kal sham ko hi uss taraf ravana kar diya tha.*" (What can I do, Cheema Sahib? The matter was so important. I'll Fax all the details later. Right now, I'm leaving this place and heading towards Babaji, but thankfully, I had already sent the other people in the evening.)

Cheema: "*Kidhar*?" (Where?)

Raju: "*Jahan pahle hota tha, 291 par* (this is the code of Jodhpur). *Ab aap unse rafta karke apni taraf wapas bulva lo. Yahan abhi kuchh pata nahin chal raha kya ho gaya. Sabhi log mehman hote ja rahe hain. Aap aisa karen, Aamir ko bhi phone kar dein ki vah bhi vahan se nikal jaaye. Apni taraf hi bula lo usko bhi aur main bhi Babaji ki taraf se aapke pass aa jaunga. Achcha main rakhta hun, zyada baat nahin karunga. Ab BD pahunch kar hi baat karunga. Salaam walekum! Allah Hafiz.*" (The place where I used to stay earlier at 291 (this is the code of Jodhpur). Now, you should contact them and bring them back to your place (Pakistan). Right now, nothing is very clear over here; everyone is being arrested. Do the same with Aamir. Ask him to leave this place. Bring him to your place and I'll also join you from Babaji's side. Okay, I won't talk much now. I'll talk after reaching Bangladesh. *Salaam walekum*! *Allah Hafiz*.)

Meanwhile, ATS informed us that they had arrested one Qasim@Ajmal near a petrol pump in the Sabarmati locality of Ahmedabad. He was interrogated. Interrogation revealed that he was launched by Azam Cheema and had crossed into India from the Jaisalmer border with the help of Pakistan Rangers three months ago. His primary task was to plot Shri L.K. Advani, Home Minister and Shri Keshubhai Patel's murders, as directed by ISI.

Raju@Abu Umer@ Usman was a key figure in the plot as he was believed to possess stocks of RDX (research and development explosive), arms and ammunition. Abu Qasim also told the police that he was also a key man in the Lashkar-e-Toiba. Abu Qasim had also undergone training in Afghanistan. After arriving in India, Qasim landed in Gandhinagar and took up a job as a marble worker in the city. But he had been monitoring the activities and movements of ministers and VIPs in the state capital since two-and-a-half months.

Later, after interrogation, Abu Qasim was taken to the Inspector-General's office by the ATS commandos and ordered to make a long-distance call to Raju @ Usman. But on the way, Qasim suddenly pulled commando P.S. Raval's carbine and tried to open fire, but another alert commando, Dinesh Jambu, immediately shot him. Qasim, who was seriously wounded, died on arrival at the Civil Hospital, Ahmedabad, at about midnight. The next day, a Press conference was organised by Shri Haren Pandya, the state's Home Minister.

□

29
Module 8—ASANSOL

The questioning of Junaid on Aamir led to the revelation that Aamir had once provided Junaid with a phone number, 0341xxxx12, in the event of Junaid desiring to get in touch with him. Mohammad. Aamir s/o Lal Mohammad Rahim Mohammed, resident of Bahiuddin Block Old, Barhanpur, West Bengal was the address that Aamir provided to Junaid as well. Because Aamir was such an egotistical person, Junaid did not call Aamir at the number listed above nor did he visit Barhanpur in order to speak with Aamir in person.

The conversation, overheard from various STD booths, revealed that Abu Abdullah, also known as Aamir, was a trained terrorist in the LeT and used to correspond with Azam Cheema and Zaki-ur-Rehman in Pakistan from Asansol, West Bengal. Abu Abdullah was originally from Faisalabad, Pakistan. About a year ago, Azam Cheema launched him in India to oversee their outfit's activities in the eastern region. In this connection Abu Abdullah@Aamir asked Zaki to provide him with the assistance of an additional terrorist, namely Abu Umer from Pakistan, as Abu Umer was desperate to join him for *jihad*.

Call 1

Aamir: "*Chachaji, chacha, mai ne aapse ek chiz mangni thi; aap vada karo ki mana nahin karoge.*" (Uncle, I wanted to ask you for something, promise me that you won't refuse.)

Zaki: "*Bata.*" (Tell me.)

Aamir: "*Nahin pahle vada karo ki aap de doge.*" (No, first promise that you'll give it.)

Zaki: "*Tu bata to sahi, pata nahin tu kya mang lega mere se.*" (Tell me what it is; I don't know what you would ask of me.)

Aamir: "*Abu Umer bhej do mere pass, yahan per bahut zarurat hai.*" (Send Abu Umer to me; there's a great need here.)

Zaki: *Usi ne kahani padhai hogi tere se. Chal mein dekhta hun. Allah Hafiz.*" (He himself must have fed the story to you. Okay, I'll see. *Allah Hafiz.*)

* * *

Abu Umer: "*Salaam walekum! Kya aapne meri baat ki Zaki Sahib se*?" (Hello, peace be upon you. Did you talk to Zaki Sahib about my problem?)

Aamir: "*Han ki thi. Vah kah rahe the ki main karta hun. Aapka ho jaega, aap befikar rahen.*" (Yes, I did. He said that he'll take care of it. You need not worry.

Abu Umer: "*Aap yah kam karva den. Mujhe pata chala hai ki Allah vahan per dua bahut qabul karta hai. Ab hamen bahut din ho gaye hain yahan per. Hamain bhi khidmat ka mauka dain.*" (You get this work done for me. I've come to know that Allah's prayers are very much accepted there. It's been a long time for us too. Give us an opportunity for doing service.)

Aamir: "*Theek hai, theek hai, aapka ho jaega. Mai ne baat kar li hai. Allah Hafiz.*" (Okay, okay, it will be done. I've talked about it. *Allah Hafiz.*)

On 24 April, 1998, his marriage was fixed with a native woman. Aamir asked Zaki about the *mehar* (obligation in the form of money by the groom to the bride at the time of marriage) to give to the bride. Zaki also informed Aamir about the arrest of Kamran. The relevant extracts of the call are as under:

Aamir: "*Salaam walekum.*" (Greetings be upon you.)

Zaki: "*Walekum salaam! Tenu mubarakan. Byaah kara*

ke dasna." (Greetings be upon you! Congratulations on the marriage. Inform after the ceremony.)

Aamir: "*Batao ki mehar mein kya daina hai*?" (Tell me, how much should I give as *mehar*?)

Zaki: "*Jo teri haisiyat ho, usi hisab se kar den. Is tarah kar sona chadha dio do tole. Kab hai shaadi*?" (Give according to your status. Like, give two tolas of gold. When is the wedding?)

Aamir: "*24 (April) ko; aaj 13 hai. Aap Azam Sahib ko bhi boliye ki kuchh paise bhijwa denge.*" (It's on the 24th (April; today is the 13th. Also, tell Azam Sahib to send some money.)

Zaki: "*Changa, main bole dewan ga. Tanu pata chal gaya uska*?" (Alright, I'll tell him to send. Have you heard about him?)

Aamir: "*O Karachiwale da?* (regarding Kamran) *Han, han.*" (The one from Karachi? Yes, yes.)

There were conversations which revealed Aamir's plan to work under cover in the business he planned to buy. Therefore, he was looking to purchase both a house and a shop in the area, so as to use the shop as a front for income. Therefore Aamir demanded Rs. 6 lakh from Cheema and Zaki. Following this, Zaki-ur-Rehman transferred Rs. 5,00,000 to him via *hawala* (in two instalments).

Call 1: Aamir to Cheema

Aamir: "*Cheema Sahib, Imaan se main aapko mila; milakar thak gaya hun. Aapka phone hi nahin lagta. Uparwala jaanta hai kitni koshish karta hun. Achcha aisa hai, mai ne dukaan aur makan ke bare mein baat kar li hai aur advance de diya hai. Aap mujhe 6 (six lakhs) bhijwa dain.*" (Cheema Sahib, I am tired of trying your phone number. God knows how much I have tried. Okay, I have discussed the shop and the house and I have given an advance. Please send me Rs. 6 lakhs.)

Cheema: "*Theek hai, main Zaki Sahib se baat karke bhijwata hun; unhin se intezaam karvata hun. Allah Hafiz.*" (Okay, I'll talk to Zaki Sahib and arrange for it through him. *Allah Hafiz.*)

Call 2: Aamir to Zaki

Aamir: "*Walekum salaam, Zaki Sahib! Main vahan gaya tha Abdullah ke pass. Usne mujhe teen (three lakh) hi diye hain, baki nahin diye.*" (Hello, peace be upon you, Zaki Sahib! I went there to Abdullah; he has given me only three lakhs, not the rest.)

Zaki: "*Theek hai, tu Cheema Sahib se baat kar na direct.*" (Okay, talk to Cheema Sahib directly.)

Aamir: "*Cheema Sahib ka phone nahin lag raha, bahut koshish kar raha hun. Aap Cheema Sahib se baat kar len.* (Cheema Sahib's phone is not connecting; I have tried a lot. You talk to Cheema Sahib.)

Zaki: "*Chal main karta hun. Allah Hafiz." (Okay, let me do it. Allah Hafiz.)*

Call 3: Aamir to Abu Umer

Abu Umer: *"Salaam walekum*!" (Hello, peace be upon you.)

Aamir: "*Abu Umer bol rahe hain*?" (Is it Abu Umer speaking?)

Abu Umer: *Hanji, hanji*." (Yes, yes.)

Aamir: "*Kya baat hui Cheema Sahib se paison ke baare main*?" (What did Cheema Sahib say about the money?)

Abu Umer: "*Meri baat hui thi unse! Unhone kaha hai aap dobara rafta karen. Vah aapko paise de dega. Aisa hai pichhle dinon rupya kafi down chal raha tha. Issliye usne rok liye the. Ab aap jakar unse baat kar lo; aapko paise mil jaenge*." (I talked to him. He said you should go again; he will give you the money. The thing is that in the past few days, the value of the currency had fallen, so he had stopped it. Now, if you go and talk to him, you'll get the money.)

After Aamir received the money, there was no further communication between Aamir and his handler in Pakistan. Due to this, the higher cadre of LeT was very upset. The challenges of operating from a remote location were compounded by the fact that we were already heavily engaged in tracking down the other modules in various states. These operations were in advanced stages and we had specific leads regarding those modules. Given the early stage of our knowledge about Aamir, we decided to share this information with the Intelligence Bureau. This was done to leverage their extensive network and capabilities, recognising that they could take any necessary action to further investigate Aamir. Despite the concerted efforts of the Intelligence Bureau, Aamir's whereabouts remained elusive. However, a breakthrough occurred in the final month of 1998 when highly confidential sources revealed crucial information. This information indicated that following a rigorous crackdown by our team, Aamir@Abdullah, along with Raju@Abu Umes and their associates, managed to evade capture and had successfully fled to Pakistan.

□

30
Conclusion

During a year-long operation in multiple states of India, the Interstate Cell (Crime) successfully busted several modules operating in Delhi, Uttar Pradesh, Punjab, Hyderabad, Andhra Pradesh, and another, which initially operated in Mumbai, later shifted its base to Jodhpur, Rajasthan, and finally tried to establish itself in Ahmedabad, Gujarat. The arrest of a total of 26 terrorists and the killing of one terrorist during an encounter affiliated with the Lashker-e-Toiba, included nine Pakistanis, four Bangladeshis and one Burmese, led to solving 42 bomb blast incidents that had afflicted the regions of Delhi, Uttar Pradesh, Haryana, Punjab, Mumbai and Hyderabad. Their possessions yielded a total of $2,200 and Rs. 1,00,000 in cash, 18 kg. of RDX, 2 kg. of PETN and 50 kg. of improvised explosives, electric detonators, an electric circuit meant for the explosion of a car bomb, hand grenades and three wireless sets, a powerful arsenal of firearms, which included one revolver, five pistols and cartridges. Furthermore, among their collection were cast iron cylinders, acids and homemade detonators – all of these items served as foreboding reminders of the potential for destruction that lay within their grasp.

Arrests Foiled

- A plan to kill Shri L.K. Advani, the then Deputy Prime Ministerand Shri Keshubhai Patel, the then Chief Minister of Gujarat.

- Immediate threats of a series of bomb blasts in Hyderabad on Ganesh Chaturthi.
- Plan to carry out an attack in Delhi, more specifically in the Cantonment area and on the Army vehicles that were parked in civic places, such as bus terminals and railway stations, and to destabilise crucial infrastructure in and around Delhi in future after receiving 200 kg. of RDX.

The victims of the bomb blast incidents and the potential targets of the terrorist group heaved a sigh of relief and closure as a result of these arrests and discoveries.

I was a witness to a spectacular span of one year in which the bustling metropolis of Delhi and towns in the NCR witnessed an astounding series of incidents of bomb blasts that had sent shockwaves throughout the region. During the initial stages of the investigation, we never received a single clue or hint that could have helped us. I was at a loss for what to do and I was unable to find any information that could be helpful. A feeling of irritation was occasionally experienced as a result of the continuous bomb blasts. But as a team leader, I had to display my capacity to guide and unite my team in order to make it possible for them to carry out their duties with the highest possible level of intelligence and cohesiveness.

In our never-ending quest to fight terrorism, we gave Pakistani phone numbers a careful screening before excluding them from consideration, relying on multiple presumptions. My team had constantly shown great performance while conducting the investigation, which was quite challenging, whether they were engaged in intense brainstorming meetings or aggressively investigating and pursuing the leads in the field. No doubt, our whole group performed as an integrated unit and worked unitedly to achieve the same objective. During the entire operation, any accidental disclosure of our plan had the potential to put the entire mission in jeopardy. Therefore, it was vital to perform an in-depth study of each step that we were required to take and to keep the details of the operation secret owing to the unknown links with ISI.

During the course of our journey, we found ourselves travelling to a variety of outstations dispersed among the various states as discussed above. Because of these outstation excursions, we frequently found ourselves emotionally detached from our cherished family and were unable to keep in touch with them on a consistent basis, especially during festivals. In times like this, it was a great challenge for me to continuously keep my team motivated and convince them to have faith in the possibility that our hypotheses might be correct. The entire team was motivated by their unflinching optimism that we would finally be successful.

Finally, working tirelessly, we remained unwaveringly committed to the cause, and after great efforts and time, my intuition was proved correct and we were at last successful in solving the mystery that had been vexing us when Harun and Musa were taken into custody. Our primary objective was to capture the key terrorist involved in a series of incidents with the utmost precision and, if possible, bring him in alive. Our determination to trace and neutralise these different modules operating within our country remained unwavering. With this in mind, I am pleased to report that our team executed a series of swift, well-coordinated operations after jeopardising their lives that ultimately achieved our mission.

It was a blessing to have a team that I could lead through long hours of laborious effort and steadfast devotion. My entire committed and enthusiastic team laboured with unyielding conviction and wholehearted dedication throughout the entire operation. An undeniable determination to catch and bring to justice those who constituted a threat to society served as the driving force behind the dogged pursuit of justice. I express my sincere gratitude to all my team members, who worked day and night by neglecting their families during those days. I express my gratitude, especially to Inspector Subhash Tandon, ASI Ashok Sharma, HC Joginder, HC Rajendra Singh and HC

Vinod Kumar, who now reside in the gentle embrace of eternity and who were once the bedrock of our shared dreams! Their contributions live on in the legacy we built together, forever etched in my heart. Their memories live on in every project and in every meeting room where we once brainstormed and laughed together. The camaraderie we shared has become a beacon of inspiration for my continued journey. Their absence is a reminder to cherish every moment and to recognise the value of those who stand by our side. The investigation into this case served as a testament to the incredible abilities of my bright officers, who have the ability to pursue elusive leads and turn an apparently impossible task into a resounding victory.

My superiors expected us to deliver great outcomes since they had faith in our capabilities in a variety of contexts. I am also indebted to my senior officers, T.R. Kakkar, IPS, V.N. Singh, IPS, B.K. Gupta, IPS, Karnal Singh, IPS and Alok Kumar, IPS, for the support, guidance and working autonomy they provided us.

It is with great pride and a deep sense of accomplishment that I share the details of a successful operation that resulted in the disruption of multiple terrorist modules operating within our borders. It is my unwavering confidence that our security agencies continued endeavours will usher in a safer and more secure future for our beloved country.

□

Gratitude

In the quiet solitude of my efforts to pen down the memory of my lifelong meaningful investigation, I find myself compelled to express a profound sense of gratitude that extends beyond the confines of this earthly realm. To my father, late Ganga Dhar and my mother, late Dharam Devi, your enduring blessings, love and wisdom continue to guide me each day, filling my heart with warmth and purpose. The blessings my parents showered upon me have become my guiding star, lighting my path through life's intricate maze. Their wisdom, now whispering in the wind, serves as a constant reminder of their enduring presence in my life.

To my dear wife Sushma, my daughters Priyanka, Iteeh and my son Shauryanker, your unwavering support during my most challenging times for about a year remained a source of strength and inspiration, especially through those days when my daughters and son were growing and required utmost care, love and attention. Their unwavering love transformed the most daunting hours of that operation into a testament to familial strength and resilience. Their smiles and encouragement were the medicine my soul needed to heal.